DATE DUE

Critical Entertainments

Critical Entertainments

MUSIC OLD AND NEW

CHARLES ROSEN

HARVARD UNIVERSITY PRESS
Cambridge, Massachusetts
London, England
2000

Library of Congress Cataloging-in-Publication Data

Rosen, Charles.
Critical entertainments : music old and new / Charles Rosen.
p.   cm.
Includes bibliographical references and index.
ISBN 0-674-17730-4 (alk. paper)
1. Music—History and criticism.   I. Title.

ML60.R7848 2000
780—dc21   99-088602

Designed by Gwen Nefsky Frankfeldt

Contents

IV Musical Studies: Contrasting Views

V The Crisis of the Modern

For Catherine Temerson and Israel Rosenfield, in friendship

It would be impossible to acknowledge all the help I received over the years from many friends and colleagues, but Henri Zerner has constantly and ungrudgingly given me invaluable advice. Above all, I must express my gratitude to Robert Silvers, who inspired and edited the majority of these articles, and was so concerned to make them intelligible.

Introduction

O F all the arts that have developed something like a complex expressive language, music is one of the most difficult to write about. Dance is the only one equally resistant (cooking may be even more difficult, but its signifying system is considerably more rudimentary). When writing about literature, one can easily quote something from the work in question. The art historian can display photographs of whatever he wants to write about. A critic of literature or art forced to rely on his readers' memories, like most writers on music, would consider himself absurdly handicapped. Reproducing a musical score is considerably less convenient than including photographs of pictures or quotations from a poem. The editor of a review is generally reluctant to print music because it will scare away almost all the readers except for a few professional musicians.

In any case, printed musical quotations are deeply unsatisfactory. Even experienced musicians do not call up all the details of a score in their imagination by looking at it with the ease of the reader of a poem. Walter Benjamin once envisaged saying everything that he had to say about an author or a work simply by stringing his quotations together in the right order without comment. That would be perhaps even more cogent for music and, nevertheless, more obviously impossible at the present time. The day may be coming when music criticism will be easily and routinely accompanied by an audible illustration of the subject in hand, but that day has not quite arrived.

I began writing about music some years ago largely to keep someone else's nonsense off my record jackets. A Chopin recording I made for Epic Records (which belonged to the CBS complex) had some notes that quoted James Huneker on one of the late nocturnes, which claimed that it "staggered drunken with the odor of flowers." This was not my view of the work. That may be beside the point: it is not clear what the use of program notes may be. Huneker's style is an invitation to the listener to dream, to dissipate attention into reverie. The writing about music that I prefer—and the performances of it, as well—fix and intensify the listener's attention. When I hear music, I prefer to lose myself in it, not to drift outside in my own personal world with the music as a decorative and distant background.

Most of the essays and reviews collected here are dominated by three concerns. The first is a suspicion of a fanatical devotion to a limited theory or system. I am equally opposed to those obscurantist musicians who despise all forms of theory, but they do not worry me or trouble my dreams. It is, in fact, the genuinely useful theories that are the problem—or at least become the problem when they are used too exclusively and too rigidly. Sociologists who believe that the history of music can be entirely elucidated by its social functions and the classes that support it without any reference to the music itself are as harmful to a sane view as the critics who believe that music stands abstractly outside of society in a world of pure forms. Intolerant anti-Schenkerians are as deplorable as obsessive Schenkerians. Of course, the temptation to yield to an absolute theory, a universal explanation, is hard to resist. It is only human to think that one has found the ultimate theory of the universe, the true nature of all possible tonal systems, the final secret of the significance of a Mozart phrase. The most pernicious theories are the ones that seem to work only too well, the tools of analysis that can be applied with such facility to any work of music, the techniques of posing a question that always come up at once with the right answer—and generally the same answer.

A second concern may be called the neglect by musicologists of the professional side of music—or, the other side of the coin, the attempt to explain music exclusively by the demands of the performers. In writing *Idomeneo,* Mozart had to deal with the prestige and waning talents of an extremely aged tenor. He partly kept the character of the voice in mind, but he did not, however, acquiesce in all the singer's demands. He even deliberately wrote some music for him that the famous tenor found unsuitable. The musicians of Vienna were as responsible for the growing fame of Beethoven as his patrons Count Waldstein and the Archduke Rudolph. Certainly as early as the fifteenth century, if not before, the interests, aesthetic preferences, and philosophical outlook of professional musicians had as much to do with the revolutionary developments of style as the desires of patrons, although both musicians and patrons lived in a world that had other aspects of culture besides music and that influenced them.

The third concern is the ambiguous relation between criticism and the experience of music. The musicology that adds nothing of substance to either performance or listening is likely to be trivial. On the other hand, the critic or historian who believes that his observations will make a profound and permanent difference to the way music is played or heard is either insolent or happily deluded. In one sense, writing about music is like playing it: a poor performance of a fine work, provided it is not absolutely incompetent, can still give great pleasure to the average music lover whose taste has not been corrupted by expertise. One might even say that the principal advantage of a great performance is not that it is so different in nature from the mediocre one, but that it is most often given by a famous performer whose prestige is impressive enough to make an audience listen with greater intensity. Even a commonplace rendition of a symphony by Beethoven gives a good idea of its power. The finest performance does, indeed, make a difference, above all for the listeners who are already familiar with the work, but not as much as is sometimes thought. In the same way, the best writing on music can make a small difference, but we must not overestimate it. Musicology can and should be read for the pleasure that it gives, not for how radically it has changed our vision of the music. In spite of this necessary skepticism (which is only a guarantee of sanity), however, we must require what we say about the music to have some tangible effect on the way we play and listen, even if that effect is not earthshaking. We can reasonably hope that what we write can sharpen the focus of our attention and even occasionally suggest an alternate point of view that renews the vitality of our experience.

I have written almost exclusively about music that I enjoy. I think it is not always understood that in the criticism of the arts, pleasure is a prerequisite for understanding. Matthew Arnold wrote: "Many things are not seen in their true nature and as they really are, unless they are seen as beautiful. Behaviour is not intelligible, does not account for itself to the mind and show the reason for its existing, unless it is beautiful. The same with discourse, the same with song, the same with worship, all of them modes in which man proves his activity and expresses himself" (*Culture and Anarchy,* chapter 5). This is basic to aesthetic judgment. At the very least, with any work that we find unsatisfactory, we must comprehend how it gives pleasure to its partisans. It is for this reason, as I remark later, that most of the claims of the enemies of modernism are worthless: they are unable to conceive how anyone can love Schoenberg or Stockhausen. The necessity to comprehend love is equally important when one deals, not with works of art, but with ideas. Without understanding how ideas come to be held and how they can inspire passion, any criticism loses its validity. That is why, in the history of music, reception and tradition must play so important a part: any account of Mozart or Brahms must attempt to comprehend, even if as a subtext of criticism, why their music excited such opposition and how that was eventually overcome.

Some of these essays, written over a period of a quarter of a century, have dated. I hope that the period flavor will be seen as an advantage, or as instructive, and have left them largely unrevised even where there are errors, preferring to add *mea culpa* in a note. There are a few exceptions: I have very slightly abridged the review of *The New Grove's* and corrected my misspellings of three distinguished musicologists (errors all the more reprehensible as two of them are friends of mine); the chapter called "The Irrelevance of Serious Music" is an amalgam of two articles written one right after the other for *Harper's* and for *The New York Review of Books;* finally, the third essay on Brahms (Chapter 11) is a reworking and considerable expansion of a review that I had intended from the first for this collection.

PART ONE

*Performance
and Musicology*

CHAPTER ONE

The Aesthetics of Stage Fright

THE physical symptoms of stage fright are those found in medieval medical treatises which describe the disease of being in love. The syndrome consists in trembling, distraction of the senses, chills and fever, nausea, and an inexplicable melancholy. Both maladies are purely cultural phenomena, not only in the sense that they are products of relatively sophisticated social orders, but also that they are in no way technically or physically necessary to those acts for which they prepare: as often as not, they may be the direct cause of a failure to perform satisfactorily.

In neither case does the malady necessarily disappear or even lessen with age, although popularly reputed to do so. The hands of the elderly pianist have almost the same tremor at the opening of a recital as those of the debutant. With age, however, the efficacy of certain magical formulas for the control of symptoms may increase as they are combined with more elaborate rituals. "Break a leg," "*Merde*," "*In bocca lupo*," "*Hals und Beinbruch*"—none of these has much force unless preceded by a complicated ceremony that varies with the individual votary: for pianists, the washing of the hands in hot water is the most common, but cracking the knuckles or yoga may be substituted provided the same pattern of behavior is adhered to at each performance.

"Stage fright is the only lucid moment in an artist's career," Moriz Rosenthal once wrote; this is the rational view, tempered only by the illuminating pun in the German word for stage fright (literally "footlight fever"). The terror before a concert, however, is not a rational response, but an act of faith which cannot be willed but is given only to the elect. It is a grace that is sufficient in the old Jesuit sense: that is, insufficient by itself but a necessary condition for success. Leopold Godowsky, according to his colleagues the greatest of all pianists when playing in private for other pianists, yet too nervous to do his best in public, was given a paradoxically crippling superabundance of grace: it is far more terrifying to play for one or two pianists than for an audience of thousands.

Stage fright is a historical phenomenon. Its origin can be related to the growth of virtuosity in performance, but it took wing only with the demand that the performer play from memory. This development dates from the nineteenth century and conceals a paradox. It makes the performance seem a spontaneous creation of the pianist himself, but woe to the pianist who deviates from the text! "Playing by heart" is a pretty turn of phrase that hides a poisonous sting. With the public demand that the pianist play from memory came the demand for textual fidelity. (The first great age of pianistic virtuosity was also the age of German textual scholarship, and Franz Liszt was himself a scrupulous editor of other composers' works. Even his notorious arrangements of Bach's organ works for the piano are, with one exception, models of strict adherence to the original text, the changes being the minimal ones required to bring works for two keyboards and pedal within the compass of two hands on one keyboard.)

The wicked ambiguity at the center of playing from memory is revealed at the start of its history. Clara Schumann was the first pianist to do away with the score at public performance, and it is in the works of her husband that the most difficult traps for the memory are set. The last piece of the *Kreisleriana* is perhaps the most famous example. While the melodic pattern of the main theme remains unaltered at each successive appearance, the bass note never comes where expected but, with continuously varied syncopation, turns up each time as a surprise. I have never heard this piece played in public without at least one memory slip.

It is only fitting, therefore, that the most famous of all lapses of memory should be ascribed, by a story perhaps apocryphal, to Clara Schumann. She is supposed to have found herself trapped inside Mendelssohn's *Spinning Song* like a squirrel in a cage, unable to find the exit as the opening theme went by yet again, and finally remembering the little alteration that leads to the final cadence only after having been round eight times. Mendelssohn, who was present, afterwards expressed his warm appreciation for her evident attachment to his work.

It is here that the latent sadism in the concept of virtuosity begins to show its head. A piano recital is a relatively civilized affair, and the open barbarism of the crowd that shouts "Jump! Jump!" to the would-be suicide standing uneasily on the edge of a roof is out of place in the concert hall. The atmosphere that turns each recital into a cruel initiation rite in which the virtuoso must prove himself only to submit to the same ritual in another town the following evening—this atmosphere is created more subtly: a judicious cough before the performer begins will often turn the trick. "If you miss the opening leap in the *Hammerklavier*, are you still going to play the repeat of the exposition?" a friend once blandly asked me as I was about to walk on stage. "Watch!" said a young man in the first row and nudged his companion brutally in the ribs just as I arrived at the culminating difficulty of the cadenza at the beginning of Brahms's B flat Concerto. The stifling air of the concert hall, the unnatural costume of the performers, the harsh lights—all this is meant to turn playing into performance, into a dramatic act midway between melodrama and the decathlon. The silence of the audience is not that of a public that listens but of one that *watches*—like the dead hush that accompanies the unsteady movement of the tightrope walker poised over his perilous space.

The cruelty of the audience is largely unconscious, of course, but it derives from an intuitive understanding of the action that takes place on the stage. They know that what they hear and see has no independent existence, but is simply the visible and audible sign of something that can reveal itself only in this fashion. They exact the tribute of stage fright without rancor as a debt, impersonally contracted and acknowledged as a matter of course. Few audiences are hostile to the performer; most reserve their resentment for the composer, the invisible puppeteer. Even hardened enemies of contemporary music mark their displeasure and show their discrimination by cheering the performers enthusiastically the moment the composer has left the stage.

But the public demands the tension of the public performance as an outward sign of the act. They know that the music is not what they hear but a point at infinity which the performer is trying to reach. There are, indeed, performers who have lost this tension, whose heartbeats do not accelerate, whose adrenaline glands do not pour their terrifying stimulant into the bloodstream. These are the musicians who, after years of unnatural labor, have come to identify their own performance with the music, have taught themselves to be satisfied with the best they can do. The distance between a good performance and the work of music itself is incalculably great; the distance between the best and the worst of a professional musician is easily within human comprehension; and there are many who are content to try to bridge the *measurable* gap.

This explains the anomaly that the absolute certainty of a botched performance can sometimes (although not inevitably) act as an anesthetic to the nerves. A piano with a defective repetition, a recalcitrant pedal—one is reduced to doing one's best, which is not a hard decision to keep to, or, better, to resign oneself to. But one's best is dwarfed by the possibilities that open up under ideal conditions: it is the fine instrument in a hall with splendid acoustics and the promise of an alert public that can really arouse terror. Some musicians like to think of themselves as carried on the waves of the public's sympathy, lapped in its love, but the love is double-faced. The popular idol is greeted as he enters with acclaim by the audience because he is, for its sake, about to expose himself to the danger of public humiliation. At any moment the singer's voice may crack on a high note, the pianist fall off his stool, the violinist drop his instrument, the conductor give a disastrous cue and irretrievably confuse the orchestra. The applause that rewards the performer who has come through unscathed is tinged with regret. "He is getting old," one pianist remarked sadly about a colleague who, on the fiftieth anniversary of his debut, had just impeccably played the same work he had massacred the year before.

The conception of what is called "classical" music is, in one respect, fundamentally perverse. Is the Serbian bard struck with paralysis as he begins to improvise his epic? Does the jazz saxophonist sweat with fright as he swings into the improvised decoration of his solo? Hardly, if at all. In any case, what terror the improvising artist may require is of a different order from the interpreter's. The "classical" musician drugs himself (with alcohol, magic, or what-have-you) for courage, the jazz musician for the strength to seek inspiration.

Since the eighteenth century, the almost absolute separation between composer and performer has exacerbated the inevitable tension between conception and realization that exists even on the level of improvisation. It has placed the work of music beyond realization but within the range of everyone's imagining. While the text is, in its absolute sense, inaccessible, it is present as a yardstick, as an instrument for judgment against which the sample made from its mold will be found inevitably wanting. The harlequin of the *commedia dell'arte*, inventing and embroidering his dialogue as he goes along, cannot be arraigned on so precise a charge as can the actor trying, without too much help from the prompter, to give significance to a text which can never gain its full meaning from one performance.

The nature of a written work implies repetition; its meaning cannot be understood in terms of a single reading. The single perfect performance of a *text* is not an unattainable ideal, but a contradiction in terms, a nonsense. The work of music is not the physical sound of a performance nor what is down on paper: the first is a mere realization, the latter only a notation. Nor is it the imagination of the composer—his inner image, so to speak—a conception not only inaccessible but indefinable as well. But neither can the work be conceived as the simple sum of all performances: it is more precisely the limit to which all performances tend.

With the "transcendental" virtuosity of Paganini and Liszt and the demands for performance from memory came the almost total decline and disappearance (in "classical" music) of the art of improvisation. Beethoven was one of the last composers to make a great part of his reputation by improvisation, and after him there was only pastiche. With the loss of improvisation, the development of centuries was completely realized, and the work of music was at last removed conceptually out of the sphere of the actual. Its essence is outside time; only its manifestation exists as a transitory event. The work is now theoretically permanent, unaffected by history. It is significant that the great revival of improvisation represented by jazz came simultaneously with a new form of permanence, the phonograph record. Here the absolutely transitory is also fixed theoretically forever. This development was followed within a few decades by its complement, pure electronic sound. Here, too, conception and performance are made one and are permanent.

The music of the eighteenth and nineteenth centuries, staple of that odd institution the concert hall, is only distorted by this new electronic immortality; its permanence lies elsewhere—in thought, not in action. Nor will this music have anything to do with a unity of idea and performance. An essential quality of the musical works of this time is the tension that comes from the unbridgeable gap between concept and realization. This tension is even built into the concept of the work, which therefore twists back upon itself. At every performance of a Beethoven sonata, the audience is aware of a text behind the sound, a text which is approached, deformed, illuminated. The significance of the music as performed starts from this tension.

The physical sign of this tension is stage fright. All manifest attempts to reduce it profane the ritual that we call the "recital." To use the score in performance is to weaken the illusion that the text is invisibly present at each moment, forced into existence by the performance. To allow the text to be used as a springboard for improvisation and invention is to destroy—even if only for an instant—its solidity. To reduce the formality of the occasion—tennis costume is obviously the only reasonable clothing for a pianist—is embarrassing precisely because it obtrudes an element of the rational into an act which makes the invisible incarnate: at an informal occasion the music tends to become that which is heard and not what is inferred behind the sound, what the actual sound even, in a sense, prevents us from hearing. It is clear that the performance must be protected from confusion with the everyday occurrence of music heard and overheard, and for this stage fright is not merely symbolically but functionally necessary, like the dread of a candidate before an examination or a job interview, both designed essentially as a test of courage. Stage fright, like epilepsy, is a divine ailment, a sacred madness.

CHAPTER TWO

The Discipline of Philology:
Oliver Strunk

In the article on Oliver Strunk in The New Grove *by Kenneth Levy, I am listed as one of his pupils. This is an honor that I do not really deserve, as I never actually took one of Professor Strunk's courses (or, indeed, any music course at Princeton, for that matter), although I sat in on some of his lectures and seminars. But Princeton University in 1950 was a much smaller institution than it has become today, and it was not through courses that most of the education took place. I asked to review Strunk's essays for* The New York Review of Books *because it seemed to me that a scholar of such extraordinary distinction should have some recognition outside strictly professional circles, and I knew that only the few musicological journals would signal the appearance of his book.*

Oliver Strunk was still alive when the following review was written, so it was not possible to convey frankly his peculiar and fundamental importance for American musicology. His undergraduate lectures were mostly soporific, and he published very little; what was printed of his work gave witness to only a fraction of his activity. He was a difficult, shy, and quirky figure with a great wit, and he was unbelievably generous. He gave away most of his research to other scholars and to his own graduate students.

On one occasion, indeed, he even gave some of his research to me, although he almost certainly knew that I would never do anything with it; he was sure it would interest me. I had a Fulbright grant for a year in Paris to work on the relation of poetry and music in the fifteenth and sixteenth centuries, which I used partly to practice the piano and play concerts in Europe. Ken Levy asked me to meet Strunk when he came to Paris on his way to Italy and take him to dinner. Strunk asked me what I was working on, and I told him that I had been transcribing late fifteenth century Credos labeled Credo de village, *and I had supposed that they were based on a chanson as yet unknown called* De Village *which I could identify, but had discovered that there was no chanson and that all the pieces were based solely on Gre-*

gorian chant Credo no. 1. Strunk laughed and said, "We've known about that in America for years." However, nobody in France knew, I replied, and added that the pieces were interesting for their peculiar harmony, as Credo no. 1 is Phrygian, ending on an E, but that the chant had many B flats, and that the late fifteenth century composers—Josquin, Ockeghem, Pierre de la Rue, and others—had tried to soften the tritone harmony that resulted with double key signatures, which created problems of musica ficta (the addition of sharps and flats to medieval and Renaissance music). Strunk said that he thought that musica ficta was like rubato in Chopin: everyone just put it in as he felt like.

This was a stimulating enough remark: after all, rubato is both free and yet guided by tradition, and it was an observation typical of Strunk's approach to musical theory. About six months later, I received in the mail a package with no indication of the sender. It contained a complete transcription in score of a mass by Loyset Compere, in which the Credo was based on Gregorian no. 1. At every point where there was a B flat in the chant, Loyset had transposed the offending phrase up a whole tone, an unprecedented procedure for the treatment of a chant at that time as far as I know. Each place where this occurred was marked with an exclamation point in the margin by the anonymous transcriber. I presume that Oliver Strunk had made this transcription many years before when he was studying Renaissance music (he had turned almost entirely to Byzantine chant afterwards), and had shipped it off to me without comment (except for the exclamation points) for my instruction.

His interests ranged over almost the whole of music, although his appreciation of the modern period may not have gone beyond Bartók. I remember he once told me that he used to own a harpsichord but had exchanged it for a piano, and when I asked why, he said that it was too difficult to sight-read the tone poems of Strauss at the harpsichord. His legacy to those that knew him and experienced his sympathy and patience was a healthy distrust of dogmatic theory and an insistence on rigorous standards in the presentation of research. I have never engaged much in research myself, and have been parasitically dependent on the work of others who do, but I felt that I owed this tribute to the man who symbolized those standards for a whole generation of scholars who work in music, and who is still remembered by so many of them with great affection.

*E*SSAYS ON MUSIC IN THE WESTERN WORLD by Oliver Strunk contains the collected essays on Western music of the most distinguished musicologist this country has yet produced. The topics in it range from medieval music to Verdi, and it is to be followed soon by a second book, only slightly larger, which will assemble Strunk's articles on Byzantine chant. Together with the introduction to a collection of facsimiles of Byzantine notation and the footnotes and brief introductions to the selections in *Source Readings in Music History* (an anthology of writings about music from the early Greeks to Wagner), these writings represent the total published work of Oliver Strunk.

This meager harvest is—to some extent, at least—deeply misleading. The footnotes to *Source Readings* betray a wealth of original research which almost alone would justify a lifetime. Strunk's influence as a teacher and as a collaborator has been as remarkable as it has been self-effacing. Indeed, the references to him in the work of other historians are, as often as not, acknowledgments of suggestions made, notes and transcriptions lent, even whole pages written for them, rather than page references to his own publications.

Now seventy-three years old, Strunk retired in 1966 after thirty years of teaching at Princeton, but he has continued his researches in Byzantine music while living in Italy, taking up residence near a church where Byzantine forms can still be heard. It is thanks to his work, above all, that we can now decipher the early notation of Byzantine chant with a reasonable assurance of getting the right notes. When Strunk began to teach, musicology barely existed in this country. He helped to create it, and has done more than anyone else to defend the quality of research.

In his writing, Strunk has never been concerned to set down a sweeping panoramic view of a period or to elaborate a large general theory; his restraint makes his work seem bloodless to some of his colleagues. What he has consented to publish is generally the irrefutable establishment of a single fact or of a new method of classifying a given material, both the fact and the method being of seminal importance. But the importance is often left to the reader's intelligence to discover: it is perhaps the one serious limitation on Strunk's work that the less one knows about a subject, the less one can learn from one of Strunk's papers on it. He takes an aristocratic view of his profession.

The style of the essays, too, is extraordinarily concise.[1] The facts are presented with a dry elegance: Strunk is reluctant to draw from them any conclusions except the most brief and obvious ones, although many of the shortest essays have had far-reaching effects and opened up new fields of research. When there is anything beyond a simple statement of the facts, it is generally to call attention to those aspects of the research which are tentative, provisional, and limited. He does not—in print—so much speculate as block incautious conclusions. The pa-

---

1. Strunk's father was William Strunk, professor of English at Cornell, whose book *The Elements of Style* has been the only enjoyable guide (with the work of Fowler) to a normative English style for generations of college students.

pers are intended to be exemplary—and they are: almost unassailable results are presented with a minimum of provocation (even when they contradict established wisdom) and a maximum of reserve. Each essay appears as solid and self-contained; its radiation is invisible.

Strunk's approach, his discipline in more than one sense of that word, may be called "philological," for lack of a better term. "Philology" has been given vague and even contradictory meanings, but throughout the nineteenth century it generally meant the study of old texts and their humane critical interpretation in the light of the culture that produced them. The texts were documents of civilization, to be deciphered, purified of the corruptions of time and incompetent scribes, and interpreted by the historical understanding. In this sense archaeology, history, and literary criticism were necessary parts of philology. "Philologist" may also mean "student of language," to be distinguished from "linguist." The philogist is interested not in language in general but in its evidence of a culture that has disappeared. The philologist, unlike the antiquarian, treasures a sense of distance from the past: he does not wish to revive it or transform it for modern use, but to comprehend its continuity with the present.

To approach music in the spirit of philology, as Strunk has done, poses peculiarly difficult problems. Music history as a subject of research is in great part a product of the Romantic revival of the Middle Ages. Since we do not know very much about classical Greek music and almost none of it has come down to us, medieval music has taken the central place in music that classical studies traditionally held in the study of literature. But as in classical studies, one of the chief problems of music history—as distinct from music theory, ethnology, and criticism—has been that of deciphering a dead language, or decoding notations whose meanings we no longer understand. For a good deal of medieval and Renaissance music, we are not always sure about the pitches that were sung, and we are uncertain about the rhythms. Nor do we know enough about how the music was performed and with what instruments.

The humanistic side of musical philology has been as important as textual studies, and they have gone hand in hand. For example, merely to understand the medieval theorists who helped us to comprehend the composition and performance of Gregorian chant, we must enter into the conflicts between rival religious orders, which are reflected in their different aesthetic ideals.

Strunk's "philological" approach may be seen at its most impressive in a brief paper of 1939, less than six pages long, called "Some Motet-Types of the Sixteenth Century." (That useful work of reference, the *Harvard Dictionary of Music,* defines the motet as follows: "As a rule, a motet is an unaccompanied choral composition based on a Latin sacred text and designed to be performed in the Roman Catholic service.") The opening sentence of Strunk's essay has a characteristically modest precision: "This paper aims to take a systematic and comprehensive but necessarily superficial look at the motet of the 16th century with a view to defining the general character and extent of the relationship between liturgical situation and musical style."

It has long been recognized that the musical style of a particular piece of Gregorian chant depends less on its text than on its place in the church service, and Strunk asks whether one can find a similar relation for the polyphonic motets of the Renaissance which replaced the chants and were often based on them. During the sixteenth century, he observes, a leveling process took place, and distinctions between kinds of motets—and, consequently, correspondences between the style of a given motet and its liturgical function—become harder to discover. Strunk concentrates on motets written toward the middle of the century, above all those of Palestrina, and demonstrates that it is still possible to observe a typology connected with the place of the motet in the service, and that genuinely different musical styles continue to characterize varieties of motets classified according to their liturgical situation.

In his preface to these essays, Lewis Lockwood remarks about this study of motets that Strunk's

> way of looking at the motet literature inevitably stressed, yet without insisting upon it, the partial preservation of earlier modes of thought and practice within a particular branch of post-medieval music. The paper thus implicitly conveyed a sense of the historical continuity between two eras while yet maintaining a sense of their distance from one another. The result is not simply a means of classification that is heuristically valuable; the essay adds to this a quality of historical richness that gives insight into the musical thought of the period and gains in force from the perception that the musicians of the period themselves had a consciousness of the past that can yet be recaptured by historians.

This sense of the continuity of the past, conveyed through the critical examination and classification of documents, is the tradition of classical philology at its most effective. Lockwood observes further of this paper:

> It shapes a concept that could lead to the emergence of a whole field of research. I put that in the conditional since even now, thirty-five

years after the publication of the essay, its implications have yet to be taken up with care and insight by specialists in the subject.

Strunk's lead has not been followed because his approach has become uncongenial to most of us today. To some, the focus appears too narrow: Strunk brings a wide range of cultural as well as specifically musical experience to bear on what appears to be at first sight the solution of a minor problem. Still, the concentration on minor problems is surely as seductive in academic circles today as it has always been. What is unfashionable about Strunk's thought is its combination of intellectual rigor with a skeptical refusal to commit himself to a particular system. These qualities are closely related: the rigor is itself a manifestation of the skepticism.

If the rigor precludes an imaginative indulgence in the large, satisfying generalizations that sweeten the teaching of history, the lack of system is even more disconcerting. It appears unscientific. Musicologists today often apply very restrictive methods to the examination of the past. They are generally very seriously committed to one system or another—to the statistical (and sometimes computerized) analysis of stylistic characteristics, to Schenkerian theories of musical form, or to psychological theories of musical perception. Such commitments are often the principal buttress of a pretension to scientific method. Basic to many of the new programs of research is the attempt to develop methods that can always be successfully carried out, whatever the intelligence of the researcher. This inevitably produces a certain proportion of uninteresting work; but one must add that the old humanistic and more intuitive methods produced their quota of foolishness as well.

Strunk's use of any system of analysis is narrow but not restrictive; his attitude is best seen in the conclusion of the essay on motets:

> To deal effectively with any large body of evidence the historian must begin by putting it in order. In many instances, as in this one, several means of ordering will present themselves. Which one he begins with may in the end make very little difference; *before he has finished he will probably have to use them all.* In stating the case for this means [i.e., the ordering of the motets according to liturgical function] I do not question the value, indeed great value, of others. But I am persuaded that the use of this means, a means in keeping with the spirit and intention of the works themselves, is the logical first step and, in any event, an essential one.

The italics are mine, and they emphasize a radical view of historical analysis, camouflaged by the reasonable tone of the style. A means of ordering is a category of analysis, a system of understanding, and Strunk's sense that all means of ordering may be necessary implies a skepticism toward each one in isolation as well as a hospitable acceptance of different modes of thought.

Both the skepticism and the hospitality to new methods are shown with greater force in Strunk's use of statistical analysis in the essay "Relative Sonority as a Factor in Style-Critical Analysis," written as long ago as 1949, in what Strunk has called the Stone Age of computing. Starting from the observation of the general and gradual increase in the use of full sonority (of complete triads) in music from the fifteenth to the sixteenth centuries, Strunk asks whether the measurement of relative sonority (the frequency of the complete triad) can "yield trustworthy indications as to date, provenance, and authorship." He then gives tables of the frequencies for a number of works ranged chronologically from 1460 to 1559: the results bear out the gradual increase but show considerable variation even in works written close together in time. A further table compares the frequencies of three sections of a mass by Josquin, one of which has been generally considered an interpolation by a later composer: the section considered spurious does, indeed, reveal a significantly greater use of the full triad than the other two.
The statistical sample that Strunk uses is small, but the variations in it are significant enough to justify his conclusions:

> To attempt now to answer the several questions raised at the outset, it may be said, I think, that with works of unknown authorship, the measurement of "relative sonority" can be used only to confirm conclusions reached by other means. With works of questioned authorship, it can be used effectively to separate the spurious from the genuine, although even here it cannot be expected to be of much help when the actual author of the questioned work is, as often happens, a member of the supposed author's immediate circle. But with works of known authorship it should prove a useful and reasonably dependable means for establishing a rough chronological sequence.

These distinctions have an importance beyond the limited field of Renaissance music, and bear upon stylistic studies in general—including those in literature as well. It is generally conceded that the study of one isolated trait tends to be unreliable, except when used in conjunction with other knowledge, but it is rare that the value and limitation of a specific statistical study are defined with such precision.

It is, in addition, by no means certain that all of our stylistic perception can be quantified or even properly systematized. Much of it depends on an appreciation of what an artist will do when working with an element that is outside his usual norms—the setting of an unusual text, the choice of a theme unlike those he habitually employs. Without Strunk's understanding of the limitation of a given "means of ordering" the musical material, these aspects of music (and they are among the most significant) are likely to puzzle us unreasonably. Checking one element against another statistically may therefore not be of much use: on the contrary, we should expect that a work eccentric to its period or to its composer's style in one respect will be eccentric in many others as well. For this reason, we may not presume that more high-powered and sophisticated use of statistics and computers will invalidate Strunk's sober conclusions. In assessing statistics, we must be prepared (as Strunk remarks in this paper) to take into account the specifically musical problems of each individual work, as well as environmental and individual differences between composers.

The reserve in Strunk's use of new techniques is in accord with his austere view of the profession of music historian. The modesty of his presentation and the reasonableness of his approach arise from his refusal to take the short cuts, the one-sided views that both the dilettant and the fanatic require in equal measure. His tough reasonableness is seen at its most ironic and most affable in an intervention (not printed in this volume) during a symposium on instrumental music in 1957.[2] As in the paper on relative sonority, the subject was the stylistic character of a work of music, the "internal evidence" which enables us to date a work and attribute it to a composer.

The problem raised was the troublesome one of those dubious anonymous works attributed to a composer like Haydn because they resemble some of his music, or are found in a collection that contains some of his authenticated work, or because he has copied out a work for use in performances or study. H. C. Robbins Landon, one of the distinguished Haydn scholars of our time, cited a symphony that appeared stylistically to be clearly by Haydn at the beginning of his career, and that was discovered more or less by accident to be by a very minor figure like Carlos d'Ordoñez. Robbins Landon concluded that the internal evidence of the music itself was unreliable: what was needed in every case was external evidence—documents, manuscripts dated and signed, contemporary catalogues with the composers clearly identified. He called for the compilation of a giant locator catalogue of all the eighteenth-century works available in manuscript or printed sources in libraries, monasteries, publishers' lists, etc., that

2. *Instrumental Music*, edited by David G. Hughes (Harvard University Press, 1959), pp. 53–56.

would give the opening measures for each work and thereby facilitate the attribution of doubtful works. This would, of course, be an ideal system for identification by computers.

Strunk, whose work on Haydn was done mostly in the early 1930s when he was chief of the music division of the Library of Congress, emphasized at length the dangers of trusting to documents, that is, to external evidence alone, and remarked:

> The way in which Mr. Landon proposes to deal with these questioned works is, of course, the best one. There is nothing more satisfactory than to assign them to the man who actually wrote them: that ends the whole argument. But it is a very expensive way of doing it. It costs a lot of money; it costs a lot of time; and it costs a lot of effort. And, one wonders sometimes if the most spectacular results it achieves—as in the case of the "Jena" Symphony[3] —are really worth it. . . .
>
> A fine instance of what happens with external evidence was suggested to me the other day by Mr. Hertzmann: the Bach *Lukaspassion*. This is a work that is unquestionably in Bach's autograph. The watermarks are of no help, and the paper is absolutely correct: it is a Bach autograph from the 1730s. There is only one thing peculiar about the external evidence: it does not say on the title page that it is by Bach, and I gather from Mr. Mendel that this would be a rather unusual thing in a Bach autograph. The internal evidence, however, will not fit at all. Not only is it inconceivable that Bach could have written it in the 1730s, but it is also hard to believe that he could have written it at any time. . . .
>
> We have many other illustrations of this kind: almost every composer has written out in his own hand, on his own music paper, compositions by other people. Mr. Hertzmann told me just the other day of a curious case he had heard of recently in Italy: madrigals by Verdi—real Verdi autographs. It turns out, of course, that they are simply copies of madrigals by Palestrina. It seems that one has to use both methods, external and internal, without relying wholly on either one.

The overkill in stylistic studies has increased so much since 1957 that Strunk's final comment gains in force today:

---

3. Supposed by a few musicologists to be by Beethoven, but discovered to be the work of Friedrich Witt.

It is precisely when you are looking for something else that you find out the most interesting things. When you look for a needle in a haystack, perhaps you may turn it up by system, but often you find it simply by kicking the straws around.

It is not the drudgery to which Strunk objected; he had himself spent many years of painstaking work including the copying and transcribing of hundreds of manuscripts. What is at issue is the substitution of drudgery for reasoning—the combination of internal and external evidence and their interaction. As he commented:

Now it would seem to me that if the study of the internal evidence almost invariably leads us to the wrong conclusions, something is wrong with our methods. It puts us in the position of the man who says, "I smoke only Camel cigarettes," but who cannot tell a Camel from a Chesterfield unless he looks at the brand on the package.

Strunk emphasizes with considerable tact that the experts were largely not fooled by spurious works, and did not need to discover the name of the real composer to know that they were not by Beethoven or Haydn. I do not think Strunk was very much interested in the experts who were fooled, except in one special case for which he laid down an admirable rule:

The internal evidence is, I think, least valuable, when one tries to use it in the conventional stage of the development of a style, before real technical virtuosity and well-defined technical manners have developed. It is unreliable, too, when you work with the very beginning of a composer's career.

One might add that for a conventional stage[4] or for a very young composer with no style of his own who largely imitates many of his contemporaries it does not much matter if we get all the attributions right, which is perhaps why Strunk was unenthusiastic about the project of a gigantic locator catalogue. We ought to know much more than we do about the music of the 1750s, a period that still rests in the shadow of what comes before and after, but the attributions are not the most pressing matter: nothing much in the history of music—or of Haydn

---

4. I have my reservations about whether "conventional stage of development" is a happy expression for the late 1750s, which Strunk was discussing.

scholarship—would have been changed if it had turned out that Haydn *had*, after all, written that symphony by Ordoñez.

This is perhaps a hard saying for those music historians who think of their task almost entirely as the compilation of a composer's oeuvre in the exact chronological sequence, and for whom attribution is never to be taken lightly. The sense of what is susceptible of stylistic definition enables Strunk, in the one popular piece in his volume of essays, a brief account of Haydn, to start with the last decades of Haydn's life and only then to return to the earliest years in which Haydn's work, even when thoroughly individual, lacks the coherence of the later period.

Strunk's publications are clearly only a small part of his work and his influence. He has abandoned the results of his researches with reckless generosity to students and friends, not only by his suggestions, but by turning over extensive notes on a variety of subjects as well as transcriptions of medieval and Renaissance scores. He trained many of the most important musicologists now working in a great variety of fields: Lewis Lockwood (in the Renaissance and Beethoven), Joseph Kerman (in the Elizabethan madrigal and eighteenth- and nineteenth-century opera and chamber music), Don Randel and Leo Treitler (in medieval studies), and Kenneth Levy (in Byzantine chant), among many others. I was never really a student of Strunk's, although I knew him when I was at Princeton, but I once wrote several pages on the way Haydn's use of repeated notes in the upbeats of rondo themes enables him to create magnificent surprises in his finales, thinking this to be all my own idea. I have only remembered while writing this review that the basis for these pages came from a lecture of Strunk's heard many years ago.

PART TWO

The Eighteenth Century

CHAPTER THREE

Keyboard Music of Bach and Handel

This introduction to the keyboard music of Bach and Handel was intimately bound up with a recording project. The distinguished British pianist Denis Matthews wrote in the late 1960s to invite me to contribute a chapter to a Penguin book on keyboard music, and asked me to deal with twentieth-century music after Debussy exclusive of serialism and the avant-garde. I replied that it was the avant-garde music which concerned me the most; excluding it left me solely with Rachmaninov as an interesting figure as far as my own taste was concerned. I added—since Penguin was then mainly a British publisher—that no English piano music seemed interesting to me with the exception of Tippett, who had to be considered avant-garde.

Denis Matthews wrote back suggesting that I take the chapter on Bach and Handel instead. Since I was engaged at the time in recording for CBS all of the manual keyboard music that Bach composed during the last decade of his life, that coincided neatly with my interests. It is for this reason that the pages on Handel and Carl Philipp Emanuel Bach are much briefer than those on Johann Sebastian Bach. I have had great pleasure in reading the work of Handel and C. P. E. Bach at the piano, but have performed little of it in public. The chapter makes no pretensions to incorporate any original research, but I seized the opportunity to explain the difference between counterpoint on paper and for the ear, and to clarify the private nature of Bach's keyboard music and the consequences for his style.

B Y the early eighteenth century the *clavier*—the keyboard, in whatever form—had become the fundamental musical instrument and the center of musical life. It was a position which it held for perhaps two hundred years, only to lose it at the beginning of the present century. Its tyranny was never greater than during the High Baroque period, the age of Bach and Handel; in its role of continuo it bound together and directed the performance, not only of operas and concertos, but even of polyphonic voice motets. The great Renaissance composers had been trained as singers, but Handel, Bach, Scarlatti, and Couperin were all basically keyboard performers. In theory, eighteenth-century musical education was founded (as today's still is) on a codified and degenerate version of sixteenth-century vocal counterpoint; in practice, it consisted in the realization of figured bass and the playing of counterpoint on a keyboard. I do not mean to call in question the vocal origin—always latent and always capable of being recalled—of eighteenth-century counterpoint, but by 1700 the linear nature of vocal writing had been completely translated into instrumental terms. Even vocal ornaments had been transformed and returned to singers in an instrumental form less suited to the voice; Bach often treats his singers only as another instrument in an orchestra.

It is time to return to the old evaluation of Bach's keyboard music as the center of his work. The fashionable placing of the cantatas as Bach's principal achievement has only been harmful: it has led to an overemphasis on extra-musical symbolism, reinforced by Schweitzer's tendentious aesthetic, and to an unhappy view of Bach's musical imagination, which was fantastically rich and yet predominantly non-dramatic. Even when the emotion expressed is as terrifying and as powerful as in the opening chorus of the *St. Matthew Passion,* the procession to Golgotha, the means of portrayal are still essentially those of meditation, raised, certainly, to an intensity that music had never known before. Handel's simple and often brutal juxtaposition of masses, his use of the elements of music almost in block form, was rarely attempted by Bach, whose largest forms arise always from a concentration on the smallest details and the fullness of their expressive power. This conception of musical composition as a meditative art is particularly suited to keyboard style. Only a keyboard instrument affords at once the spontaneous intimacy of improvisation and the possibility of polyphonic texture. Both are essential to an art that derives its greatness from the latent expressive force of even the most commonplace and most ordinary musical detail, and it is in this way that Bach's art appears to be so personal even with the most impersonal material. To understand this art, we must remember that, although Bach was one of the most famous improvisers of his age, he could never begin a series of improvisations with one of his own themes—he had to start from the idea of another composer—and he disapproved of composition at the keyboard itself. Improvisation recollected in tranquillity was at the heart of his musical sensibility—free of the pressure of the occasions and circumstances for which the cantatas and some of the large chamber works were written. The keyboard music reveals with the greatest directness the movement of his thought.

A division of Bach's keyboard works into those with pedal and those without pedal is essentially an artificial one, for such a distinction would have had little significance for Bach himself. Within thirty years of his death, however, keyboard music had become exclusively manual; when Mozart called the organ "the king of instruments" he knew he was expressing an old-fashioned opinion, but Bach even had a set of pedals at home to be used with a clavichord. The *Well-Tempered Keyboard* contains one work—the A minor fugue of the first book—that, indeed, cannot be played as written without the use of a pedal keyboard. Much of Bach's music was not intended to be played on any specific keyboard instrument. The clavichord, harpsichord, organ and, at the end of his life, the pianoforte were all available to him, and we know that he used them all; many of the preludes and fugues of the *Well-Tempered* would go equally well on any one of them. Even the requirement of two keyboards does not automatically rule out the clavichord, as one could, and very often did, put one clavichord above another and play double-manual pieces on them. Essentially the clavichord was the inexpensive practice instrument for home use, while the harpsichord, far more costly even in its simplest form, was suitable for public, or semi-public, occasions. From its invention around 1720, the pianoforte was an answer to the problem already discussed at that time that the most refined nuances of tone, dynamics, and even phrasing that one had learned practicing at home on the clavichord were inaudible in public and useless on a harpsichord. (The organ, prohibitively expensive for the home except in the form of a small *positive*, inapt for the playing of most of Bach's works, was, in Germany at least, rarely used for the performance of secular music.)

It is for this reason that the old controversy about which instrument the six great trio sonatas, the C minor Passacaglia, and many other works were intended for is largely meaningless; it is not a question that could have been asked in the early eighteenth century. The trio sonatas, in particular, are essentially practice pieces, études, in short. They would have been studied on whatever instrument with a pair of keyboards and a set of pedals was handy—at home, it would most likely have been a clavichord. This does not rule out their performance on an organ when the occasion afforded one; that would be like forbidding a performance of a modern piano work on a nine-foot concert grand. The trio sonatas, like the Chopin studies, are not only finger exercises, but great music and great display pieces as well. But practicing on an organ was not as simple a matter in the eighteenth century, in pre-electric days when manpower as well as an organist was needed to produce a sound; furthermore, occasions for the public performance of secular, non-operatic music were rare at that time. The trio sonatas are not so clearly intended for use during a church service as the toccatas and fugues. It would be wrong, however, to conclude that the sonatas were written only for clavichord; there was, indeed, very little specific literature for the clavichord before Bach's death in 1750. This basic interchangeability of instrument for most keyboard music of the time must be accepted before we can begin to understand the relatively limited number of works intended for a specific instrument. It was not indifference to instrumental sound on the part of the composers that gave rise to this large repertory of keyboard music adaptable to any keyboard instrument of the time, but the impossibility of control over the conditions of performance. There were, of course, no recitals in any recognizable sense of the word; keyboard music was private.

This fundamental privacy is one source of the greatness of Bach's keyboard style; he was as essentially a private composer as Handel was a public one. The nature of this inwardness has been most often misconstrued; it is not an early nineteenth-century composer's expression of emotions too personal for completely public revelation (as in many of Schumann's and Brahms's works, which half display and half repress their sources), and even less is it the disdain and precious avoidance of public effect of some twentieth-century composers like Satie. Bach's meditative keyboard style is at once subjective and objective, and it arises from a triumphant and profound comprehension of the musical conditions of his age. Not only were most composers of the time keyboard performers, but almost every professional keyboard performer was, in the most literal sense, a composer. The teaching of music largely entailed the teaching of composition; not only the grammar of music—harmony and counterpoint—and the technique of ornamentation, reading figured bass, and improvisation, but the actual writing of music. Singers might escape the practice of composition, although even Handel's cook, who sang in his opera company, knew counterpoint;[1] and many string and wind players may not, perhaps, have used their knowledge. But there can have been very few keyboard players—even amateur players—who did not compose a few pieces. After 1720, almost all of Bach's keyboard music became didactic, or was arranged in pedagogic form; he even called most of his published works "Keyboard Exercises." They are, however, exercises to develop techniques not only of playing but also of composition, models of form that can stimulate, the works of a composer speaking to other composers.

That this was Bach's avowed intention is stated firmly in his own hand on the title-page of the Inventions, which proclaims that his purpose was only partially to provide "honest instruction" in playing music in two and three parts; it was also to teach "lovers of the keyboard . . . not only to have good intentions, but to develop them well, and . . . also to obtain a strong foretaste of composition." The *Well-Tempered Keyboard* is, in fact, the greatest pedagogic work in the history of keyboard technique; it has been a fundamental part of the education of practi-

---

1. There is no reason, as Tovey has pointed out, not to take Handel's joke ("My cook knows more counterpoint than Gluck") quite seriously.

cally every pianist since the death of Mozart. Even before it had been published, Beethoven made his reputation as a young boy by playing it. Yet it is as much or more a treasury of musical form, a textbook of composition, as a work of keyboard instruction, and in acknowledgment of this, Chopin began his own great set of studies, op. 10, with a bow to the *Well-Tempered Keyboard,* an imitation of the first Prelude in C major.[2]

This integral relationship between composition and "keyboard practice" (style and technique) makes Bach's keyboard music seem so personal and yet so objective. It is, indeed, written to act on the emotions, to move, even to dazzle; but it is not directed at an audience. It is the performer that the music is written for, and to him that the composer is speaking—the performer, who was at least half a composer himself at that time, a student of composition, or already a connoisseur. "For the young musician who wishes to learn and for the pleasure of those already skilled": the title of the *Well-Tempered Keyboard,* like the title-pages of all the published volumes of Bach's *Keyboard Practice,* asserts the ancient classical tie between the pleasure and the profit of art. "Keyboard Practice to Refresh the Spirit of Music-Lovers" was not an empty title. It cannot be sufficiently emphasized that the keyboard works are written above all for the pleasure of the performer. One small detail will show to what an extent this aspect of musical life changed within thirty years of Bach's death. When Mozart rediscovered the music of Bach and began enthusiastically to compose fugues himself, he said that fugues must always be played at a slow tempo, as otherwise the successive entrances of the theme would not be clearly heard. Nevertheless, it is remarkable how often Bach tries to hide the entrance by tying the opening to the last note of the previous phrase, how much ingenuity he has expended in avoiding articulation, in keeping all aspects of the flowing movement constant. Yet though many of the entrances in Bach's fugues are, in Mozart's terms, inaudible, there is one person—the performer—who is always aware of them. If in no other way, he can always sense them through his fingers. The physical (or, better, muscular) pleasure in playing Bach is equal to that found in any other composer, and it is closely related to the purely musical qualities of the work by the sense of a genuinely tactile tracing of a musical line.

The very reproach often leveled at the keyboard—its blending, even confusion, of separate contrapuntal lines—made it the ideal medium for Bach's art. This inability of the instruments to make in practice the clear-cut distinctions that were made in theory embodied the tendency toward a completely unified texture and the powerful vertical harmonic force that characterized so much of the music of the early eighteenth century; it is, in fact, the equivalent of figured

---

2. "Practice Bach for me" was Chopin's way of writing "Yours sincerely" in his letters to pupils.

bass. Bach's career has often been presented as a reactionary one, an attempt to retain the old contrapuntal values that were going out of fashion. It was more than that; it was a reconciliation of the most advanced and most modern harmonic experiments with the traditional linear structure. What held these forces together was his profound development of the main principle of animation of Baroque music, the use of generic motive from which everything flows and takes its shape. No composer carried this farther than Bach; even the large harmonic sequences so typical of the period appear in his music to arise solely from the single motive which characterizes each individual work. It is this that makes the music seem like a kind of improvisation; indeed, the trick of improvisation is to start with a few notes and to draw an entire piece of music from them.[3] Bach is the first major composer in history whose art is so closely allied to improvisation, and only a keyboard instrument allows for a complex improvisation controlled by one mind. No work gives a performer the illusion of improvising—of himself as composer—so strongly as a work of Bach, and perhaps this is why his music has given rise to so much gratuitous rewriting by editors.

Once the intimate setting of this art is accepted, many of the problems of playing it either disappear, or are seen in a new light. Most of Bach's keyboard work was written to be played for oneself or for a few other musicians; some of it was written almost as much for meditation as for listening. Many of the more complex details can be appreciated fully only by the performer—they can be heard, but their significance can never be entirely grasped until one has felt them under one's fingers. This implies that much of the calculation of dramatic effect necessary for public performance was never intended for the greater part of Bach's keyboard music—except in the large organ works, it tends to be felt as an excrescence, an intrusion of the performer. Even the shaping of structure and its elucidation are not crucial in private, and performances of a Bach fugue in which the theme is consistently emphasized to the detriment of the other voices can only be a travesty of a work whose chief glory lies in the relation of the voices to each other and in their interaction; it must, however, be granted that it is exactly this sort of relation that is much easier for the performer to hear (since he knows it is there) than for the listener.

The much-debated problem of added ornamentation loses a great deal of its importance when the nature of music written above all to be played for oneself is considered. The public genres of eighteenth-century music, like the Handel operas, are skeletons that need to be fleshed by improvised ornament; the condi-

---

3. The forms and the textures of the early eighteenth century altogether are closer to improvisation than those of any other time in Western music before jazz; in spite of Mozart's and Beethoven's fame as improvisators their "planned" forms differ radically from their "improvised" ones, as we can see from written cadenzas and from their fantasias.

tions of public performance, indeed, demanded a continuously varying and ever more elaborate ornamentation. But very little of this applies to Bach, principally because when he grew older, as we can easily see from the successive versions of his works, he tended to write out the ornaments in a fairly complete form—it was a contemporary complaint that he left nothing to the performer.[4] The later works, too, are so conceived as to make ornamentation superfluous; while it is possible to ornament the repeats of the dances in the early suites, it is far more difficult to find a varied ornamentation for the repeats in the Goldberg Variations that would not seem intrusive, so much do the original ornaments seem an indissoluble part of the conception of the melodic arcs. With *The Musical Offering* and *The Art of the Fugue,* the question of ornamentation has, in most cases, become irrelevant.

Bach was not the first composer to write out the ornaments in full—there were precedents for this, cited by his defenders in answer to the attacks during his lifetime. This full notation springs, in part, from the nature of Bach's music: its display of art, its classic combination of instruction with pleasure. But it is also related to Bach's situation as *Kapellmeister* of a provincial town. Leipzig, the most important of the cities in which he was employed, had not even the prestige of the musical culture of Dresden. Handel, on the other hand, was accustomed in London to performances by international virtuosi; his singers would have been outraged by any attempt to prescribe too closely their style of performance and the ornaments they employed. We must not, however, assume that only the notation of Bach's music is the result of his reliance upon provincial musicians, and that we can perform it today with quite the same freedom as Handel's; the essence of the music itself lies in that fuller notation. If improvised ornament received such a definitive form under his hands, we can only be thankful for his failure to obtain a more illustrious post. A great part of what we know about early eighteenth-century performance comes, indeed, from Bach's fully notated scores.

We do not know exactly how many of the later works of Bach were begun earlier, and only revised, arranged, and collected later; many of them exist in several versions, and we have certainly lost a great many of the early manuscripts. Even the theme of the Goldberg Variations, published in 1742, was written by 1725 at the latest; it would be impossible to prove that none of the variations was written many years before publication. What is certain is that the last thirty years of

---

4. "Every ornament, every little grace, and everything that one thinks of as belonging to the method of playing, he expresses completely in notes." Scheibe, 1737 (in *The Bach Reader*, ed. Arthur Mendel and Hans T. David [W. W. Norton, 1966], p. 238).

Bach's life were spent in ordering his entire musical output, collecting old works and putting them together with newly written ones to fill out the monumental schemes that he had drafted. He revised old cantata movements and set them side by side with new compositions to form a Mass, and he rearranged a series of chorale preludes as a complete Mass as well. In these schemes no distinction was made between old and new works; some of the pieces in the second book of the *Well-Tempered Keyboard,* collected in 1744, were almost certainly written before many of those from the first book, dated 1722. An attempt to trace a strict chronological development of Bach's keyboard works would be highly problematical at best, and the results more than doubtful. It would not justify upsetting Bach's own order.

Bach's great systematic arrangements have a musical value in themselves, in spite of the fact that the ordering has, in general, very little to do with performance of the music; even the Mass in B Minor may have been as little intended for performance at one sitting as the Organ Mass (or Part III of the *Keyboard Practice*), for which "anthology" would be the closest description. Not that Bach was incapable of the creation of an organic work of massive dimensions, as the great *Passion according to St. Matthew* can testify, but neither the B Minor Mass nor the *Well-Tempered Keyboard* are such works. In one sense, "anthology" does not do justice to the full significance of the ordering, which indeed transcends the individual parts. How little this significance has to do with actual performance, however, can be seen from the original edition of the Organ Mass, framed by the E flat Prelude at one end and the fugue (the *St. Anne*) at the other; the fact that these two pieces belong together in performance gives meaning to the device of printing them so far apart with the Mass between them. Of course, performance—private, not public—was not out of the realm of possibility for many of Bach's great collections; he himself was known to have played through the entire *Well-Tempered Keyboard* for a pupil. It would, however, be an absurd distortion of the work to claim that it was principally intended for such a unified performance, although it exists as a unity even if it takes one year to play through it, and draws part of its meaning from that unity.

We must beware of calling such orderings intellectual or even theoretical; the existence of musical significance which transcends the immediate audible experience is essential to Bach's style. I do not imply anything mystical, or anything that is beyond our ordinary experience of music; only that some of the most important forces in the development—the actual movement through time—of a work of Bach are latent in its material without becoming audible until the moment that he chooses to make them so. The forces shaping the movement of a work by Beethoven or Mozart are far more immediately audible. The dissonance in the seventh bar of the *Eroica* audibly implies the modulation to F major that

Example 3.1

Beethoven only makes when he repeats the passage hundreds of bars later; the movement to G flat major in the slow movement of Mozart's G minor Symphony begins in the second bar. The material of the great classical composers is directional—we can hear the opening of the *Eroica* moving towards something, even if we cannot name it, and its arrival, presented as a surprise, is also a logical satisfying of a dynamic tonal impulse, the resolution of a tension.[5] But if what is to happen in a work of Mozart and Beethoven is already to some extent audible in its opening, there is absolutely nothing about the theme of the Fugue in B flat minor from the *Well-Tempered,* Book II (Ex. 3.1) that allows us to *hear* that it can be played in stretto at the ninth at the distance of one beat. Yet this quality of the theme, together with the even more complicated possibility of playing it in stretto with its own inversion in double counterpoint at the tenth, is essential to the shape of this fugue. All this is latent in the theme, but not audibly active when we hear it. Static as this kind of structure essentially is, the stretto has an impressive and exciting musical effect comparable to the most dynamic structures of the later classical period. In this comprehension of these latent musical relationships, in his ability to draw from them all their power and significance, Bach was without equal in the history of music. The great collective structures— his arrangement of a considerable part of his life's work into formal musical patterns—are the large-scale equivalent of these latent relationships.

Many early works were, however, left uncollected, perhaps many more than have come down to us. One of the earliest, written when Bach was nineteen, is the *Capriccio on the departure of a beloved brother,* one of the freshest and most delightful works by a young composer. Although there are a few moments of awkwardness, it has a naïve, spontaneous humor that appears only rarely in Bach's later work; with its picturesque qualities, its tone pictures, its gaiety, it is the work of a young talent that could have developed a much more popular manner. Another beautiful work is the so-called Fantasy in C minor, which is really a movement in early "sonata form" (i.e., with the tonal structure and thematic pattern of a dance movement, but with a more dramatically expressive character): this short

---

5. This is not mere hindsight: it is only harder to appreciate tonal relations after a century of chromaticism and a half-century of atonality and blurred tonality.

but powerful work was to be the prelude to a fugue, which remains in fragmentary form (was it really never finished, or is the only manuscript that has come down to us an incomplete fair copy?) The unfinished fugue has some of Bach's most daring harmonic progressions. In addition to these better-known works, there are a number of early toccatas, most of them vigorous, splendidly imaginative and prolix. A little-played but concise and impressive work is the Fantasy and Fugue in A minor (BWV 904); the massive sonorities of the opening and the long melodic line of the fugue are as suited to the organ as to the harpsichord.

The most important, and the most astounding, of these isolated works is the famous *Chromatic Fantasy and Fugue*. As Forkel, the first biographer of Bach, wrote, the "fantasia is unique, and never had its like." In spite of its size and the passion that fills it, it may have been written specifically for the clavichord, perhaps the only work of Bach intended for the clavichord alone. In some ways it is the most advanced of Bach's keyboard works, the closest in style to the expressive clavichord pieces of the 1760s and 1770s, the ancestor of the passionate, mannered, and fantastic improvisation of Philipp Emanuel Bach. The expressive recitatives are particularly effective on the clavichord with its capacity to reproduce vocal nuances; the final burst of octaves at the end of the fugue is the only example of such an effect in Bach, and suggests a keyboard instrument where no doubling was possible.[6] The fugue, however, has the spacious structure and the public brilliance of the great organ fugues and is as inexorable in its movement as the fantasy is varied.

Some of the collective works were published by Bach himself, but there would be little point in considering them as in any way distinct from the unpublished sets. The engraving of Bach's music was not a profitable venture; many works may have come into being in the hope of publication, and were then left expediently in manuscript. In any case, wide circulation in manuscript was very common throughout the eighteenth century, for literature as well as music. There are more eighteenth-century manuscript copies of the *Well-Tempered Keyboard* still in existence today than there ever were sold first-edition copies of *The Art of the Fugue*, and there were certainly hundreds more that have been lost; it was a famous work long before its first printing in 1801.

Pupils who came to study with Bach were started on the two-and three-part Inventions (or Sinfonias, as he himself called the latter). They are, indeed, the most deliberately instructive of all his works. They were arranged by the composer in different orders, the most interesting being the original one: first, all the tonalities that have tonic chords with only white keys, in ascending sequence

---

6. This, however, is not conclusive evidence that only a clavichord was intended. Scarlatti's works are full of octaves, and there is no doubt that they are for harpsichord.

(C major, D minor, E minor, F major, G major, A minor); and then, in descending order, the other tonalities easily playable by a young musician (B minor, B flat major, A major, G minor, F minor, E major, E flat major, D major, C minor). In this way, the problems of fingering would go from the easy to the more complex.[7]

The Inventions appear for the first time in the little book for Wilhelm Friedemann, Bach's eldest son, and this is the only manuscript of Bach to give us some of his indications of fingering (although in other pieces than the Inventions). Bach has, indeed, been given the main credit for modern keyboard fingering, a claim that goes too far, for others had used the crossing-under of the thumb before him, and the examples we have of his fingering are not as advanced as some (his son, Philipp Emanuel, in particular) would like to have us believe. These fingerings were written down when Bach was over thirty-five years old, an age after which he is not likely to have changed his technique.

With all their clearly technical purpose, no other finger exercises in musical history—not even the Chopin Studies—have the unaffected grace and sweetness of the Inventions. Only a gentle gravity betrays their didactic intention. They were explicitly written to foster not a virtuoso technique, but a singing style of playing. The ornamented versions of several of them were written later; there is no reason to doubt that the ornaments were added according to the capacity of the student, and it is by no means certain that an unornamented performance would not have been completely acceptable. It must be remembered, too, that the art of improvising ornament was an essential part of musical education.

Throughout, the two- and three-part writing theoretically remains absolutely pure: there are never more than two (or in the Sinfonias, three) notes played or held at the same time. But this apparent purity is in fact doubly corrupt (both through the larger harmonic movement, and the inner implications of each voice), and the corruption is the source of the rich power of these works. The two and three voices are not genuinely independent, and they rarely imply less than four-part counterpoint. The way the theoretical independence is offset by the imposition of what may be called an anti-polyphonic conception of musical form can be seen in a passage from the E major Sinfonia (Ex. 3.2) where the melodic line appears—but in *notation* only—to cross from voice to voice, starting in the treble and going to the bass. In reality, it is heard as a completely integral line; it moves from one voice to another only when it touches the notes of the main harmony, and these notes are then successively held down, so that the melodic line acts to provide its own figured bass. In short, this is not true three-part

---

7. Chopin's belief that F sharp major is the easiest of the scales and that one should start with it is an exceptional view, although a wise one, and based on more modern ideals of virtuosity.

Example 3.2

Example 3.3

writing, but a melodic outline accompanied by three- and four-part harmony. The retention of theoretical purity, however, is not just a display of ingenuity, but an inner contradiction; the interplay between these forces informs every measure of these works.

The richness of harmony comes from Bach's ability to imply two and even three voices with only one. In the history of music only Mozart has equaled him in the art of using a single vocal line to trace the fullest harmonic sonorities. Bach's mastery can be seen in the briefest quotation (Ex. 3.3). Here, the upper voice is really three voices, and the A sharp in the right hand is not continued until several notes later; it lingers in our ears after it has stopped sounding because it is an unresolved dissonance. It is, in fact, dissonant to its own next note, for a single line of Bach provides its own tensions and resolutions. This is the technique that makes the solo violin sonatas such convincing works. It has often been noticed that Bach's fugue themes provide their own bass, and they very often provide perfectly worked-out inner voices as well. That is why they are so expressive and so complete in themselves.

In other words, the individual voices work within a larger system of harmonic movement which transcends their integrity; and, in addition, this integrity is broken down from within by the same system. Yet the ideal of contrapuntal purity in the Inventions (and in other works, like the Goldberg Variations and *The Art of the Fugue*) does not thereby lose in power. It gains instead a pathos—an unattainable goal that is kept alive by the pretense of achieving it. Bach's career was an unavailing protest against the powerful harmonic forces represented in Rameau's new theory, forces of which he was himself such a master. In the Inventions, we are carried along by the surge of these forces with a movement that is consistent and unified: almost in direct opposition, the thin, pure integrity of the individual lines is eloquently sustained as if against heroic odds.

The *Well-Tempered Keyboard* is a monument to the ambiguity of tonal relations. It is not only the fact that all twenty-four major and minor keys are each represented here by a prelude and fugue that makes equal temperament indispensable; even if every piece were transposed into C major and C minor, they would still not be possible in just intonation. There is no space here to discuss just how equal Bach's system of tuning a keyboard really was, for this is a complex and perilous subject. But there is no doubt that he demanded enough equality in all his works—keyboard works or any others—for the ear to confuse E natural and F flat, for example, for the most far-reaching enharmonic effects to be possible. Tonal harmony is, of course, partly based on the natural physical series of overtones, and partly developed independently as a symbolic language. Bach's harmony is, in one sense, not only unnatural but anti-natural; it insists on confounding what nature has kept separate, and in so doing, incomparably enriches the expressive range of music. The great advance in musical style is not the possibility of playing in any key, but the possibility of passing rapidly from one to another—above all, the possibility of blending flat and sharp modulations (i.e., modulations at the limit of the subdominant and dominant directions).

Experiments with equal temperament date back at least to the sixteenth century, and many Renaissance pieces assume a certain amount of equality in order to be sung or played at all intelligibly. Nor is the *Well-Tempered Keyboard* the first collective work to exploit equal temperament; there were already precedents before 1720. But Bach's music is the first to make consistent and continuous use of the complete range of expressive modulation that comes from the falsification of just intonation. The *Well-Tempered Keyboard* is the celebration of this newfound "unnatural" power.

The encyclopedic nature of the work is not just a consequence of its didactic purpose, but a demonstration of the freedom that comes from equal temperament. The first book was compiled in 1722 from works, uneven enough in style (although not in mastery) to imply that they were written over a period of many years. There are fugues as concentrated and subtle as the C sharp minor, coarse and dramatic as the A minor, abstract and enchanting as the A major, lyric and loosely organized as the D sharp minor. The range of the preludes is certainly as great, from the pure improvisation of the first in C major and the rambling grandeur of the E flat major, to the profound Sarabande in E flat minor, and the delicate charm of the F sharp major. Both preludes and fugues are essentially "character pieces"; vivacity of sentiment is their reason for existing.

The *Well-Tempered Keyboard* is so familiar to us today that it is difficult to realize how it opened up the entire field of tonal musical expression. Indeed, Bach's contemporaries and immediate successors did not fully comprehend this in spite of the innumerable copies of the work that circulated, and of its fame and importance for keyboard style and teaching. Music took a different turn, toward the rendering not of sentiment, but of dramatic action. Only by the late 1770s, when both Mozart and Haydn were trying to recapture the lost riches of the polyphonic style, was the importance of the *Well-Tempered Keyboard* finally understood; not only did Mozart study the work, he even arranged several of the fugues for string trio and string quartet—music was at last becoming more public, and the intimacy of these pieces was not considered a hindrance to concerted performance. By the early nineteenth century, they had become part of the foundation of the first Romantic generation's style, as important for the music of Chopin as for Schumann and Mendelssohn.

The second book of the *Well-Tempered* was compiled twenty years later, and differs only in being generally a little more sober, more inward, less ostentatious and, perhaps, less various as a whole. It is equally glorious: the great Ricercar in B flat minor, the double counterpoint at the tenth and twelfth of the Fugue in G minor, the rich chromaticism of the Fugue in A flat major may have peers but no superiors. There is little point in singling out individual pieces from collections where each one gains so much from its presence in the larger framework. I should not wish, however, to endorse the theory that the order of the preludes and fugues was set with an eye to performance; beyond the calculated improvisatory simplicity of the first two preludes of Book I, the place of any work in the ordering does not seem to me to have in any way determined its character. The order is not a temporal one—the twenty-fourth prelude and fugue do not really come *after* the first one—but a simultaneous radiation from a central idea. The order not only transcends performance, but has nothing to do with it—all of which, however, does not take away from the magnificent effectiveness for performance of each individual piece.

The first works that Bach chose for publication were the harpsichord Partitas, one of three sets of six dance suites for keyboard that he put together at some time during the 1720s. The other two sets are the English Suites and the French

Suites; it would be unprofitable to ask which came first—claims of precedence have been advanced for both, and some of the Partitas, as well, must be dated years before their publication. The English Suites, so called, it seems, because they were written for an English nobleman, are no less French than the French Suites—more so, in fact, as their courantes have the characteristic 6/4 against 3/2 opposition of the French form (a cross-pulse rather than a cross-rhythm), while the courantes of the French Suites are in the smooth running Italian style. The French Suites are, in general, less elaborate, beginning directly with the allemande without any introductory piece; they are also easier and less brilliant. We know that Bach used the suites for teaching: students were given them when they had mastered the Inventions, probably beginning with the French and going on to the English. The six Partitas exhibit the greatest variety of organization and of style.

The suite is the most useful and most characteristic form of court music. Did Bach choose a set of six for his first publication in order to further his attempts to exchange his post at the Leipzig Church of St. Thomas for a court appointment such as he had had previously at Cöthen, where he spent the most fruitful years of his life? The dance suite is the closest the High Baroque came to public, secular music for a solo keyboard; although keyboard recitals, of course, did not yet exist, the popular dance-forms permitted the suite to bridge the gap between private, learned music and the larger concerted forms, and they were indispensable at semi-private musical occasions. Bach's suites turn, in fact, both ways: they are often as fully and as richly worked out polyphonically as the fugues of the *Well-Tempered,* and they attain easily the variety and even the orchestral effects of the concerto grosso.

The basic outline of the suite was a simple succession of dances to which, as suited the additive sensibility of the Baroque composer, other dances could be attached or inserted. The fundamental skeleton was allemande, courante, sarabande, minuet, and gigue. A gavotte or a bourrée could be inserted, generally after the minuet; a great variety of other dances or dancelike movements were possible: passepieds, badineries, rondos, airs, etc.; and variations (or doubles) of the dances could be added. The basic order has something of the slow-fast-slow-fast arrangement of the baroque four-movement sonata. It is out of this very loose form that the later eighteenth-century sonata develops, more influenced by the articulated dance forms than by the more fluid movements of many of the sonatas of the first half of the century.

The allemande and the courante generally belong together, often beginning with the same melodic pattern.[8] The allemande is always a smooth, evenly flow-

8. Sometimes whole suites were unified in this way, but it was not a practice of Bach.

ing piece—the French style of performance, with its tendency to add a lilting ir- regularity of rhythm, was expressly forbidden by Couperin in his allemandes, and this dance has always the air of a quiet prelude. The French courante with its elaborate rhythmic oppositions and its texture could be replaced by its Italian namesake, with a brilliant, rapid, and even motion. The sarabande was generally the expressive center of the work, and the minuet has the place that it retained in the late eighteenth- and nineteenth-century quartet and symphony. The forms of all these dances are, almost without exception, that of early "sonata form" in two sections, each repeated, the first going from the tonic to the dominant, and the second from the dominant back to the tonic. The pattern of the second part is largely symmetrical to the first, although it is most often somewhat more elab- orate, with the melodic fragmentation and the rapid, sequential half-modula- tions of a development section combined with the repetition of the pattern, gen- erally before the return to the tonic. Speaking with historical hindsight, the dance forms were the most modern and the most progressive of the time.

In most respects, Bach's treatment of these forms was the reverse of progres- sive. He consistently avoided the articulation of phrasing that Scarlatti used so brilliantly, and that was to become so fundamental in the style of the second half of the century. There is, indeed, periodic and symmetrical phrasing in Bach, but it is generally hidden under the overlapping and continuous rhythmic flow. The articulation of form is also minimal; while the move to the dominant is often marked by new melodic patterns, and even by a subtle increase of motion, the return to the tonic is never a dramatic effect, rarely set off from what precedes it, but is rather a gradual drift as part of a seamless structure. The last quarter of each dance is often not the resolution that the later classical style was to find so indispensable, but the occasion for some of Bach's most poignant harmonic ef- fects. The symmetry of the two halves is also High Baroque, with inversion play- ing an important role, although here Bach often begins to work out something like the later classical form, using the inversion of the theme as a development, and reintroducing the original form with the return to the tonic—in this respect he even outpaces Scarlatti in his anticipation of later developments.

In general, however, the articulation of phrase and structure natural to the dance which, emphasized and dramatized, led to the great achievements of the late eighteenth century, was a facet of the suite that Bach was chiefly concerned to minimize in his wish for a unified and always expressive ebb and flow that is rarely allowed to disturb the continuity of movement. The climactic tensions do not often rise much above the general, compared with the dramatic strokes in the minuet of a Haydn or a Mozart symphony, but the constant intensity in the piece as a whole is much greater. Only after his mastery of part of Bach's contrapuntal technique did Mozart occasionally attempt and achieve this consistently high level of intensity throughout a work.

Bach's most original contribution to the keyboard suite was his development of the opening movement; five of the six Partitas, and five of the six English Suites, have massive and brilliant first movements. Many of them transfer to the single keyboard not only the grandeur but the specific effects of contemporary orchestral style. A passage (Ex. 3.4) from the splendid opening movement of the English Suite in G minor shows how a Baroque composer could achieve a crescendo before the Mannheim orchestra had trained themselves for their famous effect. To use the two keyboards of a harpsichord when playing a piece like this is to ruin Bach's conception, which is not "terraced dynamics" at all; the contrast between solo and tutti sections is built into the writing, when it is played simply on one keyboard, by the simple thickening of sound. Pianists frequently make similar nonsense when they equalize all the dynamics and forget that on a harpsichord four notes are louder than two, and that Bach was relying on this to make a point.

The typical Baroque sonority, in any case, is not "terraced dynamics," as is so often thought; except in the concerto grosso, a contrast of loud and soft is the exception rather than the rule, a luxury rather than a necessity. The most common dynamic system at that time is a consistent level with the small but subtle range of nuances that both the clavichord and the harpsichord (used with unchang-

Example 3.4

ing registration) were capable of. Registration stops were changed manually in Bach's time (except, perhaps, for a few harpsichords in England which introduced pedals for that purpose). An assistant to pull the stops, used for the more elaborate organ toccatas and preludes, would have been ridiculous for playing a suite of dances. The range of stops available on even the most expensive harpsichords was small; the sixteen-foot was not widespread until Bach's death. I do not imply that the style of music followed the nature of the instrument: quite the reverse. It is a change in style that forces the invention of new instruments. Not only are all of Bach's orchestral effects ideal in most of these opening movements with the relatively unified sonority of one keyboard of a harpsichord; they are also only distorted by the gratuitous addition of a second dynamic system.[9]

These grand openings—the Sinfonia of the C minor Partita, the Overture in French style of the D major Partita, the concerto forms of many of the English Suites—completely transform the keyboard suite. Before Bach, suites were often anthologies, grouped by key, from which one could play as few or as many dances as one liked. Bach may have treated his own in that way—the A major English Suite has two courantes, the second of which has two doubles; a selection may have been intended here. In any case, some of his suites were written by accretion, and earlier versions have fewer movements. But the new, massive introductions of these works announce a new conception of unity, answered by the complementary development of the finale. The gigues take on a completely novel brilliance and weight, and are often fugues as rich and serious as any that Bach wrote. Some of these virtuoso gigues are also harmonically among his most daring essays, with dissonances that reach anything else his century attempted, and they have a rhythmic fury that is almost unique in his work.

How exceptional "terraced dynamics" were is shown in Bach's second publication, Volume II of *Keyboard Practice,* devoted only to works for double keyboard, the French Overture and the Italian Concerto—both open imitations of orchestral style. Separated by this requirement from the six Partitas (Volume I of *Keyboard Practice*), they were intended to form a group with them, as Bach transposed the original version of the French Overture from C minor to the less convenient B minor so that the eight works of the two volumes should cover all the keys of A, B, C, D, E, F, G, and H.[10] Even with the most courtly of his works, the encyclopedic purpose was not absent. In addition to the basic tonalities, he also covers the opposing national styles of the eighteenth century. These eight

9. However, one copy of the A major English Suite suggests the use of two manuals in that work.

10. B in German is B flat, and H is B. (The transposition to B is less practical on the harpsichord than C, as the lowest note on the instrument is a G. This puts the low dominant of B, i.e., F sharp, out of reach.)

works are, like almost all of Bach's keyboard music, intended as exemplars. The extraordinary variety of forms in the Partitas was as much for instruction as amusement—not that the two were very different for Bach.

In the works of Volume II, a double-keyboard harpsichord is used for a contrast between solo and tutti sections in concerto style, for echo effects in the French Overture, and for imitating the sound of a solo line over accompanying instruments in the Italian Concerto. Bach's command of the ornamental grandeur of the orchestral French style did not always require two manuals: the opening of the D major Partita is also in French style, and needs only one manual. And it is amusing to note that the echoes at the end of the French Overture are not naturalistic, but decorated echoes. The two keyboards are here an essential part of the decorative conception of the work. With the Italian Concerto Bach not only recreated a convincing opposition of solo and tutti, in concerto grosso form, but surpassed all his Italian models. All the Vivaldi concertos he had arranged for keyboard in his youth had taught him style, but no Italian contemporary was capable of the combination of unity and imaginative vigor, of consistency and variety displayed by the outer movements, and, above all, of the immensely long sustained arabesque of the slow movement, one of the most profound creations of the century.

The concerto grosso form of the central fugue of the French Overture and of the outer movements of the Italian Concerto—the alternation of a short orchestral tutti with solo episodes derived from it—is the natural form of the High Baroque. The contrast between ensemble and solo sections was never intended to be an emphatic one; it was an art that developed its effects cumulatively, with a slight and continuous rise and fall of intensity, rather than one with a clear dramatic outline. This alternation of ensemble and solo sections is also the shape of most chorale preludes, which move between the *cantus firmus* and derived or contrasted episodes. Even Bach's fugues fall into this form: it is reported that he insisted on the need to embellish a fugue with episodes, and the alternation of these episodes with the entrances of the themes is his most characteristic form, closely related in shape to the concerto grosso.

The polarity of the Italian and French styles is at the heart of Bach's work; as a German, he was in the enviable position of being able to balance their claims equitably. The difference between Italian and French styles is chiefly rhythmic. Italian rhythm looks outward: it falls into simple, even groups, which are then contained in larger units. The Italian Concerto opens immediately with two absolutely clear four-bar phrases; the periodic grouping by phrases imposes a broader pulse on the basic one, and a larger-scale dramatic movement is possible within this framework. French rhythm looks inward: it subdivides, and there is a consequently heavy use of syncopation, reinforced by lavish ornament. French style is, therefore, relatively static compared to the more vigorous Italian manner, which, indeed, carried the seeds of the future within it. Bach is the only composer who represents a genuine synthesis of both national styles (apart from religious music, the German tradition had very little strength at that time). Even the other great German, Handel, while his mastery of the French tradition was undeniable, relied principally upon Italian forms. Bach was able to combine the expressive ornamental weight and grace of French style with the sustained line and dynamic rhythm of Italian music; except for the operatic field, where Handel and Rameau were supreme, and the still infant proto-classical "sonata" style, Bach summed up the entire musical life of his time. The French Overture and the Italian Concerto are a declaration that he assumed the role consciously. Bach's aesthetic was an exhaustive one, as if he were driven in all that he did to cover everything, to work out all the possibilities: all the tonalities, all the genres, all the styles, all the permutations. His daemon is a key to the magnitude of his achievement, as well as to its form. The great cycles are not only an ordering of his life's work but of his era as well.

The third volume of *Keyboard Practice* came out in 1739 and contained largely organ music: chorale preludes based on the words of the Mass. But it also contained the Four Duets, examples of pure two-part writing which, in daring and sophistication, surpass the Inventions. Nothing can better emphasize Bach's consideration of all his keyboard music, with and without pedals, as a unity than their publication here.

In the last ten years of his life, Bach's style became intensely concentrated; the great collective works now developed from a tiny kernel, each one drawn from only a single theme. He wrote four variation sets for keyboard: the Goldberg Variations for harpsichord with two keyboards; *The Art of the Fugue* for single keyboard (except for one fugue for two keyboards, four hands); the Chorale Variations on *Vom Himmel Hoch* for organ with two keyboards and pedals; and *The Musical Offering*, in which the two ricercars are for single keyboard without pedals. These four sets are at once the most personal and the most generalized of Bach's works, models of contrapuntal ingenuity and composition that still speak to anyone who plays them with an intimacy and an expressive directness that have no parallel elsewhere in the eighteenth century.

The elegance of the Goldberg Variations is its glory: it is the most worldly of Bach's achievements, with the Italian Concerto. The theme dates back to a little practice-book that Bach compiled for his second wife many years before, a sarabande, richly ornamental and deeply expressive. The thirty variations are on the bass of the theme, and they come in triads: one brilliant variation for crossing hands, one canon (starting with a canon at the unison, and going through all the intervals until the ninth) and a "free" variation—a siciliana, a fugue, a French overture, or an accompanied solo. The final variation, in place of the expected canon, has a quodlibet: two comic songs combined over the bass of the theme. At the end, the sarabande is repeated. The two central canons, at the fourth and the fifth, are each inverted canons; the last canon, at the ninth, provides its own bass, and does not need a third voice. The variety of mood, rhythm, style, and sonority is dazzling.

If Goldberg's birth certificate is read correctly as 1727, he must have been fourteen years old when, as one of Bach's pupils, this greatest of all Baroque virtuoso works was written for him to play for his patron, Count Kaiserling. Essentially a creation of the comic spirit, it also contains some of the most moving passages that Bach ever wrote. A survey of most of the forms of secular music of Bach's time, an encyclopedia like most of Bach's published works, it represents the art of ornamentation at the highest point it ever reached. Baroque variation is above all the art of ornamentation, and here everything is written out, every grace made manifest.

Even if the variations were intended to be treated only as an anthology, even if Bach's age would have offered no public, and few semi-public, occasions for playing the compositions as a whole, no large keyboard work of comparable size before Beethoven achieves such unity in the modern sense. The minor variations are strategically placed to vary the harmony. A massive French overture opens the second half of the work. The use of two keyboards offers a variety of sound effects, particularly in the accompanied solos (in the other double-keyboard variations for crossing hands no great contrast is intended;[11] the virtuosity provides its own interest). Above all, there is a real sense of a finale; after the profoundly tragic twenty-fifth variation, the music gradually increases in brilliance until the great comic quodlibet, and the quiet return of the theme. Except for the *St. Matthew Passion*, in no other work is the depth of Bach's spirit so easily accessible, and its significance so tangible.

On 7 May 1747, at Potsdam, King Frederick the Great personally condescended to play on the pianoforte a theme of his own for Bach to improvise into a fugue. The Silbermann pianoforte was the King's favorite instrument; he is reported to have acquired fifteen of them. Bach improvised a three-voice fugue, and was later asked by Frederick for the seemingly impossible: a fugue on the same theme in six voices. Bach hesitated—the royal theme was too complex for such improvisation—and improvised a six-voice fugue on a theme of his own.

11. Several of these variations even bear the indication "for one or two keyboards": to play a real forte on Bach's harpsichord, one had to couple the keyboards by pulling one on top of the other and pressing down two keys at once. The direction told the player to play these variations on only one keyboard if he had the strength and the agility.

On returning to Leipzig, however, he took up the King's challenge in the wonderful, long six-voice ricercar of the *Musical Offering*, the Prussian Fugue, as he himself called it. It is a miracle of art, in its compression of the richest and most elaborate harmonies in six real parts into the space of two hands.[12] Architecturally, it is at the same time the simplest—no stretto, no inversion, no countertheme, nothing but six entrances, and six further playings of the theme, once in each voice, embedded in the most varied and expressive episodes—and the most imposing of all Bach's fugues. All the majesty and lyricism of Bach's art are concentrated in this work.

The three-voice ricercar is generally assumed to represent, at least in part, the first fugue that Bach improvised for the King: its character is indeed improvisatory, lighter and more colorful than its great companion, but with several striking harmonic effects. Both pieces were published in *The Musical Offering*, along with a trio sonata and several canons, all based on the theme; the Prussian Fugue, although written on two staves, was printed in score to display the perfection of the part-writing. The two ricercars are the only works of Bach that pianists are entitled, with any historical justification, to claim as their own. We must remember, however, that the eighteenth-century piano had a thinner and clearer sound than the modern one, and that there was nothing about the style of the music or the practice of the time to preclude playing them on any other keyboard instrument. One important quality of the Prussian Fugue is veiled on the organ: the expressive attack or accent when five or six voices move together; and there are many places in this work which are beautifully calculated to this end. Harpsichord, clavichord, and pianoforte do more justice to this great work, and it is only fair to add that Frederick the Great, to whom it was dedicated, would have listened to it played on a pianoforte. Pianists should be more jealous of their first masterpiece, still one of their greatest.

It is by now generally recognized that *The Art of the Fugue* was also intended for the keyboard—eighteen of the most complex contrapuntal works do not fall only by chance within the compass of two hands (the one exception—a three-voice mirror fugue—being arranged by the composer himself for two keyboards, four hands).[13] The only question is: was it also intended for anything except a keyboard? The publication in score proves nothing; the preface added by Marpurg in 1752 to the original edition tells us that this was for the convenience of reading. Anyone who has read the work from score at the keyboard will testify to

12. It was one of Philipp Emanuel's proudest boasts about his father that this fugue was for two hands alone.

13. The theory that *The Art of the Fugue* is either abstract or intended for instrumentation is an early twentieth-century muddle; the first great biographer of Bach, Spitta, classified it as a keyboard work, as we do again today.

the great advantage of the score over the piano reduction, and its aid to clarity and understanding. Arrangements and transcriptions were certainly common enough during Bach's lifetime, and he himself transferred many pieces from one medium to another. It should be added, however, that these transcriptions were never concerned with fugues as fully worked out and as severe in character as the Prussian Fugue or the similar ones in *The Art of the Fugue.* This kind of music was exclusively keyboard in character throughout the first half of the eighteenth century. The delightful and varied textures of the trio sonata from *The Musical Offering* show clearly what Bach, at that time of his life, thought ensemble music should be. All the fugues that Bach or Handel wrote or arranged for ensemble are in a more concerted and brilliant style, with far less of the serious or "learned" character of most of the pieces in *The Art of the Fugue.* Works as meditative and as contrapuntally rich would have been lacking in decorum in the guise of ensemble chamber music (or orchestral—the difference was hardly visible then). There is no instance of Bach's writing this kind of contrapuntal work except for keyboard. Nor was there any place for such music in early eighteenth-century musical life, where anything even as semi-public as ensemble music was allowed its earnest side, but rarely the completely undramatic seriousness of the six-voice ricercar or *The Art of the Fugue,* which is, in genre, style, and technique, keyboard music through and through.

What keyboard, as usual, does not matter. As in *The Well-Tempered Keyboard,* one fugue of *The Art of the Fugue* needs a final pedal note; one canon goes beyond the range of the average clavichord. None of this would have deterred any of the rare purchasers of the original edition (only forty people bought a copy), even if he had had only a single clavichord. He would have placed his copy on the music rack of whatever keyboard was available, and read through the work, grateful for the clarity of the printing in score. Is the music for study or for playing? This question, still posed by some writers, allows a false choice; *The Art of the Fugue* was meant to be studied by playing it, to have its marvels seen, heard, and felt under one's fingers. Some of the fugues are among Bach's most effective, and should take their place in the concert hall, but it is inconceivable that the composer ever intended a complete performance of twenty works in the same key and on the same theme, most of them, too, in the same rhythm. *The Art of the Fugue* was meant to be played over a period of time (which does not in the least distract from its unity). Apparently simple, subtly complex, with the ease of a lifetime's experience in every line, it must, indeed, be played many times before its deceptive lucidity can be penetrated.

The work was never finished; its plan, basically simple, was altered during composition, and the order of the first edition is certainly wrong. Like a gigantic set of variations, each piece is based on the same theme. There are (1) four sim-

Example 3.5

Example 3.6

ple fugues (two on the inversion of the theme); (2) three stretto fugues (the second a French overture in style, and the third with the theme in augmentation, diminution, and at the original speed simultaneously); (3) two double fugues (double counterpoint at the tenth and at the twelfth); (4) two triple fugues (the second with the themes of the first inverted); (5) four canons; (6) two sets of "mirror fugues" (each fugue with its double, which completely inverts every note of each voice); (7) and last, an unfinished quadruple fugue (there was to have been a second quadruple fugue, which was never begun). The final section of this fugue—the combination of the first three themes with the main theme of the work—was still to write; Bach became blind as he finished the third part of the fugue based on the letters of his own name. The manuscript breaks off just as the composer had, in effect, put his signature to the work that was the summation of his art.

The style of *The Art of the Fugue* is that of a counterpoint exercise; the theme is simple, the textures largely unchanging, uncontrasted. There are almost no dramatic effects; the most fantastic modulations take place discreetly, and the sequences are continually varied with a delicacy unparalleled in Baroque music. All the intensity lies in the individual lines, severe and expressive throughout. In Example 3.5 the power of sliding through several tonalities—touching them lightly and quickly—is seen with an ease afterwards lost to music until Chopin's chromatic polyphony revived it, and the texture has a transparency that makes light of the contrapuntal ingenuity. In the stretto shown in Example 3.6 there is all the melting smoothness of the finest Renaissance vocal writing, although not only are the soprano and alto in canon at the fourth, but the tenor and bass together are in strict canon at the octave with the upper voices at the distance of only one beat, an intricacy of relationship belied by the simplicity of effect. A few pieces have a more brilliant aspect: the stretto fugue in the French manner, the mirror fugue arranged for two keyboards; but in general there is a unity of style that Bach never attempted in his other collective works, as if here everything were concentrated on the single details, the subtlety of the accents, the purity of linear tracery. There is no more deeply moving music.

If Handel's keyboard music has so small a place in our estimate of his achievement, that is in part because he wrote so little of it down. Famous as a harpsichordist and as an organist, he left few pieces for keyboard alone, and even fewer of these can lay any claim to being in a finished state. Of the sixteen suites, only the first eight were prepared for publication by Handel himself; the rest are a hodge-podge of pieces put together out of works composed for different reasons—for teaching or as the basis of improvisation—some sketchy, carelessly written, and only half finished. Among the works published without Handel's consent, there are, of course, a few beautiful things, including the lovely theme that Brahms used for a set of variations.

Handel was the greatest master of the public genres of the High Baroque: opera, oratorio, outdoor festive music. The genius of these works lies in the large conception and in the vigor and force of the details, rather than their refinement. To a certain extent, the subtlety and the nuances were left to the performers, the singers in particular. No composer before Beethoven had Handel's command of large-scale rhythm, which is perhaps why Beethoven thought him the greatest composer of all. Handel's music turns outward; it is written directly at the public, and his finest works have an unlimited, if sometimes coarse, power, and an exhilaration and an excitement that Bach never tried to attain. More than in any other music, Handel's supremacy has suffered from difficulties of performance: the need for larger ensembles than Bach demanded, a dependence on virtuosity. Nineteenth-century styles of playing and singing and, more recently, pseudo-eighteenth-century performance practice, have only served to obscure his greatness further.

The first book of Suites, published in 1720, remains his only major contribution to contemporary keyboard literature. The Six Fugues or Voluntaries of 1735 are, as the title indicates, more organ works than anything else, although there was nothing to prevent their performance on any other keyboard as they are entirely manual; they are vigorous, loosely constructed, and effective. The first eight suites, however, are unduly neglected today, although some of the pieces in them, the E minor fugue which opens Suite IV in particular, are among the finest that Handel ever wrote. It is a pity that, of all these suites, only the one in E major, with the set of variations popularly called the "Harmonious Blacksmith," is familiar to concert-goers.

Not even those suites are completely notated; the opening prelude of Suite I, for example, is merely a sketch for an improvisation. A great many of the dances need not only ornamentation, but inner voices as well, for only the bare outlines have been traced. However, in a few cases, Handel has written out a fully ornamented form as a guide. The opening adagio of Suite II is complete with every note of its luxuriant ornamentation; as decoration it has never been surpassed for grace and simple expressiveness, not even by Bach. The whole of Suite II is impressive, with its brilliant allegro, the dramatic and lavishly decorated recitative-like second adagio, and the final hornpipe fugue. It is less a suite in the modern sense than an early four-movement Italian sonata.

Unlike Bach, Handel generally followed the tradition of beginning the allemande and the courante with the same motive. His suites are less elaborate, with fewer movements, and the gigues, far from being severe fugues, are unashamedly popular in style. Some of the pieces date back to 1705, but the English influence

Example 3.7

is already evident in many of the dance movements which must have come somewhat later. The rhythmic sweep is remarkable throughout in the calculation of the sequences, which are used with an imaginative vitality superior to all Handel's Italian and French contemporaries, and in the brilliant use of octave displacement for surprise and accent, as in a passage from Suite II, shown in Example 3.7, where the music is twice impelled urgently forward by the unexpected leap to another register. Also beyond the grasp of any other composer of the time is Handel's dramatic juxtaposition of different kinds of texture. Compared to the dramatic power of a phrase near the beginning of the fugue from Suite VIII, shown in Example 3.8, Scarlatti's abrupt changes of texture are more playful, and more refined. Handel's boldness is never witty. In the opening adagio of this F minor Suite, he is capable of sustaining a lengthy slow-moving progression with all of Bach's intensity; no one ever avoided a cadence more naturally or more convincingly than Handel, and he achieved breadth and grandeur of phrase with a simplicity that has been the envy of all composers.

With the death of Bach and Handel, the end of the High Baroque synthesis came quickly; in their last years they were almost alone in sustaining it. How the style fell to pieces, how musical thought became fragmented, can be seen with Bach's children. Three of them became fine composers, and they appear to have divided up the realm of style, each one cultivating only a small plot of ground. Wilhelm Friedemann, the eldest of Bach's children, continued an eccentric and highly personal version of the High Baroque; the forms and, above all, the rhythmic movement are uncontrolled but there are moments of a bold and passionate sensibility. Johann Christian, the youngest, is the hardest to appreciate, for his music seems bland in comparison to that of the great generations before and after him. But he is responsible for much of the exquisite balance of the later classical style. In Mozart's music, the symmetry—which lies under all he wrote—is delicately varied, sometimes hidden; but he would never have attained this without the model of Johann Christian, whose exemplary feeling for proportion was a creative force that was crucial in the change that came over European music. His clarity and feeling for the articulation of form were as important in the development of the late eighteenth-century sonata as were the works of his more appreciated brother, Carl Philipp Emanuel.

The latter, is, to us, the most interesting of the Bach children, the master of a style which we may call, for lack of a better name, North German mannerism. His keyboard works are almost all entirely for the clavichord—specifically so, full of an ardent, intimate sensibility suited to that instrument. His music is dramatic, his feeling for tonal relationships bold, striking, and not quite coherent. His rhythmic organizations are still less satisfactory, and he passes abruptly—sometimes with a splendid, but momentary, dramatic effect—from a baroque sequential continuity to a classical periodic articulation. What is most dated in his music is the ornamentation, almost always applied, and rarely growing from

Example 3.8

Example 3.9

within; he tried to do with decoration what Haydn, who was so indebted to him, was to learn to do with structure. Philipp Emanuel's forms have corresponding virtues and vices; they are daring, imaginative, and illogical. His conception of the rondo is an improvised fantasy on one theme that wanders through several keys, with striking effects. He helped free the dramatic sensibilities of the next generation, and his eccentricity kept alive the ideal of serious expression at a time when music threatened to become only pretty, forcedly naïve, or comic. The end of the slow movement of the Sonata in D minor (written in 1766, but not published until 1781) is an example of this exacerbated sensibility (see Ex. 3.9). The dissolution of the rhythm at the end is as remarkable as the violent contrasts of texture and the dramatic control of the line. His large output of keyboard music—fantasies, rondos, and sonatas—disappoints only because it creates and implies the highest standards; otherwise it gives nothing but pleasure. It is ironic to think that the development of a new, completely balanced and unmannered style (in the work of Mozart and the mature Haydn) was to coincide by a few years with the rediscovery of Sebastian Bach and Handel by Viennese musicians around 1780, after a generation in which Bach's children had each preserved a part of the tradition.

CHAPTER FOUR

The Rediscovering of Haydn

THE history of music proceeds by revaluation: the standard procedure is to discover greatness in the obscure, merit in the despised. Dethronings are more rare: generally the discredited monarchs topple without having to be pushed; past glories melt like the snows of yesteryear.

There is not, of course, much point in dragging an old manuscript out of obscurity only to affirm that it is of exceedingly little interest. The musicologist generally prefers to believe that when his researches do not heighten our appreciation and enjoyment of the familiar, they at least give us new objects of admiration. Occasionally a historian tries to prove that some works with claims to our respect—like one of Haydn's cello concertos or Mozart's *Symphonie Concertante* for winds—are impostors, written by anonymous or little-known hacks. These attempts are, however, rare: given his choice, the historian would rather discover a symphony by Joseph Haydn than prove that one of those now in the canon was composed by his brother.

The most famous of these revaluations, the revival of J. S. Bach by the early nineteenth century, is a myth: Bach had never been forgotten, his music was greatly admired from his death in 1750 until the end of the century, and the keyboard works were studied and played. Little had been published, but manuscript copies were common enough. The romantic revival of Bach was basically a campaign of publishing, coupled with a series of performances of the choral works, which had remained largely ignored.

The great achievement of the musicology of the nineteenth and early twenti-

Originally written in 1979 as a review of H. C. Robbins Landon, *Haydn: Chronicle and Works*: Vol. 2: *Haydn at Eszterháza, 1766–1790*; Vol. 3: *Haydn in England, 1791–1795*; Vol. 4: *Haydn: The Years of "The Creation," 1796–1800*; and Vol. 5: *Haydn: The Late Years, 1801–1809*.

eth centuries was the reappropriation of the medieval and Renaissance heritage. Then came the turn of the important early baroque figures, like Monteverdi; his fame was firmly reestablished by the 1930s. After the Second World War, all these movements continued, and new areas were opened up. Haydn's great piano trios are at last being heard from time to time in concerts. Mozart's *Così fan tutte* returned permanently to the repertory after more than a century of misunderstanding. Similar efforts have been made recently on behalf of Mozart's mature *opere serie, Idomeneo* and *La Clemenza di Tito,* but with significantly less success, neither having gained a foothold in the permanent repertory of more than one or two houses.

Perhaps the greatest commercial success in all these movements of rehabilitation is the revival of the minor composers of early eighteenth-century instrumental music—the so-called baroque and rococo styles. The music is mostly easy to listen to (a kind of eighteenth-century Muzak), recordings can be played without distracting the listener from other tasks, and the ensembles employed are small and economical.

The chief beneficiary of this movement has been Vivaldi; many of his five hundred concertos are now frequently performed. Luigi Dallapiccola's acid remark about Vivaldi, often repeated, is misleading. He claimed that Vivaldi wrote not five hundred concertos but the same concerto five hundred times. This really ought to be stood on its head. Vivaldi was full of many different ideas, most of them striking, full of genius. His problem was one of structure.

It would be more accurate to say that Vivaldi had five hundred ideas for a concerto, and that none of them ever was fully worked out. It is only after his wonderful opening bars, his extraordinary beginnings (which taught J. S. Bach so much), that his concertos bog down and begin to resemble each other in the deployment of harmonic clichés—clichés which would not matter (as they do not matter in Handel) if the large harmonic form were coherent and interesting, the clichés given a sense of direction and movement instead of a feeling of jogging on a treadmill.

Vivaldi's operas are coming in for attention now: the same faults and virtues are manifest there. The arias begin strikingly, but continue with little of Handel's energy, Bach's intensity, or Alessandro Scarlatti's subtlety. These deficiencies are less crippling here: an aria is generally much shorter than a concerto movement. In comparing Vivaldi to Bach and Handel, some of his admirers (Marc Pincherle, for example) either refused to face his weaknesses, or else— what is worse —they never understood the strengths of the already established masters. Anyone, however, who has been through the numbing experience of a

program devoted entirely to the works of one of Vivaldi's minor and justly obscure contemporaries like Albinoni will gratefully acknowledge Vivaldi's finer
talent.

The most fruitful sources for the historian seeking to make an important change
in our way of looking at music today are by no means the genuinely obscure
works never touched by appreciation, but those works—and sometimes whole
genres and styles—much celebrated in their own time, which have suffered a
long eclipse. The revival of forgotten glory, the resuscitation of dead prestige—
this is the kind of achievement that is not only relatively easy to pull off but also
attracts the most attention. The renewed interest in the nineteenth-century virtuoso salon music came up in the 1970s above all as a manifestation of anti-
modernism, a hatred of the avant-garde; the new and similar taste for official art
shown by historians of painting has its counterpart as well in the musicological
attempts to revive the *opera seria* of the early eighteenth century, the official
court style of that time. The contempt in which these styles were held until recently is not an obstacle to their revival, but a stimulus and even, paradoxically,
an aid: it gives them a kind of avant-garde status of their own. An exhibition of a
salon painter like Bouguereau or a performance of a Scharwenka piano concerto
is a kind of joke provocation, a parody version of the Armory Show or the riot at
the premiere of *Le Sacre du printemps.*

What we are often asked to do in these revivals of forgotten masterpieces is
forget all the history that has happened since the once-admired works were first
revealed to the public, immerse ourselves in the age that created them, recapture
the astonished admiration of the contemporaries, and erase the decades and
even centuries of neglect and contempt. This historicist approach demands a
considerable effort of sympathy and imagination. It may be called a necessary
preliminary to understanding.

The danger of the approach lies in the belief that it leads directly to understanding—even, in the most naïve view, that understanding consists exactly in
the imaginative attempt to retrieve the ideas and attitudes of a past age. The fallacy that supports this comfortable philosophy of history is the simple faith that
an artist is best understood by his contemporaries. This may be true for artists of
very little interest (although I doubt it), but the most rapid glance at the history
of music shows that a composer of any stature, even when he was appreciated by
his contemporaries—as he generally was, in spite of the romantic myth of the
unknown genius—was generally radically misunderstood, misread, and misinterpreted by them. It lies with posterity, not to decide on greatness (posterity can
at times be as fickle as fortune), but to clear up the inevitable foolishness which

surrounds the work during the life of its composer (adding, no doubt, some new foolishness of its own).

The post-history of a work of music—the history of its reception, its changing prestige, its influence—is perhaps even more important for critical understanding then a study of its sources or an account of its actual creation. The work is more than a passive victim of its history. It not only actively provokes the interpretations and the misinterpretations that are visited upon it, but it often incorporates them into itself so that the post-history may become an inevitable part of experiencing the work. The late Beethoven quartets, for example, have become very easy to listen to in the twentieth century, but I do not think that it will ever be possible to hear them without some consciousness of their reputed century-old difficulty: these late quartets have assumed the historical character of difficult music.

The historian who tries to reappraise a once-celebrated genre, like the liturgical music of the late eighteenth century for example, has a responsibility to deal with the condemnation that fell upon it by the 1790s, becoming almost universal after 1800. Not even the works of Mozart and Haydn escaped censure. It cannot be reasonably assumed that the censure was merely a piece of ill-luck extrinsic to the works themselves. The genre was fated to be condemned: how good it is today after more than a century of neglect is another matter, although not one to which the decline of its prestige in the nineteenth century can be pushed aside as irrelevant.

Often enough the later neglect or misunderstanding of an important work can be taken care of without much fuss. The low esteem in which Mozart's *Così fan tutte* was held in the nineteenth century was quite simply owing to its immoral and cynical libretto. Even here, however, the condemnation is instructive: the cynicism and the artificiality of the libretto were already out of date when Mozart set it in 1789, a throwback to the French comedies of some forty or fifty years earlier. It is this artificiality which makes it the most symmetrical of all Mozart's stage works, and the only one of the great comic operas to allow no echo of the political events in the world outside. This gives the music its idiosyncratic quality, one somewhat harder to appreciate than that of the other important operas: there is a good deal of pastiche and parody in many of Mozart's operas, including *Don Giovanni* and *Die Zauberflöte*, but in none is the pastiche so openly ironic as in *Così fan tutte*. Much of it is simply a direct parody of operatic style: the irony comes from the evident delight taken not only in the mockery but also in what is being mocked.

The spirit of criticism takes an odd revenge on historicism. Those who dismiss the later history of a work or a style too lightly, who try to lose themselves in an earlier age, who shut their eyes to what followed, and who attempt only to grasp the conditions in which a work could come into being and the significance found in it by the composer's contemporaries—these lovers of the obsolete and the forgotten end by misrepresenting the very thing they were trying to reproduce so faithfully, and by muddling the period to which they so austerely confine themselves. Rejecting the interpretations of the present, they miss the intentions of the past.

Some of these problems may be seen in the present efforts to rehabilitate parts of Joseph Haydn's work—those parts as yet largely unappreciated—in Robbins Landon's new, monumental biography. His efforts are above all on behalf of two genres: the operas and the masses. With the operas, I fear he is heading for a defeat. As for the great religious works of the end of Haydn's life, Robbins Landon is right in his championship, but wrong about the nature of the criticism that has been leveled against them.

Only a few decades ago there were still immense tracts of unexplored Haydn. The operas were largely unknown, and the 126 trios for baryton were unpublished and unexamined before Oliver Strunk looked at them while at the Library of Congress (the baryton—a large six-stringed viol—was the favorite instrument of Haydn's patron, Count Esterházy). The chronology of the 104 symphonies was not well understood, and scores and instrumental parts of a large number of them were unobtainable. One attempt to publish all of them failed halfway through for lack of funds. Another did not even get so far.

That we are better off today is owing in large part to the work of Robbins Landon, who has devoted his life principally to Haydn. His finest achievement was the first complete publication in the 1960s of all 104 symphonies. This edition had the great merit of returning not only to the manuscripts but also, if somewhat unmethodically, to sets of contemporary orchestral parts, with the conductor's markings. Several volumes are already out of print, but those who were prudent or enthusiastic enough to buy them at once can now survey the whole of Haydn's symphonic output. There is, finally, a complete Haydn edition under way at Cologne (containing of course a rival edition of the symphonies), and it looks like being completed in reasonable time. It will soon be possible to assess all of Haydn's works that have come down to us.

To his other researches Robbins Landon has added a new biography of Haydn in five volumes, the last four of which have so far appeared. This important book will be useful to scholars for at least a half-century to come, but it is difficult to say just what kind of book it is. Robbins Landon knows a tremendous amount about Haydn, and he has dumped almost (but not quite) everything he knows pell-mell into these volumes. They are a cross between a catalogue of works and a collection of documents, all combined with the commonplace book of a man who has spent many years with Haydn, and jotted down ideas and notions as they occurred to him.

The documents are so numerous and so valuable that it is a pity Robbins Landon stopped short of putting in absolutely everything. So many contemporary critical accounts of Haydn are given that one regrets the ones that are omitted. The size of the work is already elephantine; another volume would hardly make much difference. As it is, each reader will find something in this profusion. The catalogue is also very useful.

The weakest part of the book is the analysis of the works. It is not that Robbins Landon does not often find something important to say about the music; much of what he writes is sensitive and penetrating, and it is all informed by a great love of Haydn and an enthusiasm which would be infectious if the book were not so disorganized and unsystematic. The real difficulty is a technical vocabulary of analysis which is slovenly. For Robbins Landon, "F sharp," for example, can be a note, or the triad of F sharp major, or the key of F sharp major.[1] Without a score, it is often impossible to tell what he intends. He writes like a man going quickly through the pages of Haydn's works and pointing out to a friend the passages he likes the most.

The world of music is in Robbins Landon's debt, so there is no point in insisting on such imperfections. One can, however, regret the uneven proportions, with volumes 3, 4, and 5 each covering only four to eight years while volume 2 takes on a quarter of a century, 1766–1790, fascinating years—among the most important not only for Haydn's personal development but for his importance in history, for his influence on his contemporaries, and for the musical life of the late eighteenth century. In the period between 1766 and 1785 Haydn developed the first string quartets and symphonies which still remain in the repertory today, and produced an extraordinary number of operas by other composers as well as himself at the little court of Esterháza. Haydn's last years are better documented, no doubt, but Robbins Landon surely knows even more about the earlier and middle periods than he is willing to tell.

Now that the operas of Haydn are at last being published, we find them full of good things—how could it be otherwise? How would it have been possible for a

---

1. See, for example, page 245 of volume 5, where a modulation is described in which F major is listed twice; the first time it should be F minor, and is a key; the next it is a chord and should be V^7 of B flat.

man of Haydn's genius to have written thousands of pages of operatic score without allowing his genius to shine through? It is the nature of this genius that is in question. With all the greatness of the symphonies, quartets, and piano trios, Haydn was a small-scale composer—or, better, a middle-scale one. Mozart's ability to control a whole opera in his head at once was beyond him. On a somewhat smaller level, Haydn could be more daring and more shocking than Mozart. His use of silence is the most dramatic in the history of music. His sudden changes of harmony often take one completely unaware, and the orchestration is often intentionally astonishing—in its combinations of solo wind instruments it comes closer to Mahler's technique than any other music before the twentieth century.

The weakness of Robbins Landon's brief for Haydn's operas is apparent at once in his discussion of the operatic finale—the group of ensembles at the end of an act that follow each other without any intervening recitative. The finale was the great glory of Mozart's operatic style. Robbins Landon would have us believe that the large-scale quasi-symphonic finale was invented not by Mozart but by Haydn.

This is to misunderstand Mozart's originality. Similar sets of ensembles, more or less unified by beginning and ending in the same key, existed two or three decades before either Haydn or Mozart wrote them. It is the nature of the coherence of the tonal structure of Mozart's finales that was revolutionary. The archetype is the finale of the second act of *Figaro*. Hermann Abert pointed out the extraordinary symmetry of the different parts long ago:

E♭—B♭—G—C—F—B♭—E♭

The E flat, B flat / B flat, E flat mirror pattern at the opening and closing provides a frame, but what is even more remarkable is the inner structure. The first two keys are tonic and dominant, related as in a sonata. This initial opposition is followed by a leap to a more remote key (G major), and this change to a distant tonality is also typical of the central section of a sonata form. From then on—G, C, F, B flat, E flat—each key is the dominant of the succeeding one, leading naturally and convincingly back to E flat. In short, the form begins with a classical opposition of tonic and dominant, makes a single dramatic modulation, and then moves simply and convincingly back to the opening. Moreover, the texture starts as a duet, becomes a trio, quartet, quintet, and then a septet as the action becomes more and more embroiled.

Nothing like this is found in Haydn. Robbins Landon, claiming that "the basic organization, also the application of symphonic devices to large-scale vocal forms, is the same in both works,"[2] offers us the following pattern from *La fedeltà premiata*, Act I:

B♭—G major—G minor—E♭—C major—A♭—G minor—B♭—G minor—B♭

The framing device is partially achieved, but the inner coherence is a series of symmetrically arranged harmonic shocks, very different from Mozart's single dramatic leap followed by a progressive movement back to the opening tonality; in particular, the oscillation between G minor and B flat at the end is an example of Haydn's small-scale sense of movement.[3] (The finale of Haydn's second act has a more symmetrical scheme, but the tonal relations are even less coherent.) And, most important, the correspondence between texture and action we find in Mozart is lacking. A rehabilitation of Haydn's operas is not worth much if it entails a misapprehension of Mozart's achievement.

Operatic finales may have been first written in the 1740s, probably by Galuppi. In one sense, however, Mozart invented the operatic finale—the finale as a large-scale coherent musical form, which makes a musical sense that is almost independent of the text. The organization of a Mozart finale is not merely a set of key relations, but a sense of key movement, an ordered progression back to the tonality of the opening. For this order, and for its simplicity and efficiency, there is no known precedent, nor was Haydn's technique capable of supplying one.[4]

Haydn's masses are a different matter: his operas were largely ignored, but his masses were censured. Most of the masses were composed at the end of Haydn's life after all the quartets and symphonies had been written, at the moment of his greatest mastery and when his reputation was at its height. He had retired from his provincial post at Esterháza, and the son of his old patron Count Esterházy paid him a pension dependent only on his writing two masses a year. The young count's musical interest lay almost entirely in religious works. Haydn, deeply religious himself, accepted the commissions gladly; he devoted his last years of

2. See *Haydn: Chronicle and Works* (Indiana University Press, 1976–1980), Vol. 2, p. 544.

3. Haydn's scheme, in fact, is typically more daring as well as less effective than Mozart's. Where Mozart has only one surprising modulation by a descending third (B flat to G), Haydn has four of them, followed by a harmonic shift even more eccentric (A flat to G minor). It is precisely the richness of Haydn's imagination that makes his structure less grand than Mozart's, the interest concentrated on the individual moment.

4. Most discussions of precedent are, in any case, of very little interest: D. F. Tovey once remarked cogently that a musical idea belongs properly not to the composer who invented it but to the one who first used it effectively.

composition largely to choral music—six masses for Count Esterházy and the two oratorios *The Creation* and *The Seasons* for the Baron van Swieten. Then there followed a melancholy half-dozen years when Haydn, still full of musical ideas, was too old and too weak to compose, too feeble to go to the piano and work out his ideas, the way he had composed all his life.

The censure of the Haydn masses is called "Victorian" by Robbins Landon, and he reproaches me with great courtesy for having perpetuated the charge (in a book I wrote some years ago) that these works are too operatic for a religious service. The operatic nature of the liturgical music has never particularly bothered me, nor could it bother anyone who enjoys Verdi's Requiem. The real difficulty with some of Haydn's masses is not that they are too operatic, but that they are, at least in part, not operatic enough, not symphonic enough, not anything enough—that is, they do not have the highly idiosyncratic style of the other genres, and they do not have much of a strongly characterized style of their own to compensate. They are often timidly symphonic, tepidly operatic, and—in desperation—strongly archaizing when nothing modern will seem to do.

"Victorian" is a misleading word: it suggests that the censure began much later than it did. Robbins Landon wishes—and, I think in the end, justly—to revise what was once the standard critical opinion of these masses, to make us see how masterly they really are. But the opinion will not be simply set aside unless we see how it arose—and unless we see that it is, in fact, contemporary with the works themselves and reflects the problems that Haydn had, quite consciously, to deal with.

Robbins Landon quotes a few laudatory reviews of the masses and omits much of the contrary critical opinion, dealing summarily with what he does mention. Strong dissatisfaction with rococo church music had already begun in the last decades of the eighteenth century. Modern style seemed inappropriate for the words of the mass. Archaizing is already found by the early 1780s in Mozart's great unfinished Mass in C minor, with its magnificent imitations of Handel. Other composers went much further. The last years of the century saw a revival of the style of Palestrina, and an interest in *a cappella* writing: the chief exponent was Joseph Haydn's brother Michael.

One low estimate of the Haydn masses printed by Robbins Landon may be found in a brilliant series of articles on the development of German music in the eighteenth century that appeared in the *Allgemeine Musikalische Zeitung* in 1801. They were written by Triest, about whom nothing is known, not even his first name, except that he was a preacher in Stettin; but these articles are held up as a model of criticism by the most important early nineteenth-century dictionary of music, Gerber's. Triest arranges Haydn's works in order of importance. First come the symphonies and quartets; next comes the piano music (although, Triest says, some connoisseurs would prefer not only the piano music of Mozart and of Clementi but even that of the young Beethoven, if he would only lose some of his savagery); last and least are the operas and religious works. To have singled out Beethoven as early as 1801 shows Triest to be astute and well informed.

One sentence of Triest's article, which introduces the judgment of Haydn, is revealingly mistranslated by Robbins Landon. He renders it:

> And so I fear not, if I set up the following classification of Haydn's works against the opinion of the majority of connoisseurs and critics.

The original reads:

> *Und so fürchte ich denn nicht, gegen das Urtheil der meisten Kenner und Kritiker anzustossen, wenn ich folgende Klassifikation der Werke Haydns aufstelle.*

Correctly rendered, this is:

> And so I have no apprehension of going against the judgment of the majority of critics and connoisseurs if I set up the following classification of Haydn's works.

That is, Triest is claiming that his rating is identical with the judgment of most musicians, but Robbins Landon, whose German is much better than mine, refuses to understand him. Within a few years, the condemnation of the masses is confirmed; with all his reverence for Haydn, E. T. A. Hoffmann is apologetic about them. The disapproval of the liturgical music even begins to reflect on the oratorios: poets are better guides to cultivated opinion on music than critics, who generally have an axe to grind, and in Ludwig Tieck's discussion of music in his influential *Phantasus* of 1811, even *The Creation* of Haydn is condemned along with all of his religious music.

The contemporary criticism of Haydn's liturgical style was not so much that it was operatic but that it was trivial. If these works are to be, not reinstated (their reputation was never high in spite of a few good press notices), but revalued, offered once more with their great merits at last fully revealed, then we need not a rebuttal of the charges against them but an explanation of how the charges could have arisen, of what critical expectations Haydn had to meet and to satisfy.

The eighteenth-century composer of Catholic religious music faced contradictory aesthetic requirements. The Church officially wanted music that was festive: others, and the composers themselves, wanted music that was expressive, that aptly fitted the words of the mass. As an analogy, we may point to the conflict in Renaissance Italian architecture, when the architects wished (for both aesthetic and philosophic reasons) to build churches with a centralized form, and the Church wanted a long nave for processions, and a form that divided the priest from the laity. The setting of *Gloria in excelsis Deo* could be both grand and expressive. The problem was, above all, the Credo and the opening movement: a jolly, festive setting of *Kyrie eleison* ("Lord have mercy") seemed a contradiction in terms.

Of all the historians of music, only Hermann Abert in his great book on Mozart has dealt interestingly with this point, although briefly. Alfred Einstein dismissed it quickly, but not before pointing out that criticisms of trivial or indecorous Kyries began early in the century. Unfortunately, modern ideas of an eighteenth-century mass are based largely on Bach's Mass in B minor: very few contemporary works have the expressive intensity found there. Most are brilliant and grand in a perfunctory way—perfunctory, because an uninhibited use of the operatic style that was second nature to most composers of the time weighed on their conscience when a religious text was at hand. They occasionally did it—the greatest example is the coloratura aria with a cadenza for soprano and solo winds that Mozart wrote in his C minor Mass as a setting of *Et incarnatus est:* it would be silly to object to this ravishingly beautiful piece, but equally silly to describe it as either decorous or adequate to the text.

Admirers of rococo church music, including Robbins Landon, like to claim for it an equal status with rococo church architecture and decoration, as well as an identical spiritual impulse: the joyful celebration of faith by the most lavish and brilliant means. The playful imagination of the eighteenth-century Austrian and Bavarian churches was similarly criticized by many contemporaries: it made the interiors of the churches look like salons, they complained. Once decidedly out of fashion, these magnificent interiors are now very much appreciated, precisely for the gaudy extravagance which caused them to be censured before. But it is just this extravagance that rococo church music lacks: it is always less brilliant, less imaginative, and less idiosyncratic than the finest contemporary achievements in opera, symphony, or chamber music, while the greatest rococo churches, like Ottobeuren, either equal or surpass in brilliance and even eccentricity the comparable examples of secular rococo decoration, like those at Nymphenburg. Rococo church music is generally timid harmonically; its orchestral brilliance is with rare exceptions a conventional use of trumpets and drums and the vocal effects far tamer than those in opera. (The late Haydn masses, harmonically and instrumentally adventurous, are no longer rococo at all, but clearly moving toward a classical solution of religious style.) Above all, church decoration and architecture are not tied to the expression of a particular text: their expressive effects are more general.

"Whoever decreed that the music must fit the text?" a music historian who loves rococo church music once remarked to me (I am forced to use this anonymous verbal quotation since a musicologist who acts on this assumption, if he has both intelligence and a sense of self-preservation, does not commit it to print). Many ages did not indeed demand this correspondence between music and words, but almost everyone at the end of the eighteenth century, including Haydn himself, felt that the music must express the text of the mass. No understanding of Haydn's liturgical style can do without some sense of this demand and, above all, some realization of the difficulty of meeting it. Late eighteenth-century style was formed largely by opera, and the phrase structure derived above all from comic opera. Haydn's music could be both dramatic and witty: it was difficult for him to be one without the other.

In addition to a contradictory aesthetic and a musical language not easily accommodated to a liturgical text, there was a third force that increased the difficulty of forming a liturgical style that was both adequate and modern: the natural conservatism of religious feeling. Just as many still prefer the King James translation of the Bible, and as W. H. Auden joined the Greek Church rather than hear Anglican prayers read in modern English, there was a strong feeling in the late eighteenth century that old musical styles were best for a religious occasion. The old styles at least had a guarantee of respectability: the real proof of gravity, then as now, was a fugue. If everything else failed in the attempt to give dignity and high seriousness to late eighteenth-century style, the fugue was the last resort.

Haydn is perhaps the greatest master of the academic fugue. In a sense, he invented it: in many respects the nineteenth-century fugue owes more to Haydn than even to Bach, although this is not often realized. Cherubini's contrapuntal style was the paradigm of academic counterpoint; he learned it from Haydn's works, and transmitted it to the nineteenth century with the power of the Paris Conservatoire behind him. Haydn's fugues are largely Handelian pastiche, but they are brilliant, powerful, and often moving. If they are less interesting than the greatest fugues of Bach and Handel, that is inherent in the nature of academic pastiche—it is a dignified and always slightly archaic form. The finest of Haydn's fugues in the masses, the oratorios, and the finales of some of the quar-

tets are so magnificent, however, that the difference between them and the greatest examples of Bach is negligible—it only comes to mind if we insist on thinking about it.

Archaizing was a makeshift, however. A truly modern religious style was more
embarrassing: it came to Haydn painfully, with none of the ease that he found in
symphony and quartet. If there are, indeed, passages in his masses that sound
trivial, that is because the ways of transforming a tiny motif within a fully dramatic texture in a symphony cannot always be used with decorum in a mass:
Haydn's style is based on the use of these small cells or motifs, and sometimes
they are left untransformed in the religious works—unexploited and consequently insignificant.

In recent years the masses have become available to music lovers in accurate
editions, many of them owing to the astounding industry and energy of Robbins
Landon. Performances have become more frequent. At a Haydn conference in
Washington in 1975, all of the late masses could be heard in succession within a
week. My estimate of these works is much higher now than it was when I wrote
briefly about them; like all lovers of Haydn, I am grateful for the championship
of the masses by Robbins Landon, J. P. Larsen, and others, but I am unregenerate
about my criticism of that time. The criticism was not, in fact, my own, but traditional; most of it was made during Haydn's own lifetime, and he was fully
aware of it. It is also clear, from the apologetic remarks he made about his religious music and his absurd contention that his brother Michael's liturgical
works were better, that he acknowledged its cogency. To a certain extent, as I
have said, the traditional criticism indicates the problems that Haydn envisaged,
and they illuminate his final triumph.

It was not, and could not be, an unmixed triumph. With these new editions,
we can now follow his development from the sweetness, the charm, and the facile pomp of the early masses (above all the *Little Organ Mass*) to the grandeur of
the late works. Even these late works do not allow the free exercise of some of
Haydn's finest and most characteristic qualities: his humor and wit, his elegance
and, above all, his eccentricity—the lightning changes of harmony and texture,
which seem unprepared and turn out later to be completely integrated into the
large form. What one misses most at times is the rhythmic variety. Substituted
for it is a driving rhythmic energy, which entails an unvaried texture that becomes monotonous only because it is not handled with the large sense of harmonic movement that one finds in Handel's equally homogeneous textures.

Dramatic variety is provided by a contrast of solo voice and chorus, in an opposition that comes from concerto technique. Haydn's concertos were never his
strong point, but here, in the masses, he has three levels of sound: solo, chorus,

and orchestra, and this gives him greater space to move about. In these late masses we can trace his increasing mastery: he uses the chorus sometimes as a larger solo group, sometimes as a *tutti* section, and achieves his most dramatic effects through contrast.

The last two masses override almost all possible criticism in very different ways. In the "Creation" Mass (so-called because Haydn quotes his own oratorio in it), Haydn throws off all inhibition in some of the movements (like the Benedictus and the *Allegro* of the Kyrie) and writes a pure symphonic piece: the scherzo-like quality of the Benedictus, light and extraordinarily witty, even popular in style, is still shocking at first hearing. The final mass, with so heavy a use of wind instruments that it is called the "Windband Mass" *(Harmoniemesse)*, is very different. In this work, Haydn at last achieves a complete integration of text and music. The opening Kyrie is no longer festive but a prayer; it satisfies the Church's requirements by its grandeur and its dramatic power. It remains slow throughout, intense, and completely symphonic: solo voices act like the solo winds, the chorus is orchestral. The form is the sonata form of the instrumental works. Yet here, if anywhere in the masses, we may say that Haydn transcended the purely instrumental style of the symphonies and quartets. The Windband Mass has no sense of constraint or compromise. It offers an abstract musical form in which the identification with the text is absolute.

CHAPTER FIVE

Describing Mozart

The book reviewed here is neither important nor even very interesting, but there is a fundamental aspect of musical biography that I wanted to discuss, and it would have been unfair, I thought, to write about it in conjunction with a fine biography. Any good book deserves to have its virtues given more prominence than its faults, and Levey's book was not encumbered with any virtues that would get in the way except a certain readability. It seems to me a fallacy of even good biographers to think that a major work of art must have a more intimate correspondence with some aspect or event of the artist's life than does an insignificant or inferior work. This belief is widespread, but I think there is no evidence for it. Levey's odd judgment that the Jupiter Symphony is a disappointing work gave me an opening to treat this subject.

THE *Life and Death of Mozart* is an absurd labor of love. The author, Michael Levey, is a Keeper of Paintings at the National Gallery in London, an art historian, and a coauthor of *Fifty Works of English Literature We Could Do Without*, but his publishers assure us on the dust jacket that his great-grandfather was an Irish musician.[1] Levey was stimulated to write this book, he believes, by receiving a popular illustrated work on Mozart in French as a present a few years ago, but his inspiration must surely date further back than that. His love of Mozart, uncomprehending and undiscriminating but clearly genuine, can be felt on every page.

Like every lover, Levey has an image of his beloved unrecognizable by a third party. His Mozart is not, of course, as different from mine as Robert Benchley's

---

1. The great-grandfather, Richard Michael Levey (real name O'Shaugnessy; 1811–1899), was, according to *Grove's Dictionary*, a conductor and prolific composer of pantomimes. He also conducted the first performance of *Puss in Boots* by Charles Villiers Stanford, written when that future academic glory of English music was only eight years old.

Mozart, who never wrote a bar of music until he was ninety ("the Mozart that I meant was Arthur Mozart, who lived at 138th Street until he died, in 1926, at the age of ninety-three"). But Levey's Mozart seems not to have written the revolutionary piano concerto K. 271 (which Alfred Einstein called Mozart's *Eroica* Symphony) or the Fantasy in C Minor (the most dramatic piano piece of the eighteenth century), the Viola Quintet in C Major (the grandest, most imposing example of chamber music before Beethoven), or even the String Trio (Divertimento) in E flat Major (the greatest work in its medium of all time)—at least, if he did, Levey has no time to mention them. His treatment of the early operas is, however, extensive, and, I hope, exhaustive.

The author's lively style, which makes his book consistently readable, displays the obtuse, good-humored elegance mastered by so many contemporary English art historians. Levey's picture of the domestic side of Mozart's life is provocative and imaginative, not to say inventive. We are told, for example, of "Mozart's precociously wide knowledge of chambermaids," and Levey enlarges this entertaining perspective by musing on its influence on the musical portrayal of chambermaids in Mozart's operas. The basis for these artful conjectures is the eleven-year-old Mozart's pleasure in receiving a verse letter from a lifelong friend of the Mozart family with a taste for poetry, a lady attached to the household of Count Felix Arco, Chief Chamberlain of Salzburg. There is no evidence for Levey's additional surmise that little Mozart was petted by servants everywhere on his travels, but all these details enliven the book by building up a picture of childish erotic sensibility.

Levey gives constant life to his narrative by a play of imaginative sympathy, which never rests content with the obvious. If the young Mozart wiped his face after being kissed by a lady harpsichordist, it is not simply because the kiss was moist—Levey's powers of visualization are already a step ahead: "she, we may guess, seemed either ugly or old, or both." The events of Mozart's life inflame Levey's fancy in the same way that tiny pieces of grit irritate an oyster. In such fashion the difficult, complex reality of Mozart's relations with his father is transformed into a colorful pattern of popular Freudianism. Unaccountably, Levey neglects the fruitful possibilities of the clearly manic-depressive element in Mozart's correspondence: a wild, exhilarated overconfidence followed some weeks later by a bitter sense of hostile conspiracy and frustration.

In dealing with Mozart's musical activity, Levey is hampered by his unfamiliarity with the musical background. He effectively narrates the reception of Mozart's new symphony in Paris: "The last movement opens in exaggerated quietness, and builds up—quickly—to a crescendo. At the *piano* passage the audience—as

Mozart had expected—shushed each other; at the *forte*, they broke into applause." But he leaves out the point of the joke (there is also no crescendo, but no matter), which is that the Paris orchestra was famous for its opening *coup d'archet*, that is, for starting a piece with a brilliant *forte* display of ensemble. "They begin together here the way they do everywhere else," wrote Mozart sarcastically, and the finale of his symphony opens with the second violins playing softly by themselves.

Levey is most interesting and most instructive where he is least original, in his attempt to deal with the problem of talking about music: How can we describe it, how can it be related to the composer's life? Here is the way Levey grapples with description:

> The first movement unfolds like a bale of shot silk, soothingly smooth and sensuously delightful, rippling as if drawn so rapidly through some ring that the very material turns liquid as it flows. Then it runs more slowly, and a different, darker hue is seen, still sensuous but sensuously rich. . . .
>
> Shot silk becomes, in the adagio, the deepest, heaviest of velvets, unfolded with almost painful slowness as the clarinet begins, and the orchestra joins in, a stately threnody. What was liquid grows thickly viscous, scarcely oozing, and appearing rather to accumulate sweetness as it is stored up, half-honey, half-amber, a precious substance mellowing in a late summer which it seems will never end.

It may be thought at first blush that this does not need criticism but defense.[2] Above all, it calls for sympathy and comprehension: as recently as ten years ago, record jackets and symphony programs were decorated with similar passages, and before they become obsolete we should try to understand what inspired them.

What is most obvious about this method of description is, of course, its use of synesthesia, particularly the appeal to the sense of touch. The materials Levey sets before us are luxury products, velvet and shot silk, which give his poetry a genuine commercial resonance. (Corduroy, although it also produces an interesting play of light, would be unwelcome in such a context.) Here we can call upon a professional and expert witness on Levey's behalf. Richard Strauss, writing about *Salome*, spoke of finding harmonies that "twinkled like taffeta."

What Levey is doing (and Strauss too) is not describing the music, at least not

---

2. I note that this passage has already caught other reviewers' attention. There are many like it in the book, but it does, indeed, represent Levey at the summit of his powers.

in the usual sense of description: the metaphors are not there to make anything more easily recognizable or to point out features of the music that had previously gone unremarked. The writing does not describe but arouses and stimulates. Levey seeks by his prose to awaken in the reader the sensations he would have if he were listening to the music. The music is being sold.

The technique is an outgrowth of what the French call *le style artiste*, developed by the brothers Goncourt, a style designed not to make the reader see or understand, but to feel—quite literally to share the sensations of disgust, fear, and desire of the characters of the novel. To write about music in this way, we must first reduce it to the sensations it produces, its purely physical effect, and try to reproduce that effect by calling into play the interchange and correspondence between the senses.

There is already a word half-naturalized in English for reproducing the immediate physical effect of art while eliminating the rest: *kitsch*. It is only a pity that the word has an exclusively pejorative connotation, as it represents something inevitably and permanently attractive: art without art, art without pain, which demands nothing of us but a wholeheartedly passive response. It is true, however, that to reduce Mozart's music to that aspect which it has in common with *kitsch* is to diminish it.

To place the music in the setting of a composer's life sets us before a more fundamental difficulty. Mozart's music is clearly intelligible without the slightest knowledge of his life. It is even doubtful that we need to know much about the eighteenth century to understand a Mozart quartet. A work by Mozart (or anyone else) is in this sense outside history,[3] and this is no accident, as it was designed to be understood beyond the narrow boundaries of the little culture in which it was created. When a composer hoped for immortality—as Mozart did—this escape from history was quite simply what he intended and worked for. What then does a knowledge of Mozart's life and world add to our comprehension or our appreciation of his music? Of course, there are trivial aspects of the music, like Mozart's little joke with the Paris orchestra, that require a specialized knowledge, but every biographer and historian hopes for something more significant and more essential.

Levey's way of handling this problem is as forthright as it is routine. For him, as for many others, a Mozart symphony is a direct personal expression, a communication from the artist to the public. He therefore seeks for a correspondence between the emotions he finds expressed in, say, the last three symphonies

---

3. As Walter Benjamin said, we can write the history of forms or the history of techniques, but not the history of works of art.

and the circumstances of Mozart's life. When he finds this correspondence—as with the tragic G minor symphony—then the work contains Mozart's "personal sensations" (to use Levey's unhappy phrase). When he does not find it—as with the E flat—then the work shows Mozart "outsoaring circumstances." There is an unacknowledged assumption in all of this that the more striking the work, the more personal it must be. It is not clear why this should be so. The Jupiter Symphony is in some ways more traditional than the other symphonies, and Levey therefore finds it disappointing, which I would have thought made him unique among writers on Mozart, but he cites some anonymous critical support for this view.

Levey is aware that this approach no longer commands the assent it once had, and he has written a defense of it:

> Such an equation has perturbed some critics who fear too pat a correlation between an artist's life and his art, but the artist's personality can hardly remain unaffected by experience. Of course, Mozart may have privately overcome—perhaps had necessarily to overcome—his actual sensations of misery and despair, before they could find any expression in the music of the G minor symphony. But it cannot be denied that he had undergone those sensations. It would be a strange obtuseness to refuse them any part whatsoever in the most starkly despairing of his symphonies; and to argue that they are not present there because they apparently play no part in either the E flat or the "Jupiter" symphonies is to show a poor acquaintance with the human mind. (Some judicious disagreement round this point is recorded by the editors of *The Mozart Companion* with their contributor E. Larsen, who is particularly anxious to believe that Mozart remained "classic" and that both G minor symphonies are just examples of Mozart "seeking to master all the varieties of expression.")
>
> It may be worth adding that even if the "Jupiter" expresses such a very different mood, this itself could be explicable by the fact that so much pain had been poured into the vessel of the previous symphony.

Here Levey has abandoned his usually straightforward approach for a more devious one. The mysterious E. Larsen may be unmasked as Jens Peter Larsen, the greatest of the Haydn scholars of this century, and it is a pity that his essay was disfigured by the footnotes that Levey admires. Larsen did not, of course, believe that Mozart remained classic in the sense that the composer's experience played no role in his art, but that the style of Mozart's symphonies, unlike that of the works of Schumann and Berlioz, does not admit an identification between the expression of the music and a particular sensation or experience of the composer.

A work by Schumann deliberately abolishes the boundary between art and life: it is full of personal allusions, scraps of themes by his wife, anagrams of the musical notes that spell out names and towns of private importance. The listener can sense, and is meant to sense, the private world behind the music. Mozart's music makes no such references, and any equation between its expressive content and a specific trauma in Mozart's life is a critical excrescence upon the work. There is nothing that allows us to associate the tragic emotion of the G minor symphony with Mozart's "black thoughts" of June 27, 1788, as Levey does; we cannot even say that they prompted its composition. A triad of works each with a different affective character was commonplace at the time. As for "black thoughts," Mozart needed no specific impulse. Even a very young child has experienced a despair as black and as deep as that expressed by the G minor symphony. What Mozart created was an artistic language to express any emotion.

If a work of art is to be considered as part of history, it must be protected by mediation, and traditionally this function is performed by the concept of style. To do away with this concept is to erase the history of art, as the concept of style simply expresses the conviction that the work of art may be *intrinsically* located in time and space. The qualities of a symphony of Mozart that enable us to date it and to ascribe it to him make it part of eighteenth-century style, of Viennese Classical style, and of Mozart's own personal style. None of these styles can justifiably be construed as admitting the expression of a private emotion. A private reference within them necessarily takes the form of wit, for they are all public styles, perhaps the greatest public styles in music. Levey does not put the works back into Mozart's life; he tries to force the life into the works, with none of the respect for their integrity and for their independent existence that they demand.

CHAPTER SIX

Beaumarchais:
Inventor of Modern Opera

Like so many other eighteenth-century men of letters, Beaumarchais wanted to reform opera. This was the grandest of all musical genres, but everyone felt it to be, for one reason or another, absurd. "There is too much music in the music of the theater," wrote Beaumarchais. "It is always overloaded; and, to use the naive expression of a justly famous man, the famous chevalier Gluck, our opera stinks of music: *puzza di musica*." In spite of the authority of Gluck, this is a writer's typical irritation: too much music, not enough action. Beaumarchais even tried his hand at writing librettos: his only published example is a ridiculous allegory called *Tarare* with characters like The Genius of the Reproduction of Beings: it was appropriately set to music by a pupil of Gluck—Salieri, who was to achieve posthumous fame as a mythical enemy of Mozart.

Nevertheless, Beaumarchais realized his ambition: he did indeed reform opera, and the reform was revolutionary and permanent. It was by setting Beaumarchais's *The Marriage of Figaro* that Mozart achieved his operatic ideals and gave himself at last the central dramatic ensemble that had to be constructed for him factitiously in *The Abduction from the Seraglio*. The experience also radically altered Mozart's style, and determined the course of opera for the next century. Part of the credit must be given to Lorenzo Da Ponte, who adapted the play for Mozart, but even more belongs to Beaumarchais himself. His theater was not transformed into opera, but was originally conceived in operatic terms, quite literally inspired by the tradition of comic opera and its unrealized possibilities.

The new edition of the works of Pierre-Augustin Caron (who later called himself Caron de Beaumarchais, after a piece of land owned by his first wife) will not do much to alter his reputation. The son of a watchmaker, he was known as a daz-

Originally written in 1988 as a review of Caron de Beaumarchais, *Oeuvres* (Gallimard).

zling polemicist, particularly when his own financial interests were concerned; he won an important lawsuit by appealing over the heads of the judges to the general public in a series of brilliant and entertaining pamphlets or memoirs, in which he dramatized his case with considerable verve. He also produced some insignificant farces, and three sadly unconvincing sentimental dramas. Finally there are the two comedies: *The Barber of Seville*, original and inventive; and *The Marriage of Figaro*, a masterpiece and perhaps the finest play of the eighteenth century.

The Barber of Seville was first conceived and written in 1772 as a four-act opera: in this form (now lost) it was rejected by the Comédiens-Italiens (that was the name given to the opera company in eighteenth-century Paris). Beaumarchais rewrote it during the following year for the Comédie Française, but difficulties with the censor postponed the production until 1775. By this time Beaumarchais had enlarged the play to five acts. The first performance, on Thursday, February 23, was a disaster. The author quickly went back to a revised four-act version which was played on Sunday, February 26 and was immediately a triumphal success.

It had not lost its character as an opera in the rewriting: not only is it full of songs, serenades, and music lessons, but many of the speeches are like arias. Figaro enters singing—and his song turns out to be an unfinished aria for the comic opera he is writing, and he continues to compose the aria throughout his long opening monologue. Don Bazile's famous description of calumny is already an aria even without the music:

> First, a light sound, skirting the ground like a swallow before the storm, *pianissimo* murmurs and then bolts, sowing as it goes the poisoned suggestion [*trait*]. Anyone's mouth can pick it up, and *piano, piano,* slip it adroitly into your ear. The evil is done, develops, crawls, walks and *rinforzando* from mouth to mouth it goes like the devil: then suddenly, I don't know how, you see Calumny spring up, hiss, swell, grow before your eyes. It bounds forward, spreads its wings, whirls, surrounds, tears away, sweeps along, bursts and thunders, and becomes, thank Heaven, a general shout, a public *crescendo,* a universal *chorus* of hate and proscription. Who the devil could resist it?

This extraordinary succession of mixed metaphors has an almost purely musical structure: Rossini's famous setting is an achievement of genius, but one can see that half his work had already been done for him by Beaumarchais.

This "aria" had been added in the five-act version of the play, but it was retained when the company went back to the shorter structure. There are three different versions of *The Barber of Seville* (four, with the lost opera): the new edition gives hundreds of variant readings, all in almost unreadable form. If publishers are going to make the variants available for the delight of scholars, it is self-defeating to print them in a way that can give pleasure to no one, and is disgustingly painful to read. I should have sacrificed the hundreds of pages of Beaumarchais's mediocre sentimental plays for a satisfactory printing of the five-act version of *The Barber*. It was undeniably less effective than the final version, but it contained lots of good things that are not in the revised version—one, indeed, so good that Beaumarchais saved it for his next play: a virtuoso aria on the use of the word "goddamn" in English.

His next play was *The Marriage of Figaro,* a sequel to *The Barber of Seville* that started as a joke. Annoyed by critics who complained that the first comedy had too simple a plot, Beaumarchais facetiously outlined a possible sixth act in the preface: a ridiculous scene in which Figaro is discovered, by a birthmark, to be the long-lost natural son of Doctor Bartholo and the governess Marceline. This extravagant parody of the silliest moments of sentimental melodrama was incorporated bodily into the new play, where it is, by a kind of tour de force, both absurd and touching. This became the occasion for Mozart's greatest ensemble, the sextet of recognition, which was the composer's own favorite number in the opera—a work of the most sophisticated irony, deeply moving and yet humorous at the same time. Only Mozart could have carried this off, but only Beaumarchais thought of it. It is a fine example of the playwright's characteristic genius, at once serious and playfully impudent. The impertinence, in fact, is what made Beaumarchais's powerful moral and political satire acceptable and dangerous.

The Marriage of Figaro was written by 1778, but the assault on the social order was considerably more outrageous than in his earlier play—or than in anyone else's earlier play—and the censorship authorities refused permission to perform it until 1784: the premiere on the 27th of April was perhaps the greatest triumph in the history of the French theater. The combination of gaiety and sedition, of daring and charm, was irresistible. (At one point the Count reproaches Figaro for his detestable reputation. Figaro has a ready answer: "And suppose I am better than my reputation? Can many aristocrats say as much?")

The premiere in Vienna of Mozart's setting followed only two years and four days later. Paisiello had already set *The Barber of Seville* in 1782, seven years after the premiere of that comedy. Da Ponte and Mozart may have wished to exploit the success of Paisiello's *Barber,* which had already been produced in Vienna, or simply to exploit the popularity of a new and scandalous work. Much—but not all—of the political satire was removed by Da Ponte, or he would never have seen the work produced in Vienna, infinitely more reactionary than Paris: but with a play so recent and so famous, a large part of the public would have known much of what was taken out.

The originality of play and libretto was immediately evident. One odd measure of this is the length. Da Ponte apologized for the unorthodox length of *Le Nozze di Figaro* (four acts instead of the usual two or three), but explained that Mozart and he were doing something absolutely new. The opera is really in two acts, but the size demanded extra divisions: when the opera was finally done in Italy, it was too much for the Italians—they did the first two acts on one night, and the last two on the following (having hired another composer to rewrite them, since Mozart's last two acts were found to be too difficult). Beaumarchais's play was already startlingly long: the première lasted four and a half hours.

Da Ponte claimed that he did not translate Beaumarchais, but imitated him; in fact, he followed the original more closely than one might have believed possible. For example, after Figaro's opening scene with Suzanne, Beaumarchais gives him a menacing tirade against the Count and Bazile, the music teacher. Da Ponte changes the terms of the threat into "If you want to dance, my little Count, I'll play the guitar for you." This, however, is an adaptation of a later, defiant Figaro, when Suzanne and the Countess disguise Cherubino as a girl to fool the Count: "Dress him, fix his hair, I'll take him off and indoctrinate him and then—dance, Monseigneur!" Many of the arias come directly from the French original: Figaro's prediction of the unpleasant military life that awaits Cherubino and the latter's expression of his adolescent eroticism are almost word for word in the play. Even more than in the *Barber,* Beaumarchais was capable here of brief moments of lyric intensity. The sentimentality in Beaumarchais's serious plays is merely embarrassing: concentrated into a few brief sentences in the comedies, it has great force and, moreover, helps to organize the rhythm of the play.

The best critical interpretation of Beaumarchais's comedy is Mozart's opera. We may extend that interpretation by reversing the terms, by observing what Beaumarchais gave to Mozart, above all those gifts that no composer had ever received from a dramatist before. We shall find that Beaumarchais was largely responsible in the end not only for *The Marriage of Figaro,* but for *Don Giovanni, Così fan tutte,* and even for *The Magic Flute* as well.

The most obvious gift is the importance given to the erotic element. Of course, love was hardly a novelty in the theater, and the wicked seducer, the languishing wife, the honest gardener's niece, and her trusty betrothed are all stock figures. Cherubino, however, is an absolutely original invention on the stage, although he springs partly from the many eighteenth-century novels and stories, semi-pornographic, about awakening sexuality. It is the ambiguity of Cherubino that is new: only thirteen, he is too young to be respectably and openly an object of desire for the Countess. Beaumarchais is quite explicit about him in the preface to the play:

> Is it my page who scandalizes you? . . . A child of thirteen, whose heart is just beginning to beat, seeking everything and discerning nothing, adoring—as one does at that happy age—a heavenly object who happens to be his godmother, is he the subject of scandal? . . . Do you say that one loves him with love? Censors, that is not the right word! You are too enlightened not to know that even the most pure love is not disinterested: one does not yet love him, therefore: one senses that one day one will love him.

This is somewhat disingenuous, and, I presume, intended to seem so, but the ambiguity of Cherubino (compounded by Beaumarchais's insistence that "the role can only be played by a young and very pretty woman") is essential to the play. The Count's insane jealousy of him is both absurd and clearly right.

At the end, when the Count, humiliated and pardoned by his wife, learns that it was Figaro who received the slap on the face intended for Cherubino, he turns laughing and says, "What do you think about that, my dear Countess?" Her reply is:

> THE COUNTESS, *lost in thought, comes to herself and says with feeling*:
> Ah, yes, dear Count, and for life, with no distraction, I swear to you.

She has not listened to a word he said, and she is evidently thinking about Cherubino. Perhaps Beaumarchais himself is thinking about the depressing sequel he was soon to write, called *The Guilty Mother*, in which the Countess has to face the consequences of having yielded for one brief night, some years after *The Marriage of Figaro*, to Cherubino's passion. But we have not yet fallen so low: the Countess's feelings are only half-conscious, half-willing.

This kind of ambiguous eroticism was realized by Mozart in music even more fully with *Don Giovanni* in the wonderful scenes with Zerlina, willing and not willing, and with all four lovers in *Così fan tutte*, where the men find their emotions brought unconsciously into play by the trick they are playing on the women. Kierkegaard thought *Don Giovanni* not only the greatest opera, but the only possible one, precisely because of the way it embodied the erotic ideal. We must acknowledge the influence of Beaumarchais: none of the previous dramatic versions of the Don Juan legend have anything like the fluidity of erotic atmosphere that Mozart and Da Ponte realized; but this is already found in *The Marriage of Figaro*, in Susanna's teasing duet with the Count in which she resists and holds out the possibility of surrender, in Cherubino's opening aria, with its breathless excitement, and, above all, in the moment of lyric peace in the middle of the fourth-act finale, when Figaro is alone on the stage, believing Susanna to be with the Count:

> All is tranquil and placid
> The beautiful Venus has gone in
> She can be caught with wanton Mars
> By the new Vulcan of the age
> In his net

Cuckoldry was never before or again set with such melancholy intensity, as by Mozart's rich, slow horn calls. This scene, a wonderful contrast to Figaro's earlier sardonic aria on women's congenital infidelity, is almost pure Da Ponte. It has little counterpart in Beaumarchais, but it depends for its effect upon the elaboration of sentiment already present. Its calm resignation enlarges still further the range of erotic feeling, and compensates for the way the Countess's ambiguous feeling for Cherubino is glossed over in the opera.

The complexity and ambiguity of sentiment in *The Marriage of Figaro* made it possible for Mozart to put on the stage, for the first time in the history of opera, really human, three-dimensional, individual characters. Even in the greatest of his earlier operas, he had not been able to do that: only Electra in *Idomeneo* has some individuality—because she is raving mad—and Osmin in *The Abduction from the Seraglio*—because as a eunuch with a very short temper and an incredibly low bass voice, he is outrageously picturesque: all the others are either the standard idealized figures of *opera seria* or the stock characters of *opera buffa*. What gives a new dimension to Figaro, Susanna, Cherubino, and the Count is that Beaumarchais conceived of action and personality as a conflict, in political terms. His personages no longer move in a vacuum.

Beaumarchais was aware of the source of his power: "I have thought," he wrote, "I still think that we get no great pathos, or profound morality, or sound and true comedy in the theater without strong situations which always spring from a social disparity [or incongruity (*disconvenance*)] in the subject we wish to treat." Social disparity is the heart of his conception of stage intrigue: like so many French eighteenth-century authors, he saw life as a conflict of classes, but he was the first to be able to present this dramatically. Earlier authors had successfully depicted the hierarchy of classes: in Beaumarchais this has become a genuine opposition, even a struggle.

It is this conflict that reveals the full-blooded individuality of his—and Mozart's—actors. There is, however, still another conflict that supports this individuality, that between class and character. "Every man," declared Beaumarchais, "is himself by his character: he is what pleases fate by his position [*état*], on which his character has a great influence." Figaro's wit, for example, depends on his impudence, and this is determined by his station in life. He can only be impudent because he is not well-born. (He turns out to be the son of a doctor and a duenna, but this is a kind of joke that no one believes: neither before nor after the recognition scene does he lay claim to privilege, although he does try to get his birth legitimized.) The social disparity makes the drama possible, a conflict between character or merit and position. Figaro is not a domestic servant, but the superintendent of the chateau and about to be named ambassadorial courier by the Count in his new official post. When Figaro defends Suzanne against the seductions of the Count, he is fighting not just for love but also, as he himself says, for his property. The disparity is simply that Figaro is too clever for his station in life, and when he triumphs at the end, he humiliates his master.

Even Cherubino is conceived in class terms: as a proof that he is not to be taken seriously, Beaumarchais points out in the preface that Figaro uses the familiar form of address to him, which he would not have dared to do if Cherubino were older. His youth consigns him to an inferior class: his erotic ambitions, however, are those of a man. His inferiority, like Figaro's, is in conflict with his sense of himself.

It is the ambiguity of class that gives Beaumarchais's characters their full humanity. His characters seem to act independently, because the conflict of character and station is a dynamic principle. His sense of each character's social position was wonderfully sharp. The music teacher, Bazile, refuses to obey an order of the Count:

> BAZILE: I did not become part of the staff at the chateau to run errands.
> COUNT: What then?
> BAZILE: With my talent as a village organist, I teach the countess to play the harpsichord, her women to sing, and the pages to play the

mandolin: my job is above all to amuse your company with my guitar, when it pleases you to order it.

In response to this, the Count sends a shepherd boy on the errand, and commands Bazile to accompany him singing and playing. "He is part of my company," says the Count brutally: "that is your job. Do it, or I'll throw you out."

Beaumarchais was proud of the extraordinary individuality of his characters. I have no style, he claimed; my characters speak for themselves. In the preface to *The Marriage of Figaro,* he writes:

> When my subject seizes me, I evoke all my personages, and put them into the situation: "Be careful, Figaro, your master will find you out! . . . Ah, countess, what imprudence, with so violent a husband." I have no idea what they will say: I concern myself with what they will do. Then, when they are in action, I write under their rapid dictation, certain that they will not fool me, that I shall recognize Bazile, who does not have the wit of Figaro, who does not have the noble tone of the count, who does not have the sensitivity of the countess, who does not have the gaiety of Suzanne, who does not have the mischievousness of the page, and above all none of them have the sublimity of Brid'oison [the foolish judge in the breach of promise scene]. Each one speaks his language.

Like Beaumarchais, Mozart was able to adjust his style both to class and to personality. He had always done this, but before *Figaro* class and character did not interact. No librettist had ever offered him a scene like the one in which Suzanne comes out of the locked room to curtsy to the Count, with that ironic combination of modesty and impudence wonderfully reflected in the accompanying minuet.

After *Figaro,* the way was clear. Class plays an even greater part, if possible, in *Don Giovanni,* as the hero relegates the lady to his valet disguised as himself while he serenades the maid, and makes love to the peasant girl and sends off her fiancé with his servants. The class structure of *Don Giovanni* is static compared with that of *Figaro,* but it is disorganized by the hero—or villain—from the beginning, where he rapes the first aristocratic lady we see him with, and insults the next one by having his servant read out his catalogue of conquests. It has often been said, correctly I think, that the ball with three orchestras on the stage at the end of Act I pictures all classes of society. I believe this view has been challenged, but I cannot think why Mozart would have a courtly minuet, a less noble contredanse, and a rustic Teutscher, all played together in elaborate counterpoint, unless he wanted a virtuoso musical representation of the class structure.

Politics had always played an important role in serious opera, but it had generally been the frivolous politics of court intrigue and the alliance of two countries by dynastic marriage. The political significance of *Figaro* and *Don Giovanni*, on the other hand, is based essentially on the popular belief in aristocratic corruption and sexual exploitation—this may appear equally superficial at first sight, but it touched deeper emotions. The political theme of *Figaro* is largely mythical: the famous *droit du seigneur*, the right of the lord to take the virginity of the bride of one of his vassals. Even if this had existed at all in medieval times, by the eighteenth century it was only a vulgar legend; nevertheless, it had genuine political resonance in the 1780s. With *Figaro*, comic opera became more seriously political than serious opera.

The libertarian ethics of the Masonic societies provides the politics of *The Magic Flute*. The wicked Queen of the Night was read, correctly or not, as the empress Maria Theresa. At the heart of the opera are the demands made by the Masonic virtues, above all those of steadfastness and fidelity, upon men and women of different conditions and talents. The opera is exceptionally humane: the clownish Papageno fails all the tests, and is rewarded with the wife of his dreams anyway.

Even in *Così fan tutte*, social disparity is crucial in giving substance to the characters. Here they all come from the same class, except for the chambermaid; but the opera pits women *as a class* against men, and the inferiority of women determines the structure. This, as we might expect, makes the women more, not less, individual, gives them greater humanity as each defines herself against a clearly oppressive masculine standard. Above all with Fiordiligi, we find a superb conflict of class (or sex) and character.

With *Figaro*, we can see that the personages of earlier operas—even the greatest by Handel and Scarlatti—were not characters at all, but a set of powerful and affecting emotions, strung together as a series of arias and organized logically by the intrigue—and then generally disorganized by the singers, who almost always substituted different arias more suitable to their voices. We are sometimes persuasively told of the consistency of character in these operas created by the composers through a consistent musical style for each singer, but that is really a proof of their dramatic inadequacy. Mozart's characters seem real because of their inconsistency, their contradictions. They reveal themselves above all by reacting to each other—not in the arias but in the ensembles and the finales. The ensembles of *Figaro* were Beaumarchais's greatest gift to Mozart.

Even before *Figaro*, the ensembles of his operas had been Mozart's special pride. With *Figaro*, however, the character of these ensembles changed radically. The quartet of *Idomeneo* was magnificent but static; it is not very different from the great quartet in Handel's *Jephtha*, in which each singer individually expresses a different isolated sentiment. One can see, however, that Mozart aspired to a more active form: at the end, the singers leave before finishing the melody, and the orchestra must round off the phrase. The quartet of *The Abduction from the Seraglio* was superficially more dynamic (the lovers are reunited, quarrel, and are reconciled), but it was obviously set up with little dramatic justification so that Mozart could have a brilliant finale to his first act. It has little relation to the intrigue, and does not advance the action. Nevertheless, the ensembles in the *Abduction* contain some of the most beautiful and striking music in the opera: they are virtuoso set pieces to display the composer's genius.

The ensembles of *Figaro* are even more impressive; they are integrated dramatically and full of action. This is evident right from the opening number in which Figaro is measuring the floor for a bed while Susanna tries on a hat. From then on we have ensembles in which people dictate letters to each other, remove dresses from a chair to discover a page hiding underneath, threaten to smash down doors, and mistakenly seduce their own wife under the impression that she is the chambermaid. There were comic ensembles with some action before *Figaro*, but nothing of even remotely comparable complexity and richness of action had ever been seen before—and above all there had never been ensembles with such full-blooded individual personalities. Character cannot be portrayed adequately through the aria: this reduces the personality only to an emotion. It is the interaction of one person with another that gives character its depth; it is only through the ensemble that music can create the illusion of real people. Mozart achieved this for the first time with *Figaro*, and he continued with *Don Giovanni*: it is in the ensembles that an elderly *commendatore* is murdered, a peasant girl seduced, a funereal statue invited to dinner, the hero consigned to hell.

Even the way to construct an act was shown to Mozart by Beaumarchais, who was unrivaled at building excitement by bringing more and more people onto the stage. This was a principle of operatic construction that held sway for more than a century, and it is basic to Verdi's technique. The second-act finale of *Figaro*, which ends with a septet, is the greatest example, and the libretto follows Beaumarchais's original very closely. The tension rises steadily as people of different stations of life and opposing interests gradually enter to create fresh difficulties. For the first time in opera, an act becomes a tightly organized, complex dramatic structure.

We might say that Beaumarchais invented modern opera with some assistance from Mozart. Mozart never surpassed the second-act finale of *Figaro,* and it influenced the rest of his operatic career. I should imagine, however, that Beaumarchais did not like Mozart's operas very much; he almost certainly thought that they "stank of music": unlike any of his contemporaries, Mozart gave interesting lines to play even to the violas and the second violins. Perhaps Mozart had misgivings about Beaumarchais's play: after all, his father, Leopold, wrote: "It is a very tiresome play and the translation from the French will certainly have to be altered very freely if it is to be effective as an opera." It was, however, Mozart who proposed the play to Da Ponte.

On one point, Mozart and Beaumarchais were in accord. The latter declared: "Music will be employed seriously in the theater when we realize that one should sing only to speak." Mozart similarly answered the elderly tenor who complained that in the quartet of *Idomeneo,* he could not produce the sustained, even tones for which he was famous: "In a quartet, the notes should be much more spoken than sung." It was paradoxically in the ensembles, which are the most elaborate structures of pure music, that Mozart perfectly realized Beaumarchais's operatic ideal.

CHAPTER SEVEN

Radical, Conventional Mozart

At the opening of the following essay, the mistake of calling Joseph II the emperor Franz Joseph is so egregious that I have let it stand in the text in the hope that the public humiliation will make me more careful in the future. Several readers wrote to signal other mistakes. Mozart's sonatas were written for a queen, not an empress, of Prussia. The composer who may have influenced Mozart was Piccinni, not Puccini: I have corrected this mistake, for which I am innocent. (Typesetters do not believe that there was a composer called Piccinni until one has corrected this several times in proof. I remember making this correction three successive times in a book published by Faber and Faber, and only succeeded in imposing it by writing it large in red.) John Yohalem kindly remarked, among other points, that E. T. A. Hoffman changed one of his middle names to Amadeus from Wilhelm, not Friedrich. A. D. Roberts reminded me that it was Edward Fitzgerald, not Bernard Shaw, who said: "People will not believe that Mozart can be powerful, because he is so beautiful." I am sure that Shaw quoted this somewhere.

A few years before Mozart's death in 1791, the emperor of Austria, Franz Joseph, received the visit of a distinguished but uninteresting composer, Karl Ditters von Dittersdorf, and asked him what he thought of Mozart's compositions. In his *Recollections*, Dittersdorf reported the conversation:

> *Dittersdorf:* He is unquestionably one of the greatest original geniuses, and I have known until now no composer who possesses such an astonishing wealth of ideas. I should wish that he were not so spendthrift with it. He does not allow the listener to breathe; for hardly have we perceived one beautiful idea, that another more splendid already

Originally written in 1991 as a review of Robert L. Marshall, ed., *Mozart Speaks: Views on Music, Musicians, and the World*; Ivan Nagel, *Autonomy and Mercy: Reflections on Mozart's Operas* (translated by Marion Faber and Ivan Nagel); and Daniel Heartz, *Mozart's Operas*.

appears on the heels of the former, and this continues without ceasing until, in the end, we can retain none of these beauties in our memory.

Emperor: In his stage works, the singers have very often complained of a single fault, that he often drowns them out with his full accompaniment.

D: That surprises me . . .

E: Some time ago I made a comparison between Mozart and Haydn. Compare them yourself, so that I can see whether yours agrees with mine.

D: (after a pause) Will your Majesty allow me to put another question?

E: Go ahead.

D: How would your majesty compare Klopstock and Gellert [two of the most famous contemporary poets]?

E: Hmmm!—both of them are great poets—one must read Klopstock's works more than once in order to understand all of his beauties—on the contrary with Gellert all of the beauties lie unveiled at first sight.

D: Your majesty has my answer.

E: Mozart is like Klopstock and Haydn like Gellert?

D: So at least I believe.

If Dittersdorf's account (dictated on his deathbed to his son) is accurate—and I can see no reason why it would not be—it appears that Mozart's and Haydn's supremacy is not simply a judgment of posterity but was evident before Mozart's death. It is interesting that the charge leveled by Dittersdorf against Mozart—too great a profusion of musical ideas—was to be one of the chief complaints about Beethoven only two decades later. The poet Ludwig Tieck, in a dialogue from his *Phantasus* of 1812, has one of his speakers claim that Beethoven "seldom continues a musical idea and settles down in it but jumps through the most powerful transitions and seeks to flee from imagination itself in restless strife." These are not hostile comments, even though the character had remarked that "if we are obliged to call Mozart insane, then Beethoven cannot be distinguished from the raving mad."

What is emphasized in Dittersdorf's discussion with the emperor is the essential difficulty of Mozart's music, and this is a point that comes up again and again in the testimony of Mozart's contemporaries. Technical difficulty in the first place: commissioned by a publisher to write six piano quartets, Mozart had to abandon the project after composing only two—the publisher found the music too difficult to sell. Even the admirers of Mozart's string quartets acknowledged that they were unintelligible unless played by virtuosos of the highest technical mastery.

This leads to the second kind of difficulty, that of comprehension. After the first performance in Vienna on May 1, 1786, of *The Marriage of Figaro,* one newspaper reported:

> Herr Mozart's music was generally admired by connoisseurs already at the first performance. . . . The *public,* however (and this often happens to the public) did not really know on the first day where it stood. It heard many a *bravo* from unbiased connoisseurs, but obstreperous louts in the uppermost storey exerted their hired lungs with all their might to deaden singers and audience alike with this *St!* and *Pst!*; and consequently opinions were divided at the end of the piece.
>
> Apart from that, it is true that the first performance was none of the best, owing to the difficulty of the composition.[1]

On the whole, Dittersdorf reflected general musical opinion, and his comparison of Mozart to Klopstock for the emperor's benefit was suggestive: Klopstock was notorious as the most obscure and complex of contemporary poets, one admired but little read.

In the next generation, although Mozart's glory was now unquestioned, the novelist E. T. A. Hoffmann, who loved Mozart so much he changed one of his middle names from Friedrich to Amadeus, was still obliged to defend him against the charge that the harmony in the operas was often so radical as to be incomprehensible for anybody except a professional musician. Hoffmann's answer was perhaps his most brilliant essay on music. He took an example of Mozart's dramatic modulation from the cemetery scene in *Don Giovanni,* the E major trio, in which the stone statue nods in response to Giovanni's invitation to dinner, and the basses of the orchestra descend to a surprising and chilling C natural.

The professional musician, remarked Hoffmann, recognizes and names the technical procedure with no difficulty: the flatted sub-mediant holds no mystery for him. The general public, on the other hand, knows nothing of the technique, but shivers with terror at the sudden harmonic effect. It is the half-educated amateur who is puzzled by the chromatic change and is not sure what to call it. The connoisseur and the completely ignorant join hands in their understanding and admiration of the drama: the pretentious amateur is left behind by the complexity of the score. It was not to the great unwashed that Mozart's scores presented problems, and it is, in fact, the most complex of his scores—the G minor and Ju-

1. From Otto Erich Deutsch, *Mozart: A Documentary Biography* (Stanford University Press, 1965), p. 278.

piter symphonies, *Don Giovanni, The Marriage of Figaro,* and *The Magic Flute*—
that have won the greatest and most enduring popularity.

Half a century after his death, Mozart's reputation for difficulty was gone. For
many of Beethoven's works, on the other hand—the Hammerklavier Sonata, the
Diabelli Variations, the last quartets—the appearance of difficulty still persists
today for both audience and performer. Mozart became an excessively easy composer, and his music thereby lost much of its dramatic effectiveness. In the late
nineteenth century, Bernard Shaw remarked that no one believed that Mozart's
music could be powerful as it was so pretty. Tieck had written that Mozart's style
united heaven and hell: in 1811, everyone knew what he meant, but I think that
few musicians or music lovers would find this intelligible today.

The bicentenary of Mozart's death was an opportunity for a reassessment. No
one would wish to accept or simply resuscitate the judgment of an artist by his
contemporaries: this would often revive only the grossest misunderstanding.
Nevertheless, we need to comprehend the reaction of Mozart's audience and, in
fact, of his colleagues. To interpret Mozart for today, we have to understand the
nature of the eighteenth-century resistance to his achievement. Some difficulties
disappear with time and familiarity; others are merely rendered invisible or inaudible.

Unfortunately, the bicentenary celebration was largely a commercial undertaking. Few advances were made in 1991 in Mozart scholarship.[2] Many books
were reissued without being brought up to date. Some of the most distinguished
scholars contented themselves with writing prefaces to facsimiles of Mozart's
manuscripts, or compiling illustrated souvenir books or short guides to all of
Mozart's compositions with anecdotal information tailored to avoid provoking
thought or any critical inquiry. There is no need to take a high moral tone about
any of this. Mozart himself engaged in a good deal of hackwork.

Serious consideration of Mozart must start even today with Hermann Abert's
great two volumes of 1924, entitled *W. A. Mozart.* Seventy years later this is still
not available in English—or French, for that matter. (The biographical section is
a rewriting of Otto Jahn's nineteenth-century book; the brilliant account of the
music is Abert's own.) Plans to translate it keep coming up but have always been
shelved by publishers, convinced that it would be more profitable to commission
either a shorter book or one with a more popular slant (although the chapter on

2. A recent book by Andrew Steptoe, *The Mozart-Da Ponte Operas* (Oxford University Press,
1988), is particularly good and original on the social background of the operas. *New Mozart Documents: A Supplement to O. E. Deutsch's Documentary Biography,* edited by Cliff Eisen (Stanford University Press, 1991) brings together many new documents on Mozart's life and the reception of his
work.

Don Giovanni was translated and published as a separate book). In spite of all the recent research, Abert has not been superseded. He knew more about eighteenth-century opera than anybody else of this time—or, possibly, of our time for that matter, and, most remarkably, he understood Mozart's music. A translation of Abert would improve the quality of writing on Mozart in English, particularly if it were possible to add annotations by a Mozart scholar to bring the book up to date.

No one would be better placed to annotate Abert than Robert Marshall. His recent studies of Mozart's manuscripts, particularly those works that Mozart began and was unable to finish, have shown a combination rare in Mozart research of intelligence, good sense, and lack of dogmatism. His new volume, *Mozart Speaks,* is one of the few useful contributions to the Mozart bicentenary. This is an anthology of excerpts from Mozart's letters arranged by subject matter, interspersed with contemporary accounts of Mozart and a wonderfully informative commentary by Marshall. It makes possible a reading of the Mozart letters that is more interesting and more instructive than a chronological one. There is perhaps no book except Abert's from which one can learn what is most important about Mozart, and of course Marshall incorporates all of the research since 1924. His book cannot be praised too highly.

The only fault I could find—and it is a small one—is that on occasion Mozart's words are accepted at face value without asking why he was writing them to the particular correspondent. Much of Mozart's assurances to his father, for example, that his music will appeal not only to connoisseurs but to the ignorant as well are attempts to calm his father's suspicious fears as well as a direct expression of faith. I believe, of course, that Mozart wanted popular success, but how much he was really prepared to sacrifice, or even to restrain his more radical inspirations, to get it is a different matter.

Marshall's commentary is valuable on almost every aspect of Mozart's music and life. What does not come out sufficiently in *Mozart Speaks*—largely because it was rarely and only insufficiently expressed by Mozart himself—was the extent of his ambition. His projects were grandiose beyond those of any of his contemporaries. First there was his display of craftsmanship. At the end of his life, he was commissioned to write six easy piano sonatas for the Empress of Prussia. One of these, in D major, K. 576, is often thought to be an independent work because it is so difficult to perform: however, it is difficult because Mozart miscalculated. The only passages that are hard to play are in two-part counterpoint, of which Mozart was the greatest master since Johann Sebastian Bach (whose two-part inventions were also written for beginners). Mozart evidently thought that if each hand had to play only one note at a time, the pianist would find the piece easy. He was wrong, partly because he wanted to display his ingenuity. Much of the two-part counterpoint is in canon form: that is, each hand plays the same melody but starting some distance apart. Mozart was intent on demonstrating his virtuosity as a composer with a single theme.

Similarly in the finale of the Jupiter Symphony: here we are dealing with five-part invertible counterpoint—that is, with five themes that can be played together with any one of them above or below any of the others. Leonard Ratner has shown, in a fascinating essay,[3] that Mozart in the coda exhausted all possible combinations. The counterpoint in the operas is even more astounding: toward the beginning of the finale in the last act of *Così fan tutte,* the lovers sing a canon as a toast to celebrate the ceremony of marriage that is about to take place—at least, three of the lovers sing the canon, one of the most exquisite and expressive of Mozart's melodies, since the fourth, Guglielmo, is still too outraged by the recent betrayal of Fiordiligi to be able to do anything except mutter that he hopes they are drinking poison.

Here, I think, is one of the keys to Mozart's supremacy—a perfect realization of an extremely conventional form followed by a dramatic transformation. He was at once the most conventional and the most radical of composers. The vaudeville at the end of *The Abduction from the Seraglio* is another example: a vaudeville is a strict form in which all the members of the cast line up and each one successively sings one stanza while all sing the refrain in chorus. In *The Abduction,* it goes along conventionally until it is the turn of Osmin, the eunuch, outraged that these wicked Christians should get off scot-free; he bursts into a raging fit and rushes off. The rest of the cast sing a brief quartet in favor of forgiveness and condemning wrath and vengeance, and then finish the vaudeville without him.

The mastery of convention is as impressive as the revolutionary daring, although the former suits modern taste somewhat less, and requires familiarity with the style to appreciate. All composers who have mastered their craft fulfill the conventions of the musical language and style of their time, but many, like Haydn and Beethoven, disguise these conventions as they realize them, turn them into something more personal and more idiosyncratic. Mozart displays the conventions nakedly: his radical ideas coexist side by side with the most commonplace ones, the latter transformed only by his exquisite workmanship.

One might say that Haydn is always unpredictable, but that Mozart always does what one expects him to do—and then immediately afterward produces an

---

3. *Compleat Mozart,* edited by Neil Zaslaw (North, 1991), p. 196.

original stroke that no other composer could bring off. In a Haydn symphony, the arrival of a new theme or the return of an old one is very often a surprise, but almost never in Mozart, where we can generally sense the return sixteen bars in advance. The lyrical theme in the exposition of the Prague Symphony is clearly prepared by a long and elaborate transition—and then, at the very last split second, we realize that the last notes of the transition are already the first notes of the new melody.

Mozart could match the achievements of any of his contemporaries, and he could even wonderfully mimic the style of past decades. It is the scope of his thought that went beyond anything seen before: even today, the ballroom scene of *Don Giovanni* seems an amazing tour de force, with three orchestras on the stage each playing a different dance in different rhythms, one for each class of society, peasant, bourgeois, and aristocratic, and each orchestra successively tuning up in harmony with the dance that has already started. Mozart's ambition challenged not only his contemporaries but posterity as well. He began a comic opera like *The Magic Flute* with one of the most elaborate fugues ever heard in an opera, and, in the second act, wrote a chorale prelude in Baroque style based on a Protestant chorale. Mozart was Catholic, but also a Freemason: Was this intended as a plea for religious tolerance in Catholic Vienna?

II

The seriousness of Mozart's transformation in opera is evident in two books which are the most substantial of the recent offerings: Ivan Nagel's *Autonomy and Mercy* and Daniel Heartz's *Mozart's Operas*. They are very different: *Autonomy and Mercy* is a concentrated philosophical work of 150 pages; *Mozart's Operas,* a large collection of essays on the Italian operas by Professor Heartz, with two supplementary essays on the German operas by Thomas Bauman,[4] is one of the most important contributions to recent Mozart research.

Walter Benjamin once wrote that to understand the late eighteenth century's conception of marriage, one must oppose *The Magic Flute* to Kant's definition of marriage (a contract between a man and a woman which allows each the use of the other's genital organs for life): this, he said, gives the two poles of Enlightenment thought. The center of *The Magic Flute* is both the ideal and the reality of marriage. Pamina and Tamino pass every test successfully and are united; but Papageno, who fails every time, is given a wife too, because he is human and that is what he wants. I cite Benjamin because I think Ivan Nagel's *Autonomy and*

---

4. Bauman is the author of a very fine recent book on Mozart's *Abduction from the Seraglio, Die Entführung aus dem Serail* (Cambridge University Press, 1988).

Mercy is strongly influenced by him, but Nagel takes a very different approach. His book starts from the observation that the last seven of Mozart's operas all end with a pardon, with the exception of *Don Giovanni*, where the hero refuses to ask for mercy. In several of these operas, the pardon is demanded by an act of autonomy in a Kantian sense. As Nagel writes:

> This act knows, wishes, *effects* that the individual, by the sheer decision to affirm his or her own truth, is able to change his destiny, to burst the prison of fate—otherwise freedom would be only an enticement to failure. . . . When Goethe's Iphigenie, Mozart's Pamina confess, celebrate their truth "even if it were a crime," they do not cause but rather compel (through the ritual of their offer to die) pardon from above.

Nagel's book is an important one, sometimes profound, always imaginative. It places Mozart's operas within the moral and political thought of his time. What is remarkable is that in doing this Nagel is able to attend to the music, even if his references to details of the actual scores may appear intermittent. As he writes:

> Criticism of Mozart's operatic forms should heed their sensuous detail, even while inquiring into the words of the libretto or the idea of the genre. The unity of idea and words (as the design for a world or the text for a coloratura) is precarious anyway. Although both idea and words precede the composition aesthetically and chronologically, their union triumphs or fails only with the birth of the music. . . . To grasp our particular problem—what opera becomes when all ideas and words begin to change—we should listen even more intently to what the sounds are telling us. We need to test whether the breakthrough of mercy (which seria, singspiel, and buffa promised and spelled out, each in a different way) has been proved true, or given the lie, by its own music.—In *Tito*, the praise of sovereignty made the music of mercy sound untrue. In *Die Zauberflöte*, the rise of autonomy helped mercy come true. This double paradox forces us to confront at last our most perplexing question: In the era of autonomy, what need is there for mercy?

It is clear that Nagel does not bend to fashion, and that he refuses to accept the present evaluation of *La Clemenza di Tito* as equal in interest to *Figaro* and *Don Giovanni*. The old view still seems correct to me: Mozart was tired, sick, and in a hurry when he wrote *Tito* and it was not a subject that he chose for himself, as he had done with the five previous operas. It is true that Mozart's music is always competent and, indeed, always beautiful, but some of it is not very interesting. Some admirers of *Tito* have tried to defend it by observing that Mozart was trying to imitate Paisiello and achieve an easy success: Paisiello's style was much less complex than Mozart's, and he avoided the famous reproach thrown at Mozart, "Too many notes." For example, he generally wrote the same line for first and second violins, while Mozart almost always made the second violins independent, and, in addition, gave the violas great importance. This richness disappears in *Tito*, which has, of course, great things: a wonderful duet, a sublime slow opening to one of the long, brilliant arias (called "rondos"), and an astonishing first-act finale—which is too short, and suddenly comes to an unexpected halt. (About a chorus in this finale, E. J. Dent wickedly but accurately remarked that it sounds as if it were composed by an English organist of the 1860s.)

Nagel is at his finest with *The Magic Flute* and *Don Giovanni*. I do not remember any book that demonstrates so well how much relevance the subject matter of an opera can have to its music. His treatment of the relations of Mozart's operas to contemporary European culture—to Goethe, Kleist, Gluck, and Beethoven—is exemplary. His only failure is with *Così fan tutte*, perhaps because the characters in this opera cannot decide their own fate but are only manipulated. The great achievement of Da Ponte and Mozart in this work, however, was to reveal how the men gradually realize that they cannot control their own feelings: their autonomy is an illusion. Ferrando, in fact, succeeds in conquering Fiordiligi only because of his shock and anguish at Dorabella's betrayal. The shock endows him with a new power reflected in his music.

Nagel understands the tragic form slightly better than the comic. Everything he says about *The Marriage of Figaro* carries weight, but he does not see the extent to which Figaro emancipates himself from the very tradition of comedy. The relation of valet and master is an ancient comic tradition, and the resentment and opposition conveyed are integral to the genre. But the relation before Beaumarchais was a stable one: the clever valet works to realize his less intelligent master's desires. Figaro, however, works against the Count. Most astonishingly, he loses control; he himself is fooled, and by the women who take over the opera. Mozart as well as Da Ponte treats the Countess and her maid Susanna absolutely as equals (there are even doubts about who sings which line in the ensembles).

III

The great strength of *Mozart's Operas* by Daniel Heartz is his understanding of how Mozart undertook the composition of his operas, his choice of subject, his interventions in the construction of the libretto, his attempts to accommodate the singers. I do not think that the complicated process of dealing with librettists, opera impresarios, and singers has ever been explained with such lucidity, or that any other musicologist has shown so deep an understanding of the various pressures on a composer in the composition and mounting of an opera. Heartz also demonstrates the planning that went into the composition, particularly the way that the different tonalities in the operas were to a certain extent laid out in advance. This has been discussed before, and perhaps more cogently, but Heartz shows that it was practiced not only by Mozart but even by Mozart's great rival, Salieri.

The difficulty with Heartz's treatment of the tonal plan is that he views it formally rather than dramatically, as a way of creating symmetries instead of articulating the action. In *The Marriage of Figaro,* for example, he emphasizes a series of juxtapositions of G major and B flat major and, as a result, he observes the dramatic introduction of G major in the finale of the last act, when the Count surprises Figaro making ostentatious love to a woman dressed as the Countess. But Heartz's static conception of tonal order has nothing to say about the preceding shift, which is even more impressive dramatically, from G major to E flat a few minutes before, when Figaro sees the Count leave with a woman he takes to be his wife, Susanna. This introduces a brief nocturne, placid and tranquil, with an orchestration of an unparalleled soft richness; the air is saturated with the sound of clarinets and horns, and Figaro muses on what he imagines to be happening.

The dramatic and musical center of the finale occurs at this moment, just before everything starts to unravel. According to the comic tradition an act of sexual intercourse should be taking place behind the scenes, with the Count still believing that the Countess is Susanna. It is a basic principle of classical comedy that all women are alike in the dark, as in Shakespeare's *Measure for Measure* and *All's Well that Ends Well.* But in fact the Countess dressed as Susanna has gone into the pavilion on the right while the Count looks for her in the woods.

Da Ponte follows Beaumarchais here: in an early sketch for the play, however, Beaumarchais had the Count and Countess leave together, although in the final version prudery or prudence intervened. In any case, the music portrays not Figaro's emotions, but the scene he imagines. The composer was less prudish than the playwright or the librettist: the sudden change to a slow tempo, the unexpected quiet, the wonderfully rich sonority—all conspire to set the imaginary erotic scene.

E flat is a key most dissonant to D major, which is the basic tonality of the finale and of the opera as a whole—the basic harmonies of each key have almost no notes in common. The two keys clash profoundly. After Mozart reached the age of nineteen he established for himself certain fundamental principles of organizing his operas tonally. Each opera begins in the key in which it will end; except when separated by recitative in the Italian operas or spoken dialogue in the German, every number must end in the key with which it began,[5] and every finale—the succession of numbers at the end of an act—must close in the key in which it opened, even if the finale includes several changes of scene. There are always two large finales in a Mozart opera, and the first one is always composed in a tonality only distantly related to the tonality of the opera as a whole. The central finale concentrates the harmonic tensions of the work, and the harmonic tension explicitly reflects the dramatic tension.

The interior form is governed by this dramatic concern. The tonal symmetry that frames the beginning and end of the opera is generally rendered easily audible by Mozart, set in relief for all to hear. The concluding scenes of *Così fan tutte* and *Don Giovanni* quote the overture, and *The Magic Flute* and *The Abduction from the Seraglio* return at the end to the sonority of the opening pages of the overture. The interior symmetries that Heartz finds so important, however, seem to me trivial: there is no point in noticing that Marcellina's and Basilio's arias in the last act of *The Marriage of Figaro* are harmonically parallel to the letter duet and a peasant's chorus in the third. These pairings only occur because they relate to the opposition of D major and E flat major, which governs the fourth-act finale, as we have seen, and which also governs the total structure of the opera— the second-act finale is in E flat major, and is the point of greatest harmonic tension. In other words, these pairings in *The Marriage of Figaro* are not mirrors of each other, as Heartz claims; they are cumulative in nature, offshoots of the harmonic plan of the opera. They have individually a local dramatic significance, and are part of the total plan. They do not refer to each other, but only back to the whole.

The question of the harmonic significance may perhaps be clarified by referring to Heartz's discussion of Susanna's aria just before the last-act finale: *"Deh vieni non tardar"* ("Come, do not delay"). This is in F major, but an earlier version of this aria (with different words but a similar content) exists, much longer and more brilliant and with none of the simple lyricism of the one now performed: the early version is in E flat and not in F. Heartz remarks: "Since [the earlier version] follows Figaro's E flat aria (or preceded it at one stage, still reflected in the autograph), the result was an anomaly; two successive arias in the same key." He suggests that Mozart wanted his soprano, Nancy Storace, to sing the simpler lyric

---

5. The first aria of the Queen of the Night in *The Magic Flute* has a B flat opening, but finishes in G minor, which has the same key signature.

form all along and hoped to bring her around and abandon her desire for a brilliant display, and that the E flat aria "was only a feint." It seems to me impossible to believe that Mozart wrote a long, elaborate aria knowing that it could never be performed.

Heartz has not remarked another impossibility: the finale begins in D major, and it could not begin after an aria in E flat. Mozart could not have intended to initiate a very large form down a half-step from what precedes it—this would make everything sound flat for several bars. Neither the original version of Susanna's aria nor the present one of Figaro, both in E flat, could immediately precede a finale in D. It should be clear that the soprano display aria in E flat was written before Mozart had decided to give an E flat aria to Figaro, and that he must have planned an aria in F or B flat for Figaro to follow Susanna's aria and precede the finale. Since Figaro's aria is about cuckoldry, E flat is the proper key as it is the traditional key for horns—the standard symbol of cuckolds. Nancy Storace was then given an aria in F; the relation of F to D major is similar to the B flat–G major pairing that Heartz finds so significant, but it is local effect, not symmetry, that determines Mozart's planning.

The only symmetry that has any importance in the tonal structure of a Mozart opera is the frame: the beginning and end of individual numbers of the finales, and of the opera as a whole. The frames are important because they establish the meaning of what happens inside. Within these frames there are only three aspects of key change that count: the dramatic effect of the movement from one tonality to another, which articulates the action on the stage; the rate of change, so that the speed of the musical action can be controlled in order to fit the drama; and, finally, the coherence of the changes, so that distant tonalities can mark the extreme points of tension and the return to the initial key is both convincing and intelligible. No other composer has ever managed to coordinate these three aspects as Mozart did, and claims made on behalf of Haydn or Paisiello always fail to take into account the supremacy of Mozart's organizing powers.

Writing about a work of music is, at least in one sense, like performing it: both writer and performer must decide which aspects of the music are the most interesting, choose which details to emphasize, and attempt to convey the vitality of the work. It is the effectiveness with which this vitality is represented that is the test of both analysis and performance. It is not the presence of harmonic symmetries in Mozart's tonal plans which is in question, or even whether they can be perceived by the listener who looks for them, but how they act within one's experience of the work. This applies even more strongly to Heartz's other preoccupation in his study of Mozart's operas: the thematic and motivic relationships. He is persuaded that Mozart uses motifs to refer to the characters in the opera or to certain ideas.

He finds, for example, a phrase in the overture to *Idomeneo* that reappears a few times (sometimes radically altered) in connection with Idamante, the young prince who must be sacrificed to placate Neptune. The phrase is ordinary enough in late-eighteenth-century style, and it is not clear why it should represent Idamante. At the time Mozart was writing, André Ernest Modest Grétry and Etienne Nicolas Méhul in France were developing the use of leitmotifs or, rather, mottoes that appear throughout an opera. In their works, however, the initial appearance of the motto and most of the later ones are isolated and set in relief. It is difficult to accede to an analysis that would make Mozart a much less effective composer than Méhul. These recurrences in Mozart may not be fortuitous—it is just possible that Mozart involuntarily recalled a trivial phrase from an earlier scene when composing a later one, but he certainly made no attempt to call it to the attention even of the connoisseurs whose opinion he prized.

That is the trouble with any criticism which discovers something in a well-known work that no one seems to have noticed before: it is not likely to be important, or to have anything to do with why the work is considered a masterpiece. The only recourse for the critic is to claim that we have been noticing it at least semi-consciously without putting it into words, that it has been acting upon us, or that previous audiences noticed it but that we have lost the knack or the understanding. The latter is what Heartz attempts to do with his favorite leitmotif, a descending chromatic fourth that he finds many times throughout Mozart's work, and, indeed, throughout the eighteenth century. In chapter 12 he writes:

> To Mozart's audience the motif meant pain, suffering, and death—it could not be otherwise, since they and their forebears had for several generations heard similar chromatic descents in mass settings to convey the words "Crucifixus, passus et sepultus est," corroborating their experience in the opera house on the demise of heroes and heroines (e.g., Dido). The descending fourth with chromatic steps is present as a bass from the first notes of the Andante of the overture to *Don Giovanni*, which is of course modeled on the music to which Anna's father, the Commendatore—slain by Giovanni at the outset, to the accompaniment of many chromatic "dying falls" in the orchestra— makes his entrance as a statue in the finale of act 2.

No one would deny that slow music in the minor is sad and that slow chromatic music in the minor is even sadder, and that slow music in the minor with a descending chromatic bass is sadder still. What is at issue is the interval of a fourth, which is the shape of Heartz's motif. I do not know how many settings of "Crucifixus" with descending chromatic fourths Heartz knows, but I have no doubt there are several. There is the Bach B minor Mass, of course, which Mozart did not know, and I presume that Heartz's Dido is Purcell's, which Mozart did not know. In these works, and most of the others with chromatic descending fourths that I am aware of, the bass descends a fourth from tonic to dominant. This is not surprising: all music in the eighteenth century goes from tonic to dominant, and a chromatic bass generally goes chromatically down a fourth from tonic to dominant. There is nothing significant or expressive about the interval of a fourth. The representation of "pain, suffering, and death" requires the minor mode as well as a chromatic descent to make its effect—and if it is "death" that is meant, then words are required as well.

Heartz, nevertheless, hears "death" with every chromatic descent, and the next step is clear: rising chromatic fourths. Some pages earlier he writes:

> In this opera [*Don Giovanni*] chromatic lines spell death, but also the related phenomenon of love death, or the sexual act, as is made abundantly clear in the great sextet . . . and where the descending chromatic line is complemented by the rising chromatic line.

And Heartz later returns to the same point:

> Sudden chromatic surges upward, such as help characterize the hopes and fears of Elvira at the beginning of the sextet, have less clear meaning than chromatic descents, yet Mozart's audience surely understood these too as affective symbols. An example from the year before *Don Giovanni* was written will help place the figure in context.
>
> For the revival of *Idomeneo* at Vienna in March 1786 Mozart rewrote the love duet to take advantage of a tenor Idamante. Near the end of the piece (K. 489), the lovers sing of their union to the words

> *Non sa che sia diletto*
> *Chi non provò nel petto*
> *Si fortunato amor.*
> (He knows not what delight is
> Who has not felt in his breast
> Such fortunate love.)

Between these innocent-sounding lines (which may be by Da Ponte), Mozart allows his orchestra a sudden chromatic ascent marked crescendo. . . . This makes the surging emotions of the lovers more explicit than do their words or the melodic lines they sing; indeed, if the same degree of passion were to be expressed in words, one suspects they would not pass the imperial censor.

Part of this chromatic surge comes from placing all the violins in unison in their lowest range. Playing on the bottom G string, they produce a gutty sound, all the more penetrating when reinforced by the violas in unison and the cellos and basses at the octaves below. The combination of the timbre, the crescendo, and the upward-striving chromatic surge bespeaks a sensuality that is at home somewhere below the *petto* mentioned in the words.

If I understand Heartz's interpretation of a rising chromatic line correctly, with his shy reference to a sensuality at home somewhere below the breast and his vague suggestion that we are dealing with censorable matters, then I think he is erecting a construction, or construing an erection, upon very flimsy foundations. I do not believe a banal chromatic rise of a fourth even played on the G string is all that exciting.[6]

Furthermore, it takes a very literal mind to argue, as Heartz does, that an occasional descending chromatic line in *Don Giovanni*'s infectiously brilliant "champagne" aria signifies anything like the sexual act, or that a simple phrase descending a C major scale from the Turkish music in *The Abduction from the Seraglio* can function, radically altered, at the beginning of *Così fan tutte* as a hint that the two young men will get disguised as Albanians later in the opera. I have no doubt that Heartz has trained himself to listen this way, and that he responds to what he is convinced is the meaning of falling and rising chromatic fourths. (He is like the man in the old Viennese joke who asked the doctor if he could take the Rorschach tests home to show the dirty pictures to his friends.) But what would Heartz do with the last page of Mozart's Viola Quintet in D major, a very jolly rondo in Haydn's style, where a series of falling chromatic fourths are answered over and over again by rising chromatic fourths?

For the late eighteenth century, extra-musical meaning in music almost always worked metaphorically; the music imitated some aspect of nature—babbling brooks, cuckoos, the patter of raindrops, the moaning of wind. By extension, bagpipes signified a rustic pastoral atmosphere; soft horn-calls implied distance, particularly when echoed. Neither rising nor falling chromatic lines

6. Abert says the rising chromatic line in the sextet is "uncanny," and so it is. Heartz absurdly reproaches him with not observing that there was "an echo" of the sextet's chromatic rise an hour earlier in the opera in Don Ottavio's aria "*Dalla sua pace*," with an entirely different sound and rhythmic shape. I think everyone would agree that Heartz is the first to make this observation.

sound like the sexual act. Heartz is succumbing to the perpetual temptation—that is, tempting only to musicologists—to decode the music, and Mozart does not need to be decoded but listened to.

How misleading Heartz's approach is may be appreciated by the way he has influenced his colleague Thomas Bauman, who writes the chapter in Heartz's book on *The Magic Flute*. He is describing the little postlude to Pamina's wonderfully despairing aria, where she announces her intention to commit suicide. Bauman has noticed that the opening of the postlude resembles a phrase in the seventeenth bar of the aria with the words "See, Tamino." He therefore calls it a "Tamino" motif and places the words "Tamino Tamino . . ." over the violin part of the opening of the postlude in his printed example (he does not seem to have noticed that the same pattern is used twice for other phrases in the aria with different words):

> The closing ritornello is deeply indebted to the aria it concludes . . . the melodic motif employed here is a direct elaboration of her interjection "Sieh, Tamino!" from the passionate middle section of the aria.
>
> For whom does the orchestra speak in these moving final measures? The obvious answer would be Pamina. As in earlier ritornellos, this passage derives a psychological subtext from key verbal phrases in her aria. In this case, however, the process is far more thoroughgoing. Tamino's name seems to repeat itself obsessively in Pamina's mind, and through the octave descent . . . his name is linked with her aria's opening thoughts of lost happiness.

Compare these remarks with Ivan Nagel's on the same aria and postlude in *Autonomy and Mercy*:

> Mozart did not have much time when he wrote *Die Zauberflöte*: some weeks left to compose, some months to live. His late style creates a fluid alternation of melodic shapes which emerge from and are submerged in one another, yet without thematic contrasts to define or hold back the flow. The music which has overcome all unrest still has no time to linger; this strangely reverses the listener's sense of time. Because the lovely flow of sound slides all too soon to an end, we experience it as if in retrospect—full of blissful regret that it is passing, that it has already passed. Thus in each moment of Pamina's aria, the melodies that move "in an undisturbed stream without any clearly defined motifs" (Jahn) yearn for the phrase which has just faded away, permitting memory to draw delight even in pain. . . .

When the music is all farewell, no threshold should warn the listener before the end and give him time to separate. Therefore the last
gesture is compressed, simplified, almost omitted. The orchestral coda
of Pamina's G minor aria lasts only four measures. Finally resolving
in despair and weariness the diminished seventh chord's tormented
question, "Fühlst du nicht der Liebe Sehnen" [If you no longer feel the
yearning of love], the orchestra confirms the ultimate answer offered
by Pamina's now mute voice: "So wird Ruh'im Tode sein." There will
be peace in death. The orchestra bows its head: amen.

Whom shall we believe, Heartz and Bauman or Jahn and Nagel? Is there "an
undisturbed stream without any clearly defined motifs," or is there a motif that
says "Tamino, Tamino" even in the orchestra? Can we separate and decode
specific meanings, or is there only a fluid alternation of melodic shapes?

The answer to these questions depends essentially on a decision how to listen to
Mozart: Which way of listening is the most rewarding, most coherent? Another
question may help to determine our answer. Does the postlude repeat the name
Tamino six times, or does it resign itself to death? Here there is no contest (and
Bauman's own excellent observations on metrics and dynamics confirm it while
denying his claim to hear the orchestra repeat Tamino's name): the metric displacement and the crescendo both attempt to resist the inflexible movement
downward, and finally yield in the last two bars.

The way to hear Mozart is not to attach a finicky set of references to the
melodic formulas, but to be aware how these formulas—largely banal, conventional, and commonplace, although there are astonishing exceptions—work
within a larger harmonic movement to allow the dramatic action to unfold, to
establish the most extraordinary dramatic strokes by rapid changes of harmony
and texture, and to allow both the passion and the irony of the music to move
easily within the spacious frame created by Mozart's manipulation and transformation of conventional form.

Mozart's melodic shapes are rarely as idiosyncratic as Haydn's, and his passage
work is almost always banal. Beethoven knew how to make the most ordinary
tonal formulas seem as idiosyncratic as Haydn's more individual motifs, largely
by a ruthless employment of accent, naked reiteration, and dynamics. Mozart
needed his motifs to sound ordinary; it allowed him to release the latent expressiveness in the tonal language with ease, so that moments of concentrated energy
could act as a shock. Heartz does not see that his liberal quotation of Mozart's
borrowing of dozens of phrases from Gluck, Piccinni, and Paisiello and from his
own earlier works does not establish Mozart's borrowing of meaning: all these
phrases show how commonplace his material was (and even more examples

could have been added from other composers, particularly Johann Christian Bach). They demonstrate his reliance on *almost* meaningless formulas, motifs that are expressive, but whose expressive content remains vague and diffuse, so that the significance would have to be drawn from each new work.

Daniel Heartz is a historian of great distinction and stature. If he goes so wide of the mark, it is because he is trying to realize an impossible dream, one that keeps returning to musicologists and even composers: to give music a very specific referential power, to enable it to act exactly like language. Richard Strauss once said that eventually one would be able to distinguish musically between a fork and a spoon. Deryck Cook in *The Language of Music* tried to identify melodic shapes which would signify specific sentiments—unsuccessfully, because he neglected rhythm, and for every one of his examples dozens of counterexamples can be found which clearly express very different sentiments.

Heartz fails to take into account the large scale on which Mozart works. It is not with tiny motifs that Mozart represents sentiment, and he does not characterize a hero in passing with four or five notes. He may indicate Donna Elvira's shudder with the gesture of a few notes in the sextet, but it takes him a long aria (turned into a trio by sardonic comments from Leporello and Don Giovanni) to begin to portray her character.

We ought not to confound the suitability of a musical phrase to render an emotion with a specific fixed meaning. A brilliant passage of coloratura is a wonderful way to express the rage of the Queen of the Night in *The Magic Flute*, but those rapid high notes do not signify rage. Chromatic lines aptly disturb the calm surface of more simple harmonies, and they are suitable to render violence, terror, erotic excitement, and despair—but they do not mean any of these emotions unless the composer, like Wagner, has deliberately isolated motif and words, and linked the two by repetition, and that is not how Mozart proceeds.

Heartz calls Bernhard Weber one of the best early critics of Don Giovanni, and quotes him: "Never can one find in his works an idea that one has heard before." Oddly, Heartz seems to be trying to prove the opposite by showing how much Mozart's turns of phrase resemble ones by Paisiello and others. Heartz is right insofar as these motifs are commonplace, the stock-in-trade of every contemporary musician—but Weber was right, too, since he was considering the music from a larger viewpoint. Nobody ever controlled music over such a long span of time as Mozart did, not even Beethoven, but it is less by use of motifs than by blocks of tonality, and by rhythm and texture. His sense of long-range movement was unsurpassed, above all in the first versions of his operas. The cuts and additions he was often forced to make for a second production invariably weaken the structure, no matter how beautiful the additions were.

A musical recall or reference in Mozart to an earlier act—or to anything outside the opera—is very rare and always unmistakable. A Mozart opera does not function like an opera by Wagner, Strauss, or Berg as a complex system of cross-references, and Heartz's attempt to construct such a system only distracts one from seeing (or hearing) how the music works.

IV

The reunion of Pamina and Tamino was, for Edward Dent, the most moving number of *The Magic Flute,* and it is the center of Ivan Nagel's meditation on this work: this is the moment when, as Nagel says, "the official myth of a man's initiation by saving a woman" reverses itself; "the woman in need of rescue becomes the rescuer." This scene is indeed, for me, the greatest moment in the opera, and in its combination of austerity and ambition, it reveals the nature of Mozart's genius. It follows the extraordinary chorale sung by two armed men, a pastiche in Baroque style and yet one of Mozart's greatest achievements in religious music. The finale of the last act, of which this scene is a part, is in E flat major, and the chorale is in the closely related key of C minor. The reunion arrives in the distant tonality of F major, and creates the greatest harmonic tension with E flat major. It is, harmonically, the culmination of the finale—what follows moves toward resolution. We do not need perfect pitch, or a memory of the basic key of E flat or any technical training to realize that something astonishing is taking place: the sudden change in harmony and texture will alert any sympathetic listener.

The opening of the reunion is electrifying in its simplicity: each lover sings nothing but a short scale and a bare cadence. There is not a trace of original melodic invention in these opening bars, nothing but the most commonplace melodic shapes. If it appears heartbreaking, that is only because of the sudden stillness, the radical change in tonality, and the soft, transparent instrumentation. Then the orchestra begins a steady, quiet pulsation, and Mozart's originality of melodic invention asserts itself in a supple form of declamation that some critics have felt as an anticipation of Wagner, as Pamina explains to Tamino how her father made the magic flute, and declares her resolution to stay at Tamino's side through the trials. The sound of the flute will protect us from the shadows of death, she sings with Tamino and the two armed men, and Mozart writes a passage that represents an overflowing happiness that even surpasses the end of the great sextet in *The Marriage of Figaro,* when Susanna realizes that Figaro has found his parents and there is no longer any obstacle to their wedding. The music seems simple, a banal figure repeated over and over as the harmony rocks back and forth between the most commonplace harmonies, tonic and dominant, and for a half-minute time seems to stop.

The richness of texture here for Tamino, Pamina, and the two armed men betrays Mozart's ambition: all four vocal parts are in double invertible counterpoint. The long phrase is sung twice: the second time Pamina and Tamino exchange their melodic lines, and the tenor and bass of the two armed men exchange theirs. I do not think that there is a single unusual or idiosyncratic motif anywhere at this point: every melodic shape is ordinary, but nothing like this section had ever been heard before. The motifs are common property, but the long sustained line, the repetitions, the fullness of texture are all Mozart's own. Marianne Moore once wrote: "Ecstasy affords the occasion and expediency determines the form."

CHAPTER EIGHT

Beethoven's Career

The following review provoked some correspondence. Stephen Basson wrote to point out that Leonore's aria in Fidelio *does not have four horns, but three horns and a bassoon. Professor DeNora wrote to defend her book (*New York Review of Books, *April 10, 1997). We are unfortunately not able to include her letter here, but I add my reply (reprinted at the end of this chapter), from which most of her arguments can be clearly recognized. I have included my reply because the subject dealt with in the correspondence is a larger and more important one than to what extent Beethoven owed his career to aristocratic patronage. What is at issue is whether music has any intrinsic qualities that can account for its success.*

I do not suggest an outmoded Eurocentric view that Beethoven's work is great for all eternity, for all cultures and all systems of values, for all possible worlds. Nevertheless, it is an error of present-day sociological analysis to claim that Beethoven survived because of decisions made at the moment by some of his contemporaries— or by posterity—for non-musical reasons. When one sees the issue from a longer-range position of the musical tradition since the Renaissance, and takes into account the musical language of the eighteenth century from Sebastian Bach to Haydn, it is evident that Beethoven handled this language with greater power and effectiveness than any other composer of his time, and at the same time—paradoxically, it may seem—radically transformed the language and its system of values. It may have taken a few decades for the world of music to realize this (just as it took a few decades for the whole scientific community to accept the work of Einstein); but the point to be emphasized is that Beethoven did precisely what European culture since the Renaissance expected a genius to do: create works that followed logically and intelligibly from the contemporary tradition, and yet transform that tradition in a

Originally written in 1996 as a review of Tia DeNora, *Beethoven and the Construction of Genius: Musical Politics in Vienna, 1792–1803.*

way that was personal and original and usable for the artists who succeeded him. That is why no legitimate assessment of Beethoven can approach him as DeNora did, attempting to evade any direct encounter with the music itself. The music has, indeed, intrinsic qualities that must be understood both from within the tradition at the time of Beethoven and from the changed system of musical values that Beethoven helped to form.

B EETHOVEN, some think, had all the luck. An ethnomusicologist, tenured at a respected university (he will perhaps be happy to remain anonymous), once asserted: "There must be hundreds of symphonies just as good as the *Eroica,* but we just don't know them." This is the naive view of history immortalized in Thomas Gray's "Elegy Written in a Country Churchyard," quoted not quite accurately by Tia DeNora on the last page of her *Beethoven and the Construction of Genius:*

> Full many a flower is born to blush unseen
> And waste its sweetness on the desert air.

It does not, however, stand up well to examination. Hundreds of symphonies by dozens of contemporaries of Mozart and Beethoven have been exhumed and republished in the last two decades, and no one has been found willing to make any extravagant claims for them.

A more refined form of this primitive theory has been elaborated in our time by cultural historians: we assume that the *Eroica* is so much better than the works of other composers simply because posterity has made Beethoven the touchstone of musical value. Dismissing the works of his contemporaries is not an independent act of criticism but only a mechanical repetition of what we have been schooled to believe. Beethoven has entered the canon; his contemporaries Joseph Wölffl and Joseph Weigl have not. Any further evaluation is merely redundant: we have been brainwashed. This view, however, is undermined by our realization that the supremacy of Beethoven was not imposed by posterity but accepted, sometimes with reluctance, by Beethoven's contemporaries. By the age of thirty-five he was the most famous composer of instrumental music in Europe, and his position has remained largely unchallenged even by those who do not care for his work.

Tia DeNora's thesis is more sophisticated than Gray's or the ethnomusicologist's quoted above, and more knowledgeable than the simplistic cultural criticism. Beethoven's reputation, for her, was created and permanently established by the society in which he worked, largely by the backing of the aristocratic class whose support he cultivated assiduously. It was aristocratic patronage first in

Bonn and later in Vienna that made Beethoven's career possible, declared him a genius, and permanently consigned to the dustbin of history contemporary rivals like Wölffl and Jan Ladislav Dussek (the latter a composer once very much admired, and who can give considerable pleasure today). Beethoven's genius was "constructed" by his society, above all by the upper class. DeNora writes:

> We have not understood Beethoven very well if we fail to realize that had he spent the decade of 1792–1802 in London (as did Dussek), his artistic output would have developed quite differently.
>
> It is unlikely that Beethoven in London would have become the prominent figure we know, even with the support of English aristocrats.

It is, of course, equally unlikely that he would have become the prominent figure we know if he had spent ten years in St. Petersburg, Naples, Boston, or wherever, if he had been a woman, or if . . . (further conditions to be added at the reader's discretion).

DeNora's book is in many ways a very good one. It gives a fascinating picture of important aspects of musical life in Vienna and of the complexities of musical politics. While very little of her research is original, she marshals the works of other students (like Mary Sue Morrow, Dexter Edge, and Julia Moore) clearly and cogently, and summarizes the present state of scholarship on Beethoven's early career with considerable skill.[1] The chapter about Beethoven's concern with the manufacture of pianos and his influence on their construction is brilliantly handled. There is a wealth of enlightening detail throughout the book, and even specialists on Beethoven are likely to gain a much greater understanding of his early years. The conclusions drawn from all this detail, however, are too often either wrong or, at best, inadequate.

The basic thesis of DeNora is

> that a serious music ideology, which took as its exemplars Beethoven and reconstituted, more explicitly "learned" and grandiose versions of Mozart and Haydn, emerged during the 1790s in Vienna, and that this ideology was primarily subscribed to by old aristocrats, not the middle class. This view runs counter to what Arnold Hauser (1962),

---

1. It is disconcerting to note that all of her references to the most important music journal from the end of the eighteenth to the mid-nineteenth century, the *Allgemeine Musikalische Zeitung*, are derived from quotations by later authors, and she misses several important references in assessing Beethoven's reputation.

Henry Raynor (1976), Theodor Adorno (1976), and a host of other scholars have had to say, on the basis of scant evidence, about the origins of serious music ideology, and, as such, it challenges received sociological wisdom and Beethoven mythology concerning the origin of the musical canon.

For the moment, we must leave aside the question to what extent works of music, or art in general, represent the philosophy or the ideology of those who are financing it or simply paying for it, although the assumption that the views of the artist, his audience, and his patrons generally coincide will not bear examination. I do not, of course, wish to question the fact that Beethoven sought the most highly placed aristocratic support for his work in order to give it the greatest possible prestige. Nevertheless, the evidence used by DeNora to determine the class of Beethoven's partisans and her interpretation of it are not convincing.

To start with, DeNora measures Beethoven's growing reputation as a young composer in Vienna almost entirely by the statistics of public performance. Most music-making in Vienna, however, took place either at home or at semiprivate performances in the salons of the more affluent music lovers and patrons. She gives various reasons to justify her decision, including the growth of public concerts and their accessibility, and adds: "Finally (and more practically), there is not enough specific information available on private concert programs (the salons), where composers and works often remain unidentifiable." I know that it is traditional in the social sciences to generalize on the basis of the available information even when that information is clearly not representative, but the conclusions are not exactly trustworthy. More than in Paris, London, or Berlin, cultural life in Vienna depended on various forms of intimate music-making. We cannot assume that the repertoire for large public concerts and private gatherings would have been similar. The program for orchestral performances is often determined by ease of rehearsal and relative familiarity of style to both musicians and public. Furthermore, the public concert at the end of the eighteenth century was still in Vienna something of a novelty compared with many of the other European centers (and, I believe, compared with New York).

The interpretation of even this very limited evidence is not always persuasive. Most of the theaters and concert halls were, as DeNora writes, managed by the aristocracy, with one exception: "The most distinctly middle class of Vienna's concert locations at this time [1791–1810] was the Leopoldstadt theater, located in Vienna's suburbs. . . . Judging from the programs listed in Morrow's public concert calendar, Beethoven was never performed at the Leopoldstadt theater."

This would, indeed, imply that popular bourgeois interest in Beethoven was minimal, since elsewhere Beethoven was the most performed composer in Vienna after Haydn and Mozart. Unfortunately, however, in the back of DeNora's book, we find a note in small print: "Because relatively few Leopoldstadt concert programs survive, generalizations about the repertory there must remain speculative." This further weakens our confidence in DeNora's assessment.

Other problems arise in determining the social class of Beethoven's supporters. Table I offered by DeNora gives us a breakdown of 186 "virtuosi, amateur musicians, and music patrons in the Viennese high culture music world, as listed in [Johann Ferdinand von] Schönfeld," the author of a musical yearbook in 1796. We get twenty-three "first aristocracy by rank," i.e., princes, princesses, counts, countesses, and one baron; eighty "second aristocracy," which includes fourteen barons and Freiherren, along with sixty-six merely with "von" in front of their last name; nineteen middle-class professionals and businessmen; and finally sixty-four "musicians." We never hear anything further about these "musicians." If they were supporters of Beethoven, they do not interest DeNora. Nevertheless, in the establishment of Beethoven's genius, they were the ones who counted the most. Support from the rich or the aristocratic was never forthcoming without professional advice.

Nor does the group of prominent music lovers with a simple "von" before their family name play any further role in spite of their considerable number. In any case, the nobility and legitimate status of this "von" cannot always have been clear. As DeNora knows, the line between "second aristocracy" and the middle class was not sharply drawn. Or even between "first" and "second." The one baron classified among the music patrons of the "first aristocracy" is the famous Gottfried van Swieten, sponsor of Haydn and Mozart, and important for the revival of interest in the instrumental works of Bach. He was one of Beethoven's principal promoters, and the First Symphony was dedicated to him. His father was Maria Theresa's physician, for which he received a title. The van Swietens were therefore a recently ennobled family from the professional middle class.

DeNora's main thesis stands things on their heads. She would like to believe in "the emergence of the serious music ideology in the aristocratic music world between the late 1780s and the early 1800s." She claims that in the campaign for serious music and against both the style of easy superficial pieces for the amateur and flamboyant virtuosity to please the mob, "the issue was simultaneously social and political because of the alignment of music patronage with the pursuit and maintenance of status." In order to maintain their dominant cultural position, her account goes, the aristocrats aided in the construction of the concept of the great musical "genius," and supported Beethoven's difficult and often rebarbative music against the more easily assimilable and agreeable works of Dussek and Wölffl.[2]

DeNora's concept of an identifiable and isolatable aristocratic taste and ideology is a constructed fiction. Her bias in interpreting what we know about the musical life of the period comes out in her comparison of the careers of Dussek and Beethoven. With Beethoven, the emphasis is on his early experience at the court of Bonn and his relatively successful attempts in Vienna to attract the support and patronage of the most prestigious and influential music lovers. With Dussek, she sets in relief his relations with the commercial music world of London, the many dedications of his works to middle-class citizens, and his work as a piano teacher. We could try a different slant with the two biographies: we might note the insulting snubbing of Beethoven in front of his colleagues by Prince Esterhazy, and recall Beethoven's notorious revolutionary republican principles, his ostentatious refusal to take off his hat at the passage of royalty. Dussek, on the other hand, worked for William V of Holland, and was a salaried musician at the courts of Catherine II of Russia and Marie Antoinette of France, becoming a favorite composer of both these queens; he was also employed for two years by Prince Radziwill. We might speculate that the coddling by royalty sapped Dussek's ambition, condemning him to be a minor composer of piano music, while Beethoven's struggle to obtain financial support stimulated him to greater efforts.

All of this, one way or the other, is largely irrelevant. Dussek chose to settle in London, an important commercial center of music, with a distinguished school of composers for the piano including John Cramer and Muzio Clementi. Another possible choice was Paris, where the interest in music devolved principally on opera, and the scene was dominated by Cherubini, Méhul, and Grétry. Beethoven's early training in Bonn was largely based on the latest Viennese instrumental style and on *The Well-Tempered Keyboard* of Johann Sebastian Bach, a work as yet unpublished which had just attracted a lot of excitement in the circle connected with Mozart, and which the young Beethoven performed complete to the admiration of the musical world in Bonn. Vienna was not only the most natural choice for Beethoven, but the most reasonable one for a young composer with great ambition: the latest developments in pure instrumental style there were attracting international attention and revolutionizing the aesthetics of music. In addition, there was the opportunity of personal contact with Haydn.

2. The most exaggerated formulation of DeNora's thesis concerns the piano contest between Wölffl and Beethoven: she claims that "the serious music ideology as represented by Beethoven can be further clarified as the property of Vienna's old and highest aristocracy."

The prestige of difficult, serious music had already developed to a much greater extent in Vienna than DeNora believes in her effort to give the credit for it largely to aristocratic machinations or to tar it with the brush of upper-class privilege. Although she refers to the complaints about the difficulty of Mozart's works during the 1780s, she does not grasp the magnitude of the objections,[3] which lasted well into the nineteenth century (there is a brilliant article by E. T. A. Hoffmann defending the complexity of Mozart's modulations against the attacks of another opera composer, Sacchini), and she takes no account of the extraordinary experiments in fugal writing in the quartets by Haydn and other composers like Florent Gassmann of the early 1770s, which turned the quartet into a learned form.

Who were the beneficiaries of the new grandiose pretensions made for the art of music? Obviously not the court or the aristocracy but the musicians, above all professional composers and performers.

II

The greatest disappointment in DeNora's account is the lack of any historical consideration of the idea of greatness in music or the other arts. The late eighteenth century does not mark the first appearance of the concept of the temperamental genius in music. The Netherlandish composers, including Johannes Ockeghem, Pierre de la Rue, and Josquin des Pres, at the end of the fifteenth century had already developed that kind of international prestige, which made them sought after by Italian courts, and they had also demonstrated their importance by an extremely complex and learned style. Moreover, this style was not merely a demonstration of craft: we have only to read the account of an early sixteenth-century critic like Glarean to see the enormous emotional impact of the music of Josquin, who reduced his listeners to tears, and who, furthermore, was known for his arrogant and temperamental refusal to write music when commissioned except when he felt like it.

The basic model of the temperamental genius, however, was to be found in the visual arts, with Michelangelo. Beethoven's persona, the figure he presented to the world of a difficult, irascible nonconformist, is clearly an imitation of the mythical paradigm of the temperamental genius refusing to bow to the authority of pope or aristocrat that Michelangelo supplied for the centuries that followed him. This would suggest that the relation of a high classical art and the artist as

---

3. How close to Beethoven Mozart continued to appear as late as 1812 is seen in a dialogue about music by the poet Ludwig Tieck in which someone says: "If we may call Mozart mad, Beethoven often cannot be distinguished from a raving lunatic."

genius to an aristocratic society is a very complex one, in which the artist's genius is a trophy for the court that hires him but also a protest against, and an undermining of, the aristocratic authority that finances the art.

The gap between trivial and serious music was established and enforced in Vienna by the musicians themselves. The first musicians' union in Vienna, formed in the early 1780s, explicitly denied membership to performers of dance music. The gradual increase in the seriousness of nonliturgical music at this time was a natural result of the decline of church and court patronage, and the necessity of guaranteeing the musicians' livelihood in other ways and increasing their social standing.

By the late 1770s, Haydn was recognized internationally as the greatest composer of instrumental music, a genre that was finally to be considered the most philosophical and noble form of music in Germany, England, and France, and even to replace opera as the vehicle of the sublime. DeNora claims that Haydn was not accepted as a star in Vienna until after his great success in London in 1791. That may be true about the way the aristocratic circles thought of him, since he was still a salaried employee at a minor court, but his reputation among his fellow musicians and amateurs had spread his fame to London and then later to Paris. In order to understand the dealings of Viennese composers with the aristocracy, incidentally, we need some discussion (absent in DeNora) of the legendary insolence of the Viennese upper classes.

Mozart's reputation as a more difficult composer than Haydn was firmly in place by the time he was twenty-five years old. His letters to his father assuring the anxious old man that his music could be appreciated by the layman should be interpreted as a way of calming paternal fears that his son's music would be accessible only to the professional musician and the connoisseur. Many of Mozart's works were considered both difficult to play and to listen to. He began the composition of six quartets for piano and strings, but after two of them had been completed and printed the publisher canceled the commission: they were too hard to play and nobody would buy them. Critics thought that he overloaded the instrumentation of his operas so that the singers could be not heard. Singers complained that his elaborate ensembles did not allow them to show off their vocal qualities to advantage. In his first opera of great importance, *Idomeneo,* there is already an aria with three solo wind instruments accompanying or, rather, vying with the singer: this opera contains some of his greatest music and was never revived during his lifetime after the first performances in the wonderful rococo court theater in Munich that seats a public of only three hundred. The following opera, *Die Entführung aus dem Serail,* has an aria which contains a full concerto for a quartet of solo winds.

We misjudge Mozart if we do not see that his ambitions and his pretensions were extraordinary. And we misinterpret the idea of musical genius if we fail to understand that what stimulated his ambitions was the consciousness of his powers, his awareness of how effectively and easily he could realize them even at the risk of losing some of his popularity. He rarely resisted the temptation, for example, to show off his contrapuntal skills, perhaps the greatest in history since the death of J. S. Bach. (As far as one can see from Mozart's correspondence, the one person close to him absolutely fascinated by fugues was not an aristocrat but his wife, Constanze.) He not only followed Haydn in writing fugal sections in the developments of symphonies and quartets, as well as fugal finales, minuets with elaborate canons, and the famous contrapuntal tour de force of the coda of the finale of the Jupiter Symphony, but he also put three orchestras on the stage in *Don Giovanni* in addition to the one in the pit, all three playing dances in different rhythms and even tuning up while blending harmoniously with the others. He also inserted a full three-part canon in a comic opera like *Così fan tutte,* while the farcical *Singspiel The Magic Flute* has an overture with a masterly double fugue and, in the second act, a superb chorale prelude in antique style: understandably, the farce has philosophic pretensions that match its musical ones, with Masonic symbolism and moral reflections.

This was the tradition in which Beethoven aspired to show his talent. To top Mozart's three-part canon in an opera, *Fidelio* has a four-part canon. Fiordiligi in *Così fan tutte* has an E major aria in grand style with two solo horns; Leonore in *Fidelio* has an even grander one in E major with four horns. It is not true that Beethoven imitated Mozart and Haydn in the early works and ceased to do so in the later ones: the influence of his predecessors continued to work upon him until his death, and, in addition, the innovations of the first works are more radical than is sometimes understood today, which explains the initial opposition to Beethoven of which DeNora makes so much. She interprets the opposition as a conflict of ideologies overcome only by the influence of the aristocracy in Beethoven's favor. The more natural explanation is that the initial opposition was a reaction to Beethoven's continuing practice of the innovative tradition of originality established by Haydn and Mozart and sanctioned by the new European aesthetics in all the arts; and it was overcome principally by greater familiarity with Beethoven's music and the support of the professionals and amateurs who were fascinated by it.

Mozart and Haydn both tried to get the backing of the most prestigious and influential members of the aristocracy in addition to their cultivation of publishers and middle-class financiers and impresarios. Mozart found support for his most serious and difficult operas, not in Vienna, where the theater was controlled by the court, but in Prague, where the opera house was managed by the municipality. Beethoven had every reason to follow their example. He sometimes went to great lengths to do this. He allowed the first performance of the *Eroica* Symphony to take place in the palace of Prince Lobkowitz; the available room was so small that it could only accommodate an orchestra of thirty-five, and even that crowded the space so that the audience had to listen from the next room. There are four independent horn parts in this symphony, but with an orchestra of thirty-five there was place only for two cellos: the opening cello theme must have sounded ineffective, and of course everyone complained that the horns were too loud.

Some but not all of the members of the Viennese aristocracy liked music. Some of these, but not all, were interested in serious and difficult music. In spite of what sociologists would like to believe, such inclinations are too individual to be tied to class. We cannot, for example, claim that admiration for a tenor like Pavarotti is typical of millionaires because the New York Metropolitan Opera relies on some indecently rich contributors to help meet its huge deficit. The administration looks for millionaires who are sympathetic opera buffs; with a little luck it finds a small number. Mozart and Beethoven looked for support in the same way, and they tried to get the most illustrious aristocratic names on their subscription lists to help sell the concert tickets and the published sheet music. It is true that a number of aristocrats must have felt that becoming a patron of advanced music reaffirmed their social position, but that is not a result of upper-class ideology but a measure of the success of musicians at promoting their own importance.

Perhaps the difficulty arises from a natural confusion of an elite with an aristocracy. The interest in difficult serious music is an elite taste. It can give great pleasure even to the point of becoming addictive. Serious music seems academic and tedious to some: on others it has an emotional impact like sex or a trip on a roller coaster. It is not tied to one level of society. Not all members of the governing class take pleasure in fugues or sonatas or serial music. On the other hand, small farmers and kitchen help have been known to respond to some of the most complex forms of art music. In fact, the reason for someone's interest in serious music, pop music, or painting, football or computer games, may be as much physical as cultural.

Admittedly, nevertheless, satisfying a desire for serious music needs leisure and generally requires money. Very few of the poor in Beethoven's Vienna (and not many today) had the opportunity to enjoy his music. A taste for serious music also tends to reinforce the class structure since it is generally considered nobler and more distinguished intellectually than rock or folk dancing. To many musicians this aspect of class is irrelevant: for others, of course, serious music may be a way of enhancing their social status. It has distinct if limited snob appeal. Nevertheless, as important as these collateral benefits may be, it is a grave error of sociologists to make them the principal driving impulsions in the development of styles and reputations. They are influential forces, but rarely determining ones.

The necessity for seeking out the support of the rich and the aristocratic certainly influenced the character of the music of Mozart and Beethoven. That, as Emile Durkheim, founding father of sociology, once remarked about someone's thesis, may be sociology, but it isn't news. The influence, however, is not as direct or as obvious as some social critics might like to think: criticism is not that easy. Beethoven's republican sentiments are clear enough in the last movement of the Ninth Symphony, in the style of the music as well as the words; but with the *Missa Solemnis,* written almost at the same time, he tried to arrange private publication for distribution only to the most select royal courts. Does this tell us something about the music, written in any case for the accession of the Archduke Rudolph to his archbishopric? It is certainly a mass never intended for ordinary performance in a church, but only for a grand celebration. We cannot make a hard and fast separation between music and ideology, but marrying them to each other is a shotgun wedding. Music is too malleable, and Beethoven over time has suited almost anyone's purpose: republican, liberal, Nazi, ivory-tower aesthete, romantic idealist, austere serialist—everyone finds himself in Beethoven.[4]

What DeNora finds in Beethoven is a man who, with the backing of the old aristocracy, condemned other composers like Dussek and Wölffl (judged very briefly by some of his contemporaries to be of equal merit) to blush unseen in permanent obscurity. The impulse behind her work is admittedly the present debate on

> artistic standards and canons of taste . . . and programs for cultural reform. . . . These programs range from suggestions for "reshuffling" personnel within the canon, to suggestions for substitutions, to appropriating official members of the canon for new social concerns, to abolishing canonic structures altogether in favor of postmodernist aesthetics and local and community arts. While these programs obviously vary in levels of ambition, they share a concern with the ways

4. The process is similar to the one that Samuel Schoenbaum observed in Shakespeare biographies. Every biographer thinks that Shakespeare is just like himself: for Leslie Stephen, he was a sensible man observant of all the intellectual currents of his time without being a fanatic; for Oscar Wilde, he was sensitive and interested in young men of the lower class, etc., etc.

exclusive or "high" cultural forms are both inaccessible and inappropriate to the lived experience of a large proportion of the people to whom they are upheld as aspirational.

How shocking the word "inappropriate" is in that last sentence is something that I am sure DeNora does not understand. Whom is she patronizing? Everyone in the arts today deplores the inaccessibility of so much of culture for a large part of the population, but who are those unfortunates in the outer darkness for whose lived experience high culture is not "appropriate," the great unwashed incapable of appreciating the most difficult of Beethoven's works? Immigrant Asians or Hispanics? Single mothers on welfare? Subway motormen? Wealthy Oklahoma ranchers? Sociologists? Cultural historians?

I presume that the coupling "inaccessible" and "inappropriate" is not simply redundant, and that DeNora does not mean only that Beethoven's music is not appropriate to the lived experience of people who have never been able to hear any of it. And I hope that she is not implying that it is inappropriate for music lovers from non-European cultures to enjoy the work of dead white males, as that would entail the equally detestable corollary that live whites ought not to listen to music from China, India, or Africa, a proposal that would cause consternation even in the ethnomusicological circles which find Beethoven irrelevant to our "lived experience."

We can see how an inappropriate use of the concept of class brings to light the patronizing attitude of a cultural critic who works in an academic atmosphere. Frank Kermode wrote recently, with what seemed like envy, that at least in music history no one was teaching students that the late Beethoven quartets were an instrument of domination over the lower orders by the Austro-Hungarian upper class. He was evidently wrong. DeNora is at pains to clarify her stand: "My intention is by no means to debunk Beethoven. Within the cultural framework devoted to its appreciation, Beethoven's music is rich and rewarding of close attention, as I continue to discover." This happy discovery sets her apart from the people for whom Beethoven's music is truly and permanently inappropriate, those of whatever economic class with no musical sensibility or interest. Their lives are enriched by other pleasures.

DeNora wishes to "treat with dignity the perspectives of those for whom (and for whatever reasons) Beethoven's talent was not self-evident," and she intends

to appreciate the accounts his listeners offered about their responses to his music, not as a window to these respondents' cultural or psychological makeup, but as a way of exploring the uses of that music in context, of exploring the definition of the music's social impact by specific individuals within a specific context.

A note on this sentence explains:

> This discourse also allows nonmusic specialists to explore music's so-
> cial meaning. I exploit this loophole: I do not offer any discussion
> (informed by twentieth-century music theoretical notions of form)
> about how Beethoven's early compositions did or did not "deviate"
> from standard Viennese practice.

This discourse does not provide a loophole. One cannot explore "music's social meaning" with no reference to the music. At least to some extent a "non-
music"(!) specialist has to come to terms with the subject. It is one thing to ignore twentieth-century notions of form, but DeNora offers no discussion of
eighteenth- or early nineteenth-century conceptions: most of her quoted documents are journalistic chatter or informal reactions to the works of Beethoven
and other composers. These have their value, even sometimes great value, but
what that value is cannot be determined without examining the music being
praised or excoriated.

We do not restore dignity to the opponents of Beethoven until we can judge how
intelligent and how relevant their comments were. For DeNora all opinions are
equal—except that praise of Beethoven is generally ascribed to a desire to flatter
Beethoven's aristocratic patrons, while praise of other composers comes straight
from the heart with no ulterior motive. Hostile criticism of a composer who
would later be accepted as a master can be obtuse or sharp. Theodor Wiesengrund Adorno's book *The Philosophy of Modern Music*, for example, is largely a
fraudulent presentation, a work of polemic that pretends to be an objective
study, and the chapters on Stravinsky are vicious and unprincipled; but Adorno
was an extremely intelligent critic, and some of his comments on Stravinsky reveal important aspects of his work unrecognized by admirers (although what
Adorno thought were crippling faults would later seem to be inspired innovations).

In the same way, attacks on Beethoven could be profound and even persuasive, and would continue to be so after his death even to the present. Most musicians (outside of Central Europe) will appreciate the brilliance of Debussy's remark at a concert during a Beethoven symphony: "Ah, the development section
is beginning; I can go out and smoke a cigarette." The way Beethoven's reputation was "constructed" is perhaps revealed best in some comments made in 1812
by a close friend of Goethe, the composer Karl Friedrich Zelter:[5] "I, too, regard

---

5. I have quoted his letter to Goethe at greater length in *The Frontiers of Meaning* (Hill and
Wang, 1994), pp. 69–70.

him with terror . . . His works seem to me like children whose father is a woman or whose mother is a man . . . I know musical people who once found themselves alarmed, even indignant, on hearing his works and are now gripped by an enthusiasm for them like partisans of Greek love." A few years later Zelter was to become the teacher of Mendelssohn, who would take the latest and most difficult works of Beethoven as models for his own compositions, but in 1812 Beethoven was a monstrosity for Zelter.

The shock of alarm and indignation followed by fascination was the basis for Beethoven's reputation. It needed familiarity to be accepted. (We may be reminded of Rimsky-Korsakov's injunction to his young student Stravinsky not to listen to the music of Debussy or he might get to like it.) The repeated performances necessary to this acceptance were provided by the musicians already under his spell—the expression is not too strong. Aristocratic ideology had very little to do with it: the few aristocrats who financed Beethoven were advised by musicians who told them where to put their money for the best cultural investment. On the other hand, the new supremacy of the art of music current in literary circles had a great deal to do with it (DeNora discusses neither the new aesthetic theories nor the considerable backing of Beethoven by poets and novelists).

It is true that some composers later to be accepted as "great" did not receive the financial backing that Beethoven did, but none of them combined a shocking and even alarming originality of improvisation and composition with a brilliant and imperious virtuoso style of performance, which got Beethoven started when he was young; nor did they arrive when the literary world was working to convince the cultivated society of Europe that music was the new archetype of Romantic art. Schubert is often cited as a composer who died in relative obscurity, although at thirty-one, the age of Schubert at his death, Beethoven's reputation had only been acknowledged for a few years—and even with all of Schubert's obscurity, the eighteen-year-old Schumann as far away as Leipzig wept all night on hearing of his death.

DeNora sincerely believes in the validity of her other candidates for greatness:

> This is not to say, however, that there were not composers who might
> have been capable of garnering a similar sort of reputation. Some, I
> think, were better suited for the part than others (Gelinek less so than
> Dussek or Wölffl, for instance).

Before this can seem anything but absurd, some consideration of the music must be offered, yet this is just what DeNora seems to want to avoid at all costs. She does, however, present us with an illuminating letter of Wölffl to his publisher, Breitkopf, about his problems in London:

> Since I have been here, my works have had astonishing sales and I already get sixty guineas for three sonatas; but along with all this I must write in a very easy and sometimes a very vulgar style. So much for your information, in case it should occur to one of your critics to make fun of me on account of any of my things that have appeared here. You won't believe how backward music still is here and how one has to hold oneself back in order to bring forth such shallow compositions, which do a terrific business here.

Beethoven, too, had to compromise his serious status: he composed a cheap "Battle" Symphony with cannon effects, collaborating with Maelzel, the inventor of the metronome; wrote easy sonatinas; made an ineffective arrangement of his violin concerto for piano (adding an interesting cadenza with kettledrums); and transcribed folk songs for an English publisher. But does anyone seriously think he would have been capable of Wölffl's servile submission to popular taste? Or that Wölffl could have risked alienating his public, as Beethoven did—and Mozart as well, it must be emphasized—in order to realize his most personal musical ideas?

DeNora and other sociologists are right: the status of Beethoven as a great composer is not a fact of nature but the result of a system of values and an ideology in which we have been educated and by which we continue to judge, think, and behave. They are wrong, however, to believe that this system of values was imposed by a single class, even a class with political authority and a lot of money. It has been elaborated over a long history, and one in which a highly specialized and complex technical musical language was developed and continuously changed as a part of a larger and more general cultural environment. Neither the more general culture nor the musical language, however, could be simply altered at will, either by a class or by an exceptional individual: both of them could only be inflected and partially reshaped.

The acknowledged genius of Beethoven is to a great extent the product of this system of values and was, in fact, demonstrable within that system. A growing familiarity with his music did not establish him as a radical and revolutionary master like Monteverdi, Berlioz, Debussy, and Stravinsky—or even Haydn—but revealed his work as the continuation and fulfillment of a firmly established tradition. The changes that Beethoven made to the musical language of the late eighteenth century, as startling as some of them may have appeared at first, were in fact conceived with reference to the local tradition, most of them being expansions of procedures already worked out and employed by previous composers in Vienna. His exploitation of the style was more powerful and more effective than that of any of his contemporaries. Starting from some of the most radical experiments of Mozart and Haydn, many of which had only recently been accepted by more conservative amateurs and professionals, he used them at greater length and with greater force, employing the larger range of the new pianos and the growing size of the orchestras.

His superiority was quickly recognized after the initial shock of the new emotional violence was absorbed. It was not simply imposed from without, although we cannot deny the influence of both Viennese society and general European culture on Beethoven's individual talent. His emotional violence, on the other hand, had little to do specifically with Viennese society, aristocratic or otherwise, but was a general European phenomenon, and needs to be studied on a larger scale than the one DeNora provides. Part of Beethoven's tremendous success must be ascribed to his being the one representative in Viennese music of the new movement of passion that swept across Europe after the American and French revolutions.

DeNora's account of the social conditions of Beethoven's rise to fame is instructive, and her synthesis of recent research is generally admirable. Any interpretation of this material, however, will remain dubious until it is put in direct touch with the music and not merely with what some people said about it. DeNora thinks our prejudice in favor of Beethoven makes it difficult to trust anything we have to say today, but her naive belief that reports of performances and critical judgments of the past can be accepted without investigation as if they all had equal weight is crippling. Then, as today, critics heard what they expected to hear. (Some of them, for example, still always hear Toscanini's tempi as fast, although his *Parsifal* was the longest in the history of Bayreuth, and many of his tempi in Brahms and Verdi were slower than those of most other conductors.) Contemporary critics expected Beethoven's music to sound difficult, and often enough they heard it as difficult even when his music was lyrical and graceful. In addition, they were, as so often, incapable of separating the defects of the execution of a new work from the intentions of the composer.

We all believe that a work of music has a meaning expressive of its composer, of the moment of its creation, and of the society in which it first appeared. In trying to pin that meaning down, however, DeNora and other social historians make two assumptions which seem at first so reasonable as to be self-evident, but which are in fact either false or at best deeply misleading. The first is that the ideology of the composer or of his music can be equated with the ideology of those who pay for it. The relation of an artist to public or private patrons is very much more complex: some artists do what is expected of them, others are not so docile; some even force their patrons to accept an art at odds with their aesthetics and their political ideals. The politics and the social philosophy of a composer or of the contemporary public do not simply determine the character of the music.

The second assumption is that the ideology of a patron of music is the ideology of his or her class. On the contrary, some patrons of music are mavericks rather like the artists they support. I do not know if one can reasonably say that the Baron van Swieten, for example, was representative of his class, whatever class that may have been. Perhaps the new sociological approach is trying to fill the gap left by the now discredited Marxist history of art, but the best Marxist criticism, like that of György Lukács, was less naive than some of the recent social interpretations in spite of their richer documentation. The social history of reception can certainly increase our understanding of music, but it provides neither a simple nor an infallible method of identifying the significance of any body of work without reference to the music itself.

It would be grand to have a social history of music, but before it can be realized, the sociologists will have to take music more seriously.

Reply to a letter by Tia DeNora to *The New York Review of Books*

I never denied that genius is a social achievement. In fact, I wrote in my review: "The status of Beethoven as a great composer is not a fact of nature but the result of a system of values and an ideology in which we have been educated and by which we continue to judge, think, and behave." I claimed only that DeNora does not understand how genius is socially constructed—to use her expression. Nor did I say that DeNora wishes to debunk Beethoven or deny his talent. She is not interested enough in his music to do either. What I challenged was her belief that Beethoven's success can be explained with absolutely no consideration whatever of his work.

When she says that she argues "that Beethoven's talent was a necessary but not sufficient cause of his subsequent acclaim," she is more than a little disingenuous. Put that way, the thesis is acceptable and even bland. Who would deny it? If Beethoven had not received support and financial aid from influential members of Viennese society, he would not have achieved the early success that allowed his career to develop so spectacularly. That, however, is not all that DeNora maintains in her book: there she astonishingly and literally insists that if the Viennese aristocracy had backed a more conventional composer like Joseph Wölffl, then Wölffl and not Beethoven would have become the great genius acclaimed by the next two centuries and that the difficult and more innovative style of Beethoven would not be the model that it is for us today. Pascal said that if Cleopatra's nose had been shorter, the whole face of the earth would be changed. For DeNora, Joseph Wölffl is Cleopatra's nose. Of course, all these ifs and might-have-beens of history skirt the absurd, but DeNora's is one of the more ludicrous.

She believes that it is "tautological" to say that "Beethoven's compositional practice was 'more powerful and more effective than that of any of his contemporaries.'" That is interesting: it means that she cannot conceive any form of musical argument that would explain Beethoven's success except the fact that he succeeded. For DeNora, no form of musical discourse has any meaning. We cannot discuss Beethoven in modern terms because they have been set by our estimation of Beethoven. She also refuses to discuss Beethoven in terms of the criticism of his contemporaries.

She writes that she does "consider the view of musicians": this is untrue—she does not consider them or listen to them, she only quotes a few of them. There is no assessment of Beethoven's critics, no attempt to determine the accuracy or the cogency of any of the contemporary evaluations, to see in what way the blame or the praise heaped on Beethoven was relevant to his music. Not all of Beethoven's enemies were stupid, not all of his idolaters intelligent, but DeNora cannot distinguish among them even on their own terms. She does not think it worthwhile to know what those terms were, because musical discourse, she clearly believes, has no practical value for understanding history.

DeNora's focus is too narrow. The "social achievement" which needs to be studied in order to understand Beethoven's success is the language of eighteenth-century music, the way it was built into society and the way it was influenced by, and influenced in turn, the aesthetics and the social action of all the other arts. The "construction of genius" cannot be studied, as DeNora does, in isolation from the construction of Western art music or, indeed, from the development of the concept of "genius" fashionable in aesthetics in the late eighteenth century. DeNora does not dishonestly eliminate any discussion of this development because it would weaken her thesis, although it would: she is not aware of these matters because she has not gone back to the original sources but relies entirely on the work of recent scholars. She sums up their work brilliantly, but that is not enough to prove the points she wishes to make.

In spite of the belief of Sir Ernst Gombrich and others, eighteenth-century tonality is not a scientific discovery but a constructed system, a complex language developed in response to social pressures and to the needs of society. It was solidly in place when Beethoven began to write: in that sense it existed as a fact. To say that Beethoven was more effective than any other composer in exploiting this system is not a tautology, but a demonstrable proposition: it can be, and was, discussed and argued in the eighteenth century. DeNora writes: "Within modern musicological circles, it is quite difficult to construct a convincing argument that the music of Wölffl, for instance, is 'better' than Beethoven's, even though some of Beethoven's contemporaries suggested just that." Not many of Beethoven's contemporaries suggested that, and not for very long. (Note DeNora's quotation marks around "better": that is because she thinks the word is strictly meaningless.) It would be difficult today to construct a convincing argument that Galileo and Copernicus were wrong and Ptolemy right, but many of Galileo's contemporaries suggested that, and not every one of them was stupid or ignorant of science. Not all aesthetic judgment is a matter of taste (and the acceptance of a scientific theory is considerably influenced by social and ideological pressure). It is a fact that Beethoven was more effective than almost anyone else at handling the socially constructed tonal system as he received it from Haydn and Mozart, and this fact was recognized very early. What gave him his ultimate superiority, however, was his radical originality. Many of his contemporaries were at first appalled—and most of them later fascinated—by his innovations, but this was expected of a "genius" as the concept was developed in literary and artistic circles in Germany and the rest of Europe. The demand for innovation that shocked and even repelled was already traditional by 1800. What DeNora does not sufficiently realize is that the controversy over Beethoven was considered as a proof of genius, and she does not see at all that by 1798 the attacks against Beethoven always treated him as a considerable figure that had to be reckoned with.

A single class—like the Viennese aristocracy—cannot permanently affect the course of music. It can only give someone five years—or fifteen minutes—of fame. The history of music is an interaction of individual talent, social pressures, and the musical system already in place. The most stable of these factors is, in fact, the musical system. Ignoring it completely, as DeNora does, vitiates every generalization. Without his powerful patrons, Beethoven could not have achieved what he did. If he had not received their support (there is that "if" again), he would have had to look elsewhere or write in isolation, and his work would most probably have been different. Schubert never received that kind of patronage, and he was not a brilliant virtuoso performer. His music found public success starting in the decade after his death, and much of his work was only appreciated almost a century later. I think Beethoven was too aggressive to wait that long.

PART THREE

CHAPTER NINE

Brahms: Influence, Plagiarism, and Inspiration

For practice I have also set to music the aria "Non so d'onde viene," which has been so beautifully composed by [J. C.] Bach. Just because I know Bach's setting so well and like it so much, and because it is always ringing in my ears, I wished to try and see whether in spite of all this I could not write an aria totally unlike his. And, indeed, mine does not resemble his in the very least.

—*Mozart to his father, February 28, 1778*

O F all classical influences on Renaissance and baroque literature, the most puzzling to assess is the influence of Plato on La Fontaine; it will serve admirably as a model for what I have to say about music. We know from La Fontaine himself that he loved the writings of Plato. After La Fontaine's death, the Abbé d'Olivet wrote that he had seen the poet's copy of Plato's works (in a Latin translation): "They were annotated in his own hand on every page, and I remarked that most of these notes were maxims of ethics or politics which he planted in his fables."[1] This copy of Plato has not come down to us.

The works of La Fontaine have been studied for allusions to Plato. There are almost none. Scholars have looked for quotations from Plato, with an almost total lack of success. But nobody ever claimed there were any. Reading Plato inspired La Fontaine not to quotation but to original thought. What this original thought was can only be a matter for surmise: in the absence of any documentary evidence, no proof of any of our conjectures is possible. The rules of evidence that enable us, on circumstantial grounds, to convict a writer of having

1. Quoted in La Fontaine, *Oeuvres diverses*, ed. Pierre Clarac (Paris, 1942), II, 984.

An earlier version of this article was presented in the 1978–79 Thalheimer lecture series in Philosophy at Johns Hopkins University. I am grateful to Daniel Heartz for drawing my attention to the Mozart letter (Anderson 292) cited in the epigraph, and to Walter Frisch for the information in note 5.

been influenced are of no use to us in this case—and it is precisely this case which is the most interesting kind.

The influence of one artist upon another can take a wide variety of forms, from plagiarism, borrowing, and quotation all the way to imitation and eventually to the profound but almost invisible form we have seen with Plato and La Fontaine. About a half century ago, literary history used to be envisaged almost entirely as a tracing of such influences, and this has not yet completely fallen out of fashion. In the history of the visual arts, it is perhaps the major form of professional activity. Certain periods provide more fertile grounds than others: above all, nineteenth-century writers, artists, and composers seem to have cultivated a knack for being influenced by their predecessors. The unacknowledged, or hidden, Shakespearean quotation is as much a trick of Hazlitt's and of Byron's styles as the hidden borrowing from Renaissance sources is a part of Manet's. Buried Romantic allusions to Shakespeare are essentially different from the often tacit references to classical poets like Horace in the words of Pope and his contemporaries. Pope modernized his sources, and his hidden references ennobled their modern context for the connoisseur. The Romantic allusions archaize and alienate: they give an exotic flavor to the familiar every-day. Manet's uses of Raphael and Titian are still today a little shocking, while Dürer's adaptations of classical Greek sculpture are dignified and uplifting.

In discussing influence in music, it would be wise to refuse in advance to consider the work of adolescent composers. With the startling exception of Mendelssohn, a very young composer has no style of his own, and he is forced to get one somewhere else. His models have largely a biographical, but not much critical, significance—he may, indeed, reject his early models by the time he reaches his majority.

Plagiarism has an interest for ethics and law, but little for criticism. Even in the case of the most notorious thefts—those of Handel and Coleridge, to take two examples—the outright appropriations are less significant than those in which the borrowed material has been transformed. Nevertheless, it is the process of transformation that raises all the difficulties for study. With plagiarism, we have two works in which some part of both is identical, a part too large for the identity to be fortuitous. This identity establishes beyond a doubt the relationship between the two works. As we move away from such simple situations—that is, as the later artist transforms the borrowed material into something more his own—this relationship is put into question. The critic must still claim an identity between something in the earlier work and the material of the new work. But what gives him the right to maintain this identity except a resemblance which diminishes as the transformation is more thorough? Sometimes a document is forthcoming in which the later artist acknowledges the source of his inspiration—and, even then, the interpretation of such an admission can rarely be straightforward. When the transformation is an almost total one, evidence for the identity is erased in a work which now appears completely original. The source is likely to seem irrelevant to the critic, because it is not clear by what method he can reach it, although in this case the source is in fact more relevant for criticism than in any other. The most important form of influence is that which provokes the most original and most personal work. If we had La Fontaine's annotations to his copy of Plato, it is by no means certain that we would understand at once what the poet saw in the philosopher.

The range of the problem may be shown first by two examples from Mozart. On May 17, 1789, Mozart wrote a fugal Gigue for Piano (K. 574) in Leipzig, the city of Sebastian Bach, and gave it as a present to the court organist. It has a characteristic opening. Haydn's Quartet in C Major, op. 20 no. 2, has a fugal gigue as a finale, and it opens similarly (as shown in Ex. 9.1). The resemblance is obvious (in the descent G-F♯-F♮-E as part of the basic structure of the tune) and trivial. Such thematic resemblances are a dime-a-dozen. We are aware, of course, that Mozart knew Haydn's op. 20 Quartets very well indeed, since he imitated them closely many years before when he began to write string quartets at the age of sixteen.

From the second part of Mozart's gigue, however, there is a striking, even astonishing rhythmic change of accent (see Ex. 9.2). If the phrasing is correctly played (which is not often the case), the ⁶⁄₈ rhythm is suddenly contradicted by a ²⁄₄—or, more precisely, cut by a ⁴⁄₈ grouping enforced by the parallelisms of two staccato and two legato notes:

More surprisingly, perhaps, there is a similar effect in Haydn's gigue (Ex. 9.2). Haydn's grouping is more complex, and a little less disconcerting: it contrasts (by two staccato, two legato, two staccato eighth-notes) a ³⁄₄ with the ⁶⁄₈ grouping of three and three. It is nonetheless startling, and once heard, it is hard to forget. Mozart evidently remembered and improved on it. Alfred Einstein writes in the third edition of Köchel: "Mozart hat mit diesem Stammbuchblatt dem Genius loci—Bach—gehuldigt, ohne eine Stilkopie zu liefern." If only Mozart had written his gigue in Esterház instead of Leipzig, it would be considered a homage to Haydn.

The connection between Haydn's Symphony No. 81 in G Major and Mozart's "Prague" Symphony in D Major, K. 504, is more tenuous but more suggestive. Haydn's symphony was written in 1783–84, at just the moment that the friend-

Example 9.1

Example 9.2

ship between Haydn and Mozart began;[2] the "Prague" was written two or three
years later. Example 9.3 shows the beginning of the two Allegros. The contrast
between Haydn's muscular opening and Mozart's restrained syncopations following the massive introduction could not be more absolute. Yet both have important and uncommon things in common: a soft ostinato on the tonic note
that continues for several measures, and the striking introduction on the flat seventh in the third measure. Significant, too, is the gradual deployment of new

2. 1784 is the most likely starting point. See H. C. Robbins Landon, *Haydn: Chronicle and
Works*, II (Bloomington, 1978), 509.

motifs as the period continues, including a completely new rhythmic texture and motif, and a cadence in the last two measures, just before the theme starts up again.

Was Mozart impressed by Haydn's quiet playing of the flat seventh against a repeated tonic in the third measure of his Allegro, and did he think he could make even grander use of the device? No proof will ever be forthcoming one way or the other, nor would it be particularly interesting if it were. We should remark, however, that the "Prague" is unusual among Mozart's works in employing a particularly Haydnesque structural effect: the return of the opening theme at the dominant to establish that key in the exposition. This is only too common in Haydn but rare in Mozart, although we may find it in the Piano Trio in B♭ Major, K. 502, written a month before the "Prague" Symphony.

There are other contacts with Haydn's technique to be found in the "Prague,"

Example 9.3

particularly in the use of ritornello effects in transitional passages and in the way the motifs are developed. A study will reveal greater differences, above all in the breadth of the conception. These differences do not demonstrate any distance from Haydn—it may have been that Haydn's example stimulated Mozart to something completely his own, that Haydn provided the most profound form of inspiration. The influence of Haydn's music on the adolescent Mozart is easy to trace; the influence on the later Mozart is largely untraceable but may have been just as important. If there was any, we cannot reconstruct the steps of Mozart's transformation, only guess at them. The solidity of the study of sources begins to dissolve as the subject becomes more significant.

II

Influence of a different nature appears in the nineteenth century, with the choice of a particular work as a structural model. An example is the finale of Brahms's Piano Concerto No. 1 in D Minor. The dependence of this movement on the last movement of Beethoven's Piano Concerto No. 3 in C Minor was remarked by Tovey, but it has never, as far as I know, been spelled out.[3] The closeness of that dependence, taken together with the fact that the two pieces sound so different that even the most cultivated listener is unlikely to be reminded of one by the other, makes this an interesting case.

The two finales may be described and analyzed to a great extent as if they were the same piece:

> Rondo form. Minor key. ¾. *Allegro* (Beethoven); *Allegro non troppo* (Brahms). 1st phrase. 8 measures. Solo piano alone. Opening theme (Ex. 9.4).

> 2nd phrase. 8 measures. Orchestra repeats the first phrase with pizzicato accompaniment. Solo plays obbligato counterpoint in octaves (Ex. 9.5).

> 3rd phrase. Second phrase of theme started by solo alone, orchestra entering in the middle of the phrase. The theme develops a short descending motif repeated several times getting softer *(calando, diminuendo)* and slower *(ritard., poco sostenuto)* (Ex. 9.6).

> Cadenza (measured in Brahms)—arpeggiated figuration descending and then ascending, ending with a scale that leads directly into the re-

3. Donald F. Tovey, *Essays in Musical Analysis*, III *(Concertos)* (London, 1936), 74, 118.

BEETHOVEN

BRAHMS

Example 9.4

BEETHOVEN

BRAHMS

Example 9.5

turn of the opening phrase, now played by the piano accompanied by
the orchestra. Beethoven's scale ascends and Brahms's descends, but
that is not an impressive transformation.

After the second theme in the mediant major, the return of the first theme is
heralded by extensive arpeggios on the dominant. The opening phrase reappears
in the solo, accompanied now by the strings pizzicato.

The middle section of the rondo is a new lyrical theme in the submediant ma-

Example 9.6

jor (A♭ in Beethoven, B♭ in Brahms), appearing first in the orchestra and then accompanied in the solo piano. A staccato fugue (*pp*, Beethoven, *sempre p,* Brahms) follows as a development (m. 230 in Beethoven, m. 238 in Brahms), beginning in the strings, the winds entering later (Ex. 9.7). Then the first appearance of the main theme in the major mode is formed with a drone bass in pastoral style (Ex. 9.8). (In Brahms, it is the mediant major, in Beethoven, more astonishingly, the sharp mediant major.) This leads to extensive arpeggios on a dominant pedal followed by brilliant passagework which prepares the return of the opening theme. After the recapitulation, there is a cadenza and a coda in major (in Brahms, a long cadenza and an extensive series of codas).

This procedure of modeling upon a previous structure is clearly explicit, and equally clearly not intended to be audible to the general public, however much it may add to the appreciation of the connoisseurs. It is akin to the dependence of the finale of Schubert's Piano Sonata in A Major, D. 959, on the finale of Beethoven's Piano Sonata in G Major, op. 31 no. 1 (a relationship demonstrated some years ago independently by Professor Edward T. Cone and myself).[4] The technique has an obvious and superficial resemblance to late medieval parody technique, which we can safely neglect here, but we need to distinguish it carefully from the nineteenth-century composer's use of *quotation,* the thematic allusion to a previous work.

Brahms was a master of allusion, and he generally intended his references to be heard ("Any jackass can see that," he is supposed to have said when one of

4. See Edward T. Cone, "Schubert's Beethoven," *Musical Quarterly* 56 (1970), 779–793, and Charles Rosen, *The Classical Style* (New York, 1971), pp. 456–458.

Example 9.7

Example 9.8

them was recognized). Opus 1 (the Piano Sonata in C Major) begins with a clear reference to Beethoven's *Hammerklavier*: that, in fact, is why it is opus 1— Brahms's career starts from this quotation (the work is by no means Brahms's first piano sonata). The Scherzo, op. 4, begins with a similar quotation; the reference is to Chopin's Scherzo in B♭ Minor (Ex. 9.9). The homage to Chopin does not stop there. A page later in Brahms's scherzo we find a passage that is freely developed from another scherzo of Chopin's, this one in C♯ minor (Ex. 9.10). With this, however, we have left behind the device of quotation, and reach a new adaptation. Still later in the Brahms Scherzo, op. 4, in the second of the two trios,

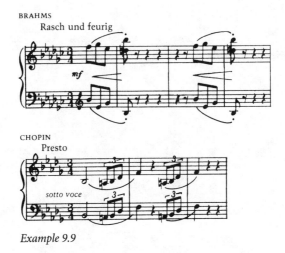

Example 9.9

Example 9.10

there is a return to Chopin's B♭-Minor Scherzo with the lovely passage shown in Example 9.11. Is this quotation or adaptation? It is derived fairly directly from Chopin. It should be clear why Brahms started his scherzo with an unmistakable allusion to Chopin: having steeped himself in Chopin's style in order to absorb a now canonic conception of the virtuoso piano scherzo, Brahms displays the thematic reference at the opening in order to signal the presence of imitation. The listener who is also a connoisseur is notified in advance that his appreciation of

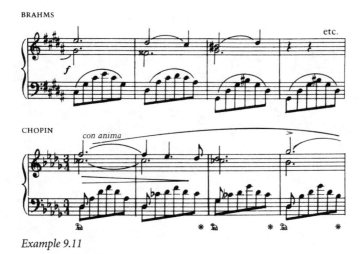

Example 9.11

the work about to be played will be enhanced if he recognizes the imitation and savors the finesse with which it has been carried out.[5]

With Brahms, we reach a composer whose music we cannot fully appreciate—at a certain level, at any rate—without becoming aware of the influences that went into its making, in exactly the same way that it is difficult to make sense of Mendelssohn's "Reformation" Symphony without recognizing the chorale tunes. Influence for Brahms was not merely a part of the compositional process, a necessary fact of creative life: he incorporated it as part of the symbolic structure of the work, its iconography. We might even conjecture that the overt references are often there as signals, to call attention to others less obvious, almost undetectable.

The two open references to Beethoven's "Emperor" Concerto made by Brahms's Piano Concerto No. 2 in B♭ Major are placed in such crucial places, so set in relief, in fact, that they must be understood as staking a claim. This work, we are informed by these open references, is intended to follow upon the tradition left off by Beethoven. Opening the first movement with a cadenza for the soloist points directly to the "Emperor": Brahms has altered the scheme only to

---

5. In light of the obvious indebtedness to Chopin, it is surprising that Brahms claimed to have known no Chopin when writing the E♭-Minor Scherzo. This is the piece that Liszt sight-read from manuscript during Brahms's legendary visit to Weimar in 1853. The pianist William Mason, who was present, reports that after the performance Joachim Raff remarked on the resemblance of the opening of the Scherzo to Chopin's B♭-Minor, but "Brahms said that he had never seen or heard any of Chopin's compositions." Mason, *Memories of a Musical Life* (New York, 1902), p. 129.

BEETHOVEN

BRAHMS

Example 9.12

Example 9.13 (continued on following page)

make room for an initial statement of the main theme by the orchestra (with additional antiphonal effects from the piano that derive from Mozart's Concerto in E♭, K. 271). Enlarging the form set by the "Emperor" to include a brief initial statement of the theme was an obvious step—so clearly the next thing to do that Beethoven himself tried this out in an elaborate sketch for a sixth piano concerto that was probably unknown to Brahms.[6]

The second reference is a thematic, as well as a structural, quotation. Compare the entrance of the soloist in the slow movements of the "Emperor" and the Brahms concertos (Ex. 9.12). Brahms adds two introductory measures, and then produces an ornamented version of Beethoven's music, a magnificent homage.

6. See Lewis Lockwood, "Beethoven's Unfinished Piano Concerto of 1815: Sources and Problems," *Musical Quarterly* 56 (1970), 624–646.

Example 9.13 (continued)

This sort of allusion is like the modernized quotation from Horace practiced by poets of the time of Pope. It creates an intimate link between poet and educated reader, composer and professional musician—and excludes the ordinary reader and listener. It also acknowledges the existence of a previous Classical style, an aspiration to recreate it, and an affirmation that such a recreation is no longer possible on naive or independent terms. The control of style is now not merely willed but self-conscious.

These overt allusions warn us of the presence of more recondite imitations. Perhaps the most interesting of the latter is the use Brahms makes of a striking passage in the coda of the first movement of the "Emperor" (see Ex. 9.13) for the identical place in his own first movement. What characterizes the Beethoven is a *pianissimo* chromatic descent followed by the first phrase of the main theme *fortissimo*, the reduction of this to a few notes, the arrangement of this fragment in a rising sequence, and the striking irregularity of the sequence in its antiphonal

Example 9.14 (continued on following page)

division between piano and orchestra. All of these qualities are faithfully reproduced by Brahms (see Ex. 9.14). In keeping with his dislike of pure orchestral effect, Brahms has slightly attenuated the antiphonal nature of the conception, although it is still clearly in evidence in his version: in place of solo against orchestra, it has become solo and strings against winds.

For the scherzo of the concerto, Brahms has no model available from the Beethoven piano concertos (although he is able to incorporate reminiscences of the

Example 9.14 (continued)

Ninth Symphony). The basic model is, once again, Chopin. We have seen that Brahms's knowledge of Chopin's scherzos was profound: here he uses the E-Major Scherzo, no. 4. Both works are built on a rigid, underlying four-measure structure in which the basic grouping of measures remains unaltered, while the phrases appear supple because they start on the second measure of a group. This imposes a long beat over the fast tempo as one hears each four-measure unit almost as one long measure, but the melodies take irregular forms within this.

Brahms's second theme is particularly striking. It appears to be an eleven-measure theme, but it clearly starts on the second measure of a unit (see Ex. 9.15),

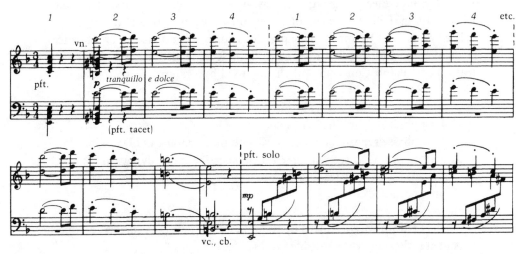

Example 9.15

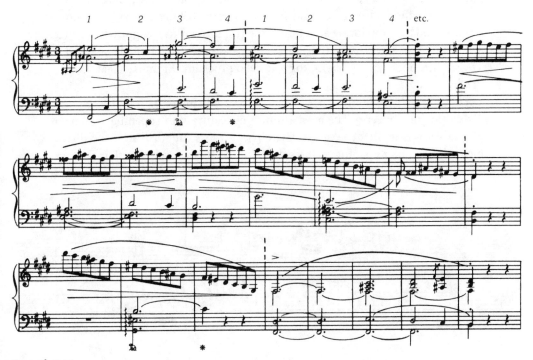

Example 9.16

which I have annotated so as to show the outer regularity of the inner irregularity. The technique is derived directly from Chopin (see Ex. 9.16). In both movements, the four-measure grouping is overridden, largely by avoiding a coincidence between the first measure of a unit and the opening of a phrase.

The first page of Brahms's finale parades a curious combination of references. The basic model for the first theme is still the scheme formulated by Beethoven in the Third Piano Concerto and already used by Brahms. To recapitulate the plan:

(1) First phrase: main theme in solo part
(2) First phrase repeated by orchestra, with monophonic obbligato in solo
(3) Second phrase in solo, accompanied, repeating motif dying away
(4) Cadenza with scale leading back to
(5) First phrase

So much is faithfully reproduced by Brahms, except that the cadenza is reduced to its final scale alone with an added trill (Ex. 9.17).

The opening phrase, however, is based on another Beethoven model, the opening of the finale of the Fourth Piano Concerto in G Major. Beethoven's phrase is extraordinary for its opening on the subdominant, reaching the tonic only toward the end of its second half. This very striking concept is plain in Brahms, and he is obviously anxious for the connoisseur to recognize the source, as he imitates the orchestration of an accompaniment by a single string line. The substitution of the viola for the solo cello proclaims Brahms's creative independence.

This is not the only time that Brahms used a scheme to be found in Beethoven's G-Major Concerto. The most astonishing feature of the opening movement of that work is its first measures. The obvious cause for surprise is the instrumentation, a quiet opening in the solo, followed by the orchestra. For the connoisseur, however, the most significant feature is the remote harmony with

Example 9.17

which the second phrase opens. It gives a wonderful sense of breadth and of space.

Brahms's allusion is for connoisseurs alone, and may be found in the first sixteen measures of the Violin Concerto. For a contrast of solo and orchestra Brahms substitutes a contrast of texture and spacing: he always disliked showy orchestral effects, and his practice of bringing in unusual instruments like the harp or triangle so that their presence at first goes unremarked has often been observed. For Beethoven's V of vi, Brahms substitutes the even more remote triad of the flat seventh degree. Achieved by much the same means, the sense of breadth and space is equally grand, harmonically more striking. (At this stage in his career Brahms's borrowings are generally heightenings: after the cadenza of this concerto, he borrows from Beethoven's Violin Concerto the device of having the main theme return softly, high on the violin's E string, but he sustains it much longer and with greater intensity.)

This last borrowing from the Fourth Piano Concerto may be doubted, and I have proposed it deliberately because it is dubious (although I cannot believe that such a parallelism could have occurred to me and not to Brahms, who knew the music of Beethoven better than any other musician in history). It approaches the sort of transformation of a model which is so complete that it is almost undetectable and certainly unprovable without a signed affidavit from the composer admitting the borrowing. This is hardly likely to turn up. What Brahms had to say about his relation to history and to the past, he let his music say for him. This goes to show that when the study of sources is at its most interesting, it becomes indistinguishable from pure musical analysis.

CHAPTER TEN

Brahms the Subversive

WRITING about Brahms's Rhapsody in G minor, op. 79 no. 2, Carl Dahlhaus makes an interesting mistake. I hasten to add that to me Dahlhaus is one of the most provocative and intelligent writers on music in this century; it is therefore all the more curious that Brahms could have misled someone so distinguished and so perceptive. The error occurs in Dahlhaus's discussion of "expanded" and "wandering" tonality (the fourth section of his essay "Issues in Composition").[1] Dahlhaus ascribes "wandering" or "floating" tonality to Wagner and Liszt, and he wishes to demonstrate that such procedures can also be found in Brahms. This he tries to prove with the opening of the Rhapsody in G minor, op. 79 no. 2 (see Ex. 10.1), though he realizes that he has not much of a case, for this passage really does sound a lot in G minor. Dahlhaus himself, in fact, finds very good reasons, from a linear point of view, for explaining why these bars are in G minor. Still, when he comes to the second theme, he claims that G minor has been so little established and the new tonality that now unfolds is so ambiguous that we accept it as D minor only because the dominant is the traditional key for a second group.

What is interesting is that in almost no piece in G minor is D minor the key for the "second group"; that we know that the second theme is in the key of D cannot be due to some kind of tradition.[2] There are a few movements in the major mode where Brahms used the minor dominant for a second group, but that is

1. In *Between Romanticism and Modernism: Four Studies in the Music of the Later Nineteenth Century*, pp. 69–71.

2. After 1800, composers occasionally used the dominant minor as a secondary tonality, but examples are very rare (e.g., Mendelssohn's String Quartet in A minor, op. 13, and the Scottish Symphony, op. 56); the dominant *major* may be found in Schubert's Piano Sonata in A minor, D. 784, and in Mendelssohn's Piano Trio in D minor, op. 49, but this relationship is equally infrequent.

Example 10.1

in fact not a tradition, but rather the breaking of one. The traditional key for the second group would, of course, be B♭ major.

The opening of this piece is so curious that it is reasonable for Dahlhaus and anyone else to be puzzled. For one thing, it begins with what appears to be a full sequence; yet, although the two opening bars sound like a sequence, one of its members is not parallel to the other, for details have been changed: the opening fourth in the bass becomes a sixth, the opening fifth in the right hand becomes a diminished fifth. Both bars are essentially V–I progressions, both with surprise resolutions. Varied sequences existed long before Brahms, of course, but it is instructive to compare Brahms's practice with that of, say, Vivaldi and Bach. Whereas in Vivaldi the sequences tend to come with unvaried rigidity, Bach usually attempts to vary his, generally by means of voice-leading, though without strong variation of harmony. In Brahms, the typical variation is more radically of a harmonic nature, as in Example 10.1.

Another peculiar thing about the opening of the Rhapsody in G minor is that almost all the cadences are what might be called "weak cadences" ("weak" in a descriptive, not a pejorative sense). The strongest form of cadence is, of course, the V–I cadence. The normal plagal cadence is already a weakened form, and there are even weaker forms of the plagal cadence. Almost all the progressions of this opening page appear to be plagal, but are in fact ambiguous. Take the one in bars 3 and 4 (Ex. 10.2). The G major chord at the opening of bar 4 is heard clearly as a tonic (as our ears have accepted the opening two beats of the Rhapsody as a V–I progression with a surprise resolution to VI); at the same time, it is weakened by the diminished seventh and sounds as the dominant of IV. The cadence is not plagal, but IV to V of IV. It is a half-cadence on a dominant, in this case a tonic chord used momentarily as a dominant to IV. This sense of going from I to V is enforced by what precedes (Ex. 10.3). This sets the pattern for the harmonic structure of the whole page (Ex. 10.4). These four half-cadences define G minor and the move to D minor completed by bar 21: the establishment of G minor is achieved not only by line, but also harmonically.

This ambiguity (plagal cadence with a touch of minor or half-close on a local dominant) may help us understand the nature of Brahms's relation to the Classi-

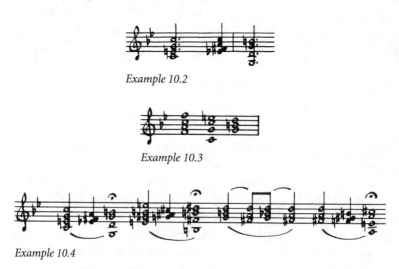

Example 10.2

Example 10.3

Example 10.4

Example 10.5

cal tradition. If we reverse each of these four cadences, we have "strong" cadences (Ex. 10.5). Cadences 1, 3, and 4 are, already in the correct order, the three cadences that open Beethoven's First Symphony: they define G as Beethoven's defined C. (Beethoven's cadences are only slightly more powerful; his three dominants are dominant sevenths.) In short, Brahms's method of establishing his tonic is a simple although radical subversion of a traditional Classical way of establishing a key. I do not mean to imply that Brahms intentionally added VI to Beethoven's IV–I–V, and then played each of the cadences backwards, but that the ambiguity that induced Dahlhaus's error does not come from a "floating" or "wandering" view of tonality, but from a thoroughly systematic and original treatment of basic Classical procedures. Reversing a Classical means of establishing a tonality allows Brahms here to define G at the same time that he establishes the move to D. This is significant, as we shall find that what is characteristic of Brahms's style is an overlapping of functions normally kept separate in Classical procedure.

These weakened cadences are typical of Brahms: when he uses tonic-dominant relationships, he tends to weaken them, and not only on a small scale, as in this piece, but on a very large scale as well. Two of the best examples occur in the first movements of the Second Piano Concerto and the Violin Concerto; both are pieces in the major in which the dominant minor is used as the second key. Perhaps there is a precedent for this, for there is a precedent for almost everything in Brahms—he was an extraordinarily learned composer, and I have become convinced that if in any instance I do not know the precedent, it is because I have not looked hard enough. Nevertheless, the use of the minor dominant as the secondary key in an exposition, and the extent to which Brahms uses it, does seem to me very innovative. And I do not think this can be related to the brief allusion to the dominant minor in the second group of sonata expositions which is frequent in mid-eighteenth-century composers such as Monn and Wagenseil and which continues as a sort of tradition (see Mozart's Piano Sonata in F major, K. 332, for an example). In a way, Brahms's use of the minor dominant is better

Example 10.6

considered as an extension of Beethoven's use of the minor in pieces such as the *Appassionata,* compositions in minor which proceed to the relative major but mix a great deal of minor into the relative major.

Another innovation of Brahms is his use of what might be called a dislocation of sense between bass and melody. Melody in eighteenth- and nineteenth-century music traditionally implied its own harmony: in other words, the harmony has two values, horizontal and vertical; in general these two are in phase. Of course a composer can also harmonize a melody in a way that is not implied by the melody itself, creating a surprise. What is interesting about Brahms is the extent to which the horizontal and vertical are out of phase, with the harmony moving on to the next step before the melody has got there. A typical example occurs at the beginning of the Third Symphony (Ex. 10.6). Even though a suggestion of F minor is in evidence in the diminished seventh chord which follows the opening tonic F major, still the minor of the second bar of the melody (bar 4) comes as something of a shock, even today when one knows the piece. I think this is very different from the way it was done by eighteenth-century composers. One does find harmonic anticipation in Haydn, Mozart, and Beethoven, so it is not absolutely new with Brahms, but the shock he derives from it is fairly new. In Mozart a change of harmony of this sort always has a very peculiar expressive value related to the intervals of the theme itself, as in the slow movement of the Piano Trio in E major, K. 542 (see Ex. 10.7, the initial, and a subsequent, harmo-

Example 10.7

nization of the opening theme). This is as astonishing as anything in Brahms, but the reharmonization is inspired by the minor seventh E down to F♯ outlined by the theme. The new harmonies only realize in advance this dissonance and its resolution to a D, but in Brahms the minor that initiates the fourth bar of the Third Symphony appears almost gratuitously independent of the melody, even though, as in Mozart, it implies what is to come in the melody. One finds the same thing, for example, in the middle section of the Ballade in G minor, op. 118 no. 3 (Ex. 10.8). The melody by itself in bars 41 and 42 implies G♯ minor, while the bass defines B major. In bar 43 the melody implies B major, at which point the bass begins to shift to G♯ minor. When the melody reaches a G♯ in bar 44, the bass moves toward F♯ major. This interplay is exceptionally fluid, and explains why Brahms's style rarely shows the hard-edged quality of the Viennese Classical tradition, where the vertical and horizontal components of harmony are much more in phase.

Once again this is a technique Brahms derived from compositions of the generation following Beethoven. Largely he takes this, I think, from Schubert, who was a master at such things. For example, Schubert has a piece of B major in which he harmonizes what ought to be a B major chord with a G♯ minor chord, the final Variation of the Andantino varié in B minor for piano four hands (the slow movement of the *Divertissement sur des motifs originaux français,* D. 823; Ex. 10.9). It is interesting that when Schubert does this, he sounds most like Brahms. I cannot comment on what direct connection this piece may have to the slow movement of Brahms's Second Symphony.

This kind of dislocation between melody and bass is something at which Brahms became very expert, and I think he went further than any other composer before him. One example, from the finale of the Horn Trio, op. 40, is particularly striking (Ex. 10.10). How disconcerting it must be to the violinist concentrating on his own melody, with the harmony it implies, to find the third bar completely reinterpreted by the bass of the piano part in a way impossible to predict from the melody. Such procedures occur in a great deal of Brahms's mu-

Example 10.8

Example 10.9

Example 10.10

sic, and what they do is to loosen the fairly strict ties in Viennese Classical style between harmony and melody.

The idea of having harmony and melody out of phase with each other is not new. Of course, it occurs in Schumann all the time. The difference between Brahms and Schumann is that in Schumann the dislocation of harmony and melody is generally systematic. In "Paganini" from *Carnaval,* for instance, the left hand begins off the beat, a sixteenth-note before the bar line and fortissimo, while the right hand begins on the bar line and piano, so that one is sure that it is the left hand which is on the bar line, the right hand which is off (Ex. 10.11). But then both hands play softly, and it is clear that the right hand is on the bar line, which seems to have shifted. Here the harmony changes systematically out of phase with the melody. In Brahms, such changes are not systematic, but fluctuate, as the example from the Horn Trio demonstrates, and bar line displacement is only momentary.

Dislocation of sense is of course a rhythmic device, and it can be used very strictly by Brahms to displace the accent. But again it is not, as in Schumann, an ongoing systematic displacement. Consider the sixth piece of Schumann's *Davidsbündlertänze*, op. 6 (Ex. 10.12). A tarantella normally has accents on the first and fourth beats, and the one on beat 4 should be quite strong (which performers sometimes forget). Yet Schumann consistently accents beats 3 and 6 in

Example 10.11

Example 10.12

the right hand, beats 2 and 5 in the left hand. This sort of systematic displacement Brahms, on the whole, avoids. Displacement is certainly present, and, I
think, probably derived from his study of Schumann, but it is very much more
fluid than in the music of his predecessor.

Returning to the opening of the finale in the Horn Trio (Ex. 10.10), we see
here what I would call a dislocation of sense between the horizontal harmonic
meaning and the vertical harmonic meaning, for, while the harmony in the upper voices goes off to vi in bars 3 and 4, the bass continues to play I–V–I–V–I. As
the passage continues, the changes of harmony occur basically on the sixth beat,
but not consistently so. Note also how Brahms puts the harmonic change into
relief by the position of the chord: root position occurs, very clearly defined, at a
point where you would not be expecting it, and the weak beats are accented by
this very strongly, though not, as I have said, with the regularity one finds in
Schumann. Indeed, Schumann would probably have carried this on until finally
you were convinced that the sixth beat was the first beat of the bar (compare, for
example, the penultimate page of the Toccata, op. 7).

The Intermezzo in C major, op. 119 no. 3, shows how these various factors can
influence large-scale structure, although in a short piece (Ex. 10.13). First of all,
the overall tonal structure is that of a fairly weak progression to relative minor
and back: it begins in C major, moves to A minor by the end of the twelfth bar,
and then repeats this exposition. In the third bar, the way in which the E minor
chord is spaced on the sixth beat causes it to receive a slight and unexpected accent. Later in the piece, at bars 29, 30, 31, and 32, this aspect is developed: new
harmonies in root-position chords appear on the sixth beat of the bar; changes
of harmony and melody occur out of phase with the basic rhythm of the piece.
In these bars the changes of harmony are also foreshadowed by the left hand on
the weak third beat in the middle of each bar: the one bass note that is held becomes the root of the harmony of the next bar.

Brahms's treatment of sequence is at its most subtle in bars 3 to 7. Bars 3 to 4
imply a rising sequential movement (see Ex. 10.14), immediately abandoned for
a descending one. The new sequence implies a simple pattern (Ex. 10.15), but
this too is inflected by Brahms. A sequence has a forward-moving energy, and
Brahms's alterations act as brakes to this motion. That is why one of his works
always seems to move more slowly than those of the Classical tradition from
which his style derives.

Brahms's treatment of dissonance subverts practices handed down from the
late eighteenth- and early nineteenth-century styles, and again he seems to
be following Schumann. Whereas Schumann, though, often leaves dissonance
hanging over unresolved into subsequent beats in a fairly systematic manner,
Brahms tends to add the dissonance just at the moment when resolution is ex-

Example 10.13

Example 10.13 (continued)

Example 10.13 (continued)

Example 10.14

Example 10.15

pected, but without, however, denying the resolution. In the sixth bar of the Intermezzo, for example, the dissonant E♭s appear just as resolution is expected. I mean this as no criticism, but in Brahms the relationship of consonance and dissonance is constantly eaten from within as if by termites. His music is full of holes, of frustrated expectations; this gives it its very unusual quality, and explains why nobody mistakes a piece by Brahms for one by the composer that he seems to be ostentatiously imitating, why Brahms never really sounds like Haydn, Beethoven, Schubert, or Mendelssohn, except, perhaps, in a few early pieces.

Brahms modulates to A minor in this Intermezzo, but the key is not fully confirmed. This confirmation is only implied—Brahms reaches A minor, then changes to the major (bar 10), as if to confirm A, but always sounds A as a six-four chord, not in a proper root position. Indeed, he never allows a clear V–I progression (until bars 24–25, when the resolution remains unharmonized). Every attempt is undercut by a dissonance that not only hangs over, but is resolved, if at all, too late to count, with the A minor and A major chords being tossed on to the end of bars 9 and 10 and colored by dissonance in bars 11 and 12.

One of the ways in which Brahms does establish A minor as a secondary key (and it is quite clearly established) is through expressive alterations of rhythm: he writes "sostenuto" over all of bar 10 and at the end of bar 12. (My readings come from the Breitkopf & Härtel collected edition, which is based on the first edition; in the autograph which Brahms gave to Clara Schumann in 1893, now owned by Dr. Friedrich G. Zeileis, Gallspach, Austria, neither "sostenuto" is present; the copyist's manuscript used as the engraver's model, now in private possession in West Germany, was not available for consultation.) The first of these establishes the key, the second occurs as Brahms quits the key. It is extraordinary how Brahms depends on the weakest possible harmonic progressions and how masterful he is at convincing us by rubato and texture that they work, as they do indeed here. (It is also interesting to see how the overlapping phrases in this opening passage subvert the usual twelve-bar structure of three four-bar phrases.)

The retransition in this piece provides another example of a false sequence, this one radically so. After a typical sequence of descending thirds (bars 35–36), Brahms begins preparation for the return, which is ultimately effected through a minor plagal cadence. In the intervening bars Brahms first moves to a root-position Db major chord, and then, in the second half of the false sequence, to F minor in first inversion. In this case, the dynamics serve to enforce the falsity of the parallelism: the peak of the crescendo emphasized a Db major chord in root position in bars 37–38, and it sounds as if Brahms is moving to an Ab major chord at the peak of the crescendo in bar 39. It is left to the bass to bring out the real harmonic progression, which is confirmed only at the last possible moment with the F on the last beat of bar 40.

The return itself is interesting. Brahms creates here on a small scale what he does in very large works, like the Fourth Symphony: an augmented return, and a particularly ingenious one. It is impossible to determine exactly where the return takes place; if we judge by the reappearance of the original rhythm, the return does not begin until bar 45. But once you have heard bar 45, and by the time you reach bar 47, you realize that this is an answer and that an elliptical return has already taken place at bars 41 to 45.

Adding to the ambiguity is the minor plagal cadence that leads to the return at bar 41; it is not until four bars later (at bar 44) that a dominant occurs, and even here there is a dislocation, for the bass of the dominant first appears as the third of an E minor chord (bar 44, beat 1), sounding quite clearly as if it is part of that chord, although its textural displacement immediately indicates that this pitch has a different meaning, that this G does not belong to the E minor chord, but is the bass for the G dominant seventh that follows. This is one of the subtlest examples of Brahms's use of this kind of displacement, and one of the wittiest: it presents us with the paradox of a dominant preparation for a return occurring four bars after the return has already begun. One might say that Brahms provides us with the dominant-tonic relationship after it is no longer necessary. That would be an exaggeration. The V^7 "preparation" is still necessary as a confirmation of the return. A basic Classical device is given once again by Brahms in reverse order, and its function becomes ambiguous. The continuity of the music is considerably enriched: the symmetry of the two four-bar phrases (41–44 and 45–48) makes us hear the V^7 chord of bar 44 as part of an already ongoing process, instead of in its traditional role as the end point of a retransition. Nevertheless, it actually fulfills its traditional function even in its displacement: we do hear bar 45 as the beginning of the reprise, and only retrospectively recognize that it had already started with bar 41.

Displacement again occurs at the end of the piece. Now, though, instead of using the dominant seventh to confirm the return to the tonic *after* the fact, Brahms sets up the dominant well ahead of time, as a pedal (bars 56 ff.). But a very peculiar process then takes place: after four bars of dominant-tonic progressions (but with resolutions on the weakest beats), he suddenly calls for two bars "un poco ritardando" (this is in the autograph version), which delays the final V–I cadence to the point where one hardly feels a need to attach much importance to it when it finally arrives, "a tempo." The return to the tonic has actually taken place during the ritardando on the six-four chord at the end of the dominant pedal (bar 62). It almost looks as if Brahms had been reading one of those Schenkerian models, in which he noticed that the important final V–I takes very little time, and so he decided he was going to get it over with as fast as possible. This gives the V–I cadence its relaxed grace. Interpretation of this passage also depends on an understanding of the traditional Viennese waltz.

One last detail: just before the six-four chord, the pitch A starts to assert itself in both treble and bass (bars 60–61) and is important until the end of the piece. Indeed, this pitch, and in this same context, played an important role at the very beginning of the piece. Its final appearance, and a prominent one, is in the "throw-away" passage which closes the piece (bars 66 ff.), where it actually gives the final cadence a kind of plagal color. The way Brahms has removed the emphasis from the firm traditional V–I cadence is the source of this page's heavy-handed but engaging charm.

What I have hoped to show with these various observations is that, although Brahms is still dealing with almost all the traditional elements of late eighteenth- and early nineteenth-century music, he tends to play with them, to manipulate them, dislocating their traditional relationships with each other and setting them off one against the other for purposes that no composer before him had ever envisaged. Brahms is both subverting the Classical tradition and at the same time exploiting it with a learning greater than that of any of his contemporaries.

CHAPTER ELEVEN

Brahms: Classicism and the Inspiration of Awkwardness

ON Easter Monday, 1872, when Brahms was thirty-nine years old, he wrote to Clara Schumann: "All winter long I have been doing counterpoint exercises very assiduously. What for? To be better able to disparage my pretty things?—I did not need counterpoint for that. To become a university professor?—no, not that either. To learn to write music better?—even that I'm not hoping for. But still in the end it's a bit tragic when one gets to be too clever for one's needs." By 1872, Brahms had become the leader of the conservative faction of European music as well as the most learned composer in the history of music. He was able to make a very good living simply from the sale of his unpublished works without relying on patronage or a salaried appointment—unlike Mozart, Beethoven, Haydn, Chopin, Schumann, Mendelssohn, or any of his predecessors whose music would remain, like his, in the repertory for another century.

Yet he was temperamentally uncertain of the value of his work. He submitted his compositions for advice from the musicians and amateurs he most respected, and often enough refused to accept their counsel. He destroyed dozens of large-scale works. His first published string quartets were preceded, he said, by twenty that have now disappeared. Trunkfuls of early works were burned. The manuscript of the Sonata for Piano no. 1, opus 1, published when he was twenty-two years old, is titled "Sonata no. 4."[1] But it is not merely the compositions of his youth that have gone forever. In 1880, when he was forty-seven, Brahms played two new trios for Clara Schumann. She preferred the one in E flat Major. He burned it. The very large number of works that have survived—121 opuses—must be about one-third of his total output. His diffidence hid an immense am-

---

1. The Sonata in F sharp Minor, opus 2, was written before opus 1, so two piano sonatas were destroyed.

bition: the revival of the classical tradition of pure instrumental music from Haydn to Schubert.

Brahms's Sonata in C Major, opus 1, opens with an unmistakable reference to Beethoven's *Hammerklavier* Sonata in B flat Major, opus 106, and combines this with the structure of Beethoven's *Waldstein* Sonata in C Major, opus 53, which begins with one phrase in C major immediately repeated in B flat major—so that the second phrase of Brahms's sonata arrives at the key of the *Hammer-klavier;* any pianist too stupid to recognize the quotation from the *Hammer-klavier* from the first bars is given another clue. When, twenty-three years later at the age of forty-three, Brahms finally published his first Symphony in C Minor, opus 68, it displayed an unmistakable reference to Beethoven's Symphony no. 9 in D Minor in the main theme of his last movement (someone remarked on this to Brahms, and he replied, "Any jackass can see that"). Since he destroyed several sonatas before publishing opus 1, and several attempts at writing a symphony before making public the C Minor, these references are like a manifesto. In spite of all his modesty and his uncertainty about his own work, Brahms wanted a public understanding that he was working in the tradition of the most prestigious monuments of classicism, and would not publish until he could stand up to the *Hammerklavier* and to the Ninth Symphony. Since he was eighteen or nineteen when he composed the C Major sonata, he understood the nature of his temperament and his task from the very beginning.

II

The awkwardness of Brahms's writing is rarely mentioned, never seriously discussed, as if it were simply an unfortunate but accessory aspect of his work—as if his music was uncomfortable to play because the composer was too profound to bother with unimportant aspects of musical composition like the convenience of the performer. Nevertheless, the awkwardness is fundamental to the music, and it is clearly deliberate. Passages awkward to play occur frequently enough in the work of other composers, but they generally come into being governed by a different logic. In Beethoven, the development of the basic ideas of a composition leads often enough to writing that is difficult and even impossible to execute gracefully: arrangements of the hands on the keyboard that force a momentary and ungraceful displacement, orchestral details that are hard to render with clarity and tonal balance. The famous opening of the Sonata for piano opus 106, for example, may be difficult, yet it lies well for the hands (the fourth beat of the first bar may stretch the right hand a little since the keys of Beethoven's piano were narrower than they are today); however, later in the first movement, as in the fugal finale, there are moments much harder to play smoothly. In Chopin, the initial bars of even the most difficult etude almost always lie well for the pianist's hands, but the chromatic developments in the interior of the work and the increase of passion lead to stretches of writing that twist the hands unmercifully.[2] In Brahms, however, it is very often the initial idea that is either uncomfortable to play or awkward to listen to, or, at times, both.

Like most composers from 1750 to 1950, Brahms was essentially a pianist. From the beginning of his career as a composer, he demonstrated a predilection for pianistic devices that cruelly stretch the hands or make exorbitant demands on the weakest fingers. The best example of the latter is his frequent employment of a trill for the fourth and fifth fingers with an added octave for the thumb:

This is from the opening movement of the Piano Concerto no. 1 in D minor, but the device can be found in the second concerto and in the second piano sonata as well. Most of the trills quoted here are negotiable although hard to play with the brilliance and grand resonance demanded by the character of the piece, but the last one in bar 116—an octave D with the fifth finger on an E♭—is wickedly difficult for the average hand as it traps the fourth finger between two black keys and makes the rapidity and sonority of the trill questionable. Many pianists, including Artur Schnabel, have rewritten these trills in the following Lisztian fashion:

but it was precisely to avoid the brilliant Lisztian sonority that Brahms asked for less effective trills which integrate more easily with the musical texture. There is also an essential aesthetic difference: the Lisztian version is easy to execute and it

2. See my *The Romantic Generation* (Harvard University Press, 1995), pp. 381–383.

sounds difficult; Brahms prefers a greater difficulty, partially concealed in order to avoid the appearance of virtuosity.

These trills are only an extreme example of Brahms's lifelong delight in a texture which alternates octaves and single notes, as in the Variations and Fugue on a Theme of Handel:

This device theoretically preserves the clarity of the contrapuntal line on paper but makes it difficult to hear as the representation of a single voice. It is awkward to execute because the single notes are given here, as in the concerto trills, to the weakest fingers of the hand, the fourth and fifth, and the single note must at least partially balance the larger sonority of the octave. However, when Brahms puts the single notes in the stronger thumb and second finger, the result is even more inconvenient for the performer, as in a spectacularly difficult variation from the Paganini Variations, Book 2, where the alternation of octave and single note continuously displaces hand and arm in a series of slight jerks which makes it difficult to reach the next note comfortably: ease of octave-playing demands a steady position of arm and wrist. This variation is so clearly an attack on this ease that Brahms placed the first two bars in his *51 Finger-exercises*, with indications of how to practice it:

Repeating either the octave or the single note slightly slows down the necessary shift of position between the two which displaces the hands, and repeating first the octaves and then the single notes slows down one shift while keeping the other up to tempo. The appearance of this variation in the *51 Finger-exercises* demonstrates the fundamental importance of this device for Brahms's piano writing.

Another finger exercise is perhaps even more instructive:

14

I can reach the span of a tenth, but I cannot satisfactorily play the finger-breaking stretches that arise from holding down the inner notes required by this exercise. Brahms must have enjoyed the suffering that this exercise causes to most pianists. Another witness to his delight in discomfort is the transcription of the Chopin Etude in F Minor, opus 26 no. 2, as one of his studies:

The tempo mark, *Poco presto,* is a stroke of Brahms's humor. It is, I think, impossible to achieve a convincing rendition of so absurd an arrangement, which makes the famous Godowsky transcriptions of the Chopin Etudes for the left hand seem relatively simple. The near impossibility, however, is its reason for existing: when we try to play it, we are meant to rejoice at what sounds and feels impossible, at the almost absurd sense of struggle which is the essence of the concept.

This arrangement reveals that Brahms's delight throughout his career in a texture of parallel sixths played *legato* is not only a preference for a certain kind of sound but a physical pleasure in awkward positions for the hand. Parallel sixths are more awkward for pianists than octaves, and writing for the piano was fundamental for Brahms (his music for other instruments constantly betrays the thinking of a pianist). In playing octaves, the thumb and fifth fingers are together either on white keys or on black keys, and hand and arm can remain steady; playing sixths, however, demands continual shifting of position. Octaves lie well for the hand if one plays them staccato or at least detached. *Legato* octaves, on the other hand, are only comfortable if they move stepwise, as in Chopin's Etude in B minor, op. 25 no. 10. When Brahms asks for *legato* octaves, the passage borders on the unplayable, as in the famous page in the scherzo of the second piano concerto:

It is not often that the indications here of *pianissimo, sotto voce,* and *legato,* which add to the difficulty, are observed in performance. Once again, Brahms avoids the octave brilliance of the school of Liszt, and writes something even more demanding because it lies so badly for hand and arm.

The four-hand version of the Hungarian Dances is occasionally awkward but not really difficult: it was intended for home use by amateurs. The two-hand version, however, is another matter. Let us compare two forms of one passage:

In the two-hand version, the left hand plays all the notes given to one of the pianists of the four-hand version, the right hand all the notes of the other. There is no attempt on the part of the composer to make the two-hand version successful in performance. Transposing it up a half-step to the black keys of F sharp major does, however, make it feasible. What Brahms deliberately produced here was staggering difficulty with little effect. That is why we almost never hear the Hungarian Dances in the version for two hands in concert: they are hard to play but are not impressive (the four-hand version is still played in private for home entertainment). It is something of a feat to compose music so difficult that makes so little impression of virtuosity, and it required a determined effort on the part of the composer to evade effectiveness. We can see that Brahms had a decided preference for an awkward difficulty over a flashy one. The Lisztian pianist triumphs with ease over difficulties that would dismay weaker mortals; the Brahmsian pianist remains engaged in his struggle, and will always seem buried in the musical material, and at moments overcome by it.

This preference for the awkward to play transfers itself to the awkward to hear. One manifestation is Brahms's use of octave displacement—that is, the sudden displacement of a musical line from one register to another. In the Rhapsody in E flat Major, op. 119 no. 4, an arpeggiated figure that descends down F–D–B♭ first appears:

(In passing, we might note that the phrase looks like Mozartean figuration, but the final A and E♮ in the first two four-note groups remain as unresolved dissonances, a thoroughly unclassical technique at odds with Brahms's revival of classicism.) This passage is rewritten later with a double displacement:

This is less convenient for the ear as well as for the hand, although more exciting. Later, the beginning of the coda displaces the notes more radically within a simple melody, employing Brahms's device of octave/single-note alternation:

The displacement adds excitement with both audible and visible drama. The passage is not, of course, hard to construe for the listener, but it conveys its meaning with a sense of constraint, as the added octaves emphasize only the weakest beats of the measure. This reduces the rhythmic force of the strong beats, but also acts at the same time as an impulsion, an infusion of energy.

The deliberate exploitation of the awkwardness of octave displacement allowed Brahms to arrive at some of his most dramatic effects. In the violin concerto, he turns an innocuous and fairly tame motif into a dramatic one, and brings out the potential for angry dissonance within the motif:

All the dramatic power of this page comes from the octave transposition. If the motif is realized in a single register, it becomes tame and insignificant:

In the same movement, Brahms presents a greater challenge and demands that the soloist overcome the awkwardness of octave displacement with grace. The following passage depends entirely for its sweetly poignant effect on the continuous shift of register, and Brahms marks it to be played *dolce lusingando*:

The shift of register both makes the passage expressive and at the same time makes it difficult to play expressively. The direction goes technically against the grain, and the lyricism is all the more impressive because of the effort involved.

It would be misleading to say that Brahms renders the realization of his musical ideas awkward to play and to hear: to put it more precisely, the awkwardness is an essential element of the musical idea. In variation no. 5 of the first book of the Paganini set, the bass plays a rising scale that goes from E to E (E F F# G G# A B C C# D D# E):

However, the rising scale is realized in a series of descents in register which it make extremely difficult for the ear to grasp. It is also inconvenient to play, as the left hand invades the area of the right hand, requiring not only a crossing of the hands but a superimposition of one over the other. The expressive cross rhythms of the melody in the right hand make this even more complex. It is doubtful if even professional musicians in the audience understand at first hearing what goes on contrapuntally in this piece.

The second part of this variation has a descending chromatic bass that is even harder for the ear to grasp:

The descent (A G♯ G♮ F♯ F♮ D) is both difficult to execute clearly and difficult to perceive, as Brahms has wickedly shaped the passage so that each note of the descent is played by the weak fifth finger, and it is also the weak release of a two-note motif in which traditional classical phrasing requires the second note, here the important one, to be softer than the first. In this instance, as in so many others, Brahms works within the classical system and against it at the same time.

This manipulation of the classical aesthetic arrives fairly early in Brahms's career with the Handel Variations, where the third variation is based entirely on the classical appoggiatura, the most fundamental element of melodic expression in Western music from Monteverdi to Schoenberg:

An appoggiatura, to fulfill its expressive function, demands an accent on the first or decorative note, which is the dissonant note, and a softer release on the second note, which is consonant, and the principle remains in force here in this variation—except that Brahms has made every appoggiatura a single note and the softer release a triad. The consonant release must still be played more softly than the expressive initial dissonance of each two-note group, but Brahms has made this difficult and awkward for the performer to achieve. It is, in fact, this awkwardness that increases the expressive potential. At the end of his career, Brahms drew a wonderfully effective pathos from this device in the slow movement of the Viola Quintet in G Major, op. 111. Putting the emphasis in the accompanying instruments on the off-beat release is anti-classical, but it takes the classical system for granted in order to work:

The importance of the awkward for Brahms may come from the Romantic tradition of the grotesque. It was through the grotesque that Romanticism made its frontal attack on the classical aesthetic. Nevertheless, the originality of Brahms is his integration of the grotesque with the classical. This explains his penchant for writing learned inverted canons in which the inverted form is so ungainly as to be unacceptable to an academic taste. There is a striking example in the Handel Variations:

Within the tradition of tonality from Bach to Chopin, a melody violates the standards of taste if it outlines a dissonance without resolving it subsequently into a neighboring tone, although the resolution may be deferred for a moment or two. The right-hand inversion here ends (bar 6) by outlining two sevenths, C/Bb and Eb/Db, neither properly resolved within the melodic outline. Playing the soprano voice by itself reveals how impossibly dissonant the melodic line is within a classical vision, in particular the way the final Db is reached by a leap upward, while the phrasing implies a graceful resolution. It is the combination with the bass, however, that renders the inversion mellifluous, in the same way that the final rising notes of the soprano part, Ab, Bb, Eb, A♮, outrageous to respectable ears when they were written, are transformed into a graceful and harmonious effect as they blend with the principal canonic voice.

Schoenberg's profound and acknowledged debt to Brahms comes, I think, in part from this daring employment of melodic dissonance. By means of the accompanying harmonies, Brahms made his dissonant melodies sound graceful and supple or mellifluous and infinitely melancholy. One important subsidiary theme of the opening movement of the great Viola Quintet in G Major, opus 111 (a work that Brahms originally intended as his farewell to music), has a dissonant, spiky outline comparable to the beautiful slow-movement fugue from Stravinsky's *Symphony of Psalms:*

The accompanying instruments resolve Brahms's melody with a rich harmony:

Nevertheless, the dissonances within the single melodic line leave a residue in the mind: the harmonic sense of the individual voice is only incompletely offset by the full score. The listener is aware, at least unconsciously, I think, of how close we come to hearing an unresolved harshness. Later modernist composers had only to imitate Brahms's melodic daring, and then omit the attenuating respectability of the harmony.

The Intermezzo in B Minor, opus 119 no. 1, is dominated largely by a succession of 11th chords, and Brahms himself called it extremely dissonant in a letter to Clara Schumann, but assured her that all the dissonances were properly introduced and resolved. It is true that preparation and resolution are carried out impeccably, but resolution is sufficiently delayed so that by the time the dissonances of the interior voices are fully resolved a new dissonant chord has already been formed:

Resolution of a dissonance within a new dissonance is a technique that Brahms could have learned from Bach or Mozart, but the heavy concentration of 11th chords within this piece is exceptional, ending in a final 13th chord, the only one in which all the voices are resolved simultaneously:

The dissonances arrive tactfully, one by one in an arpeggiation, and build up gradually as the fourth, fifth and sixth notes introduce a dissonant harmony. However, Brahms wanted them clearly heard, and told Clara Schumann that it was not enough to say that the tempo must be very slow: "every note must be played *ritardando*," he wrote extravagantly. This was the only way, he said, that the full melancholy of the music could be drawn out. The music exploits the overtones of the piano: as the arpeggiation in thirds slowly proceeds, the notes played earlier and held down begin to vibrate in sympathy, and this brings out the full resonance of the 9th and 11th chords. No one has ever surpassed Brahms in his ability to make pure diatonic harmony deeply melancholy.

Brahms disdained the complex chromatic harmony of Wagner, but his own harmony, in appearance closer to that of Mozart and Beethoven, is in fact equally radical and dissonant. He stretched the function of the most basic traditional harmonies beyond expectation, and he made weak, subsidiary harmonies suddenly play an unprecedentedly powerful role.[3] Much of his work was a systematic dislocation of classical procedures, disconcerting above all because his understanding of the earlier style was more profound than that of any of his contemporaries. That is why the revolutionary potential of his innovations was, for those that listened to them carefully, as explosive as Wagner's.

Brahms was, perhaps, the only composer who understood that reviving a tradition of the past was an enterprise that was not only difficult, but could not appear easy. A return to the techniques of Haydn, Schubert, and Beethoven made sense only if the demands of originality integral to the classical tradition were met. In the creation of large-scale works, this tradition seemed to offer for an ambitious composer the only alternative to the Wagnerian music-drama that Brahms found so unsympathetic. He loved the tradition of pure instrumental music, but he knew that it could not be simply repeated. In continuing it, he found a double route to originality: the first was the use of material unacceptable in the past. In one sense, this way had already been indicated by Beethoven, who deliberately employed material that an earlier composer would have considered too simple for complex expression: one might even say that it was not simply the complexity of Beethoven's music that upset so many of his contemporaries but the almost primitive quality of much of the basic material. It was, indeed, the contrast between the simplicity of the basic stuff and the richness of development that gave Beethoven's works their extraordinary power. Brahms chose material that even Beethoven might have considered unpromising: simple relationships that were ugly, awkward, resistant to development. He knew that the awkward could be made radically expressive, and how it could be exploited.

The simplest illustration of this is the opening of his popular Intermezzo in A Major, op. 118 no. 2:

Andante teneramente

The harmony is perfectly respectable, but the leap of a seventh could not have been placed this way by a previous generation, although Brahms introduces it with a technique derived from Schumann: the arpeggiated opening of the second bar delays the high A of the melody as if it were difficult to reach. This simu-

---

3. See Walter Frisch, *Brahms: The Four Symphonies* (Schirmer Books, 1996), pp. 49–50 and 72, for the way Brahms undercuts the traditional strong harmonic preparation of the return of the main theme in a symphonic movement by a detour.

lates the vocal difficulty of reaching a high note by placing a momentary obstacle in the pianist's way, a slight hesitation which was an essential expressive effect attached to arpeggiating chords in both the eighteenth and nineteenth centuries. The vocal model is the basis of expressive melody from the sixteenth century to the present. The hesitation softens the harshness of the seventh, makes it seem not awkward but deeply felt.[4] Through similar procedures, Brahms was able to enlarge the possibilities of expression in a largely diatonic system.

The second method of achieving originality for Brahms was to use the devices of classical tonality ambiguously, against the grain, both realizing and distorting classical stylistic procedures. The radical treatment of the opening of the recapitulation in the fourth symphony and the second cello sonata reveals his reformulation of one of the basic elements of traditional form: in both works the main theme returns much more slowly with an effect that fundamentally alters the conception of form. The Sonata in F major for Cello and Piano begins with the main theme in striking syncopation:

---

4. Moriz Rosenthal said that Brahms arpeggiated all the chords when playing the piano. There are, however, different kinds of arpeggiation: here, in the A major Intermezzo, it is intended to be slow and expressive, and I suspect that most arpeggios that are so directed, rather than improvised by the performer, were to be so played. In the original version of the *Sonetto 47 di Petrarca*, Liszt directs *"quasi arpeggiando"* in bar 10; I presume that means a rapid and almost imperceptible arpeggio is intended, and this may correspond to a style of playing common to some performers at the time. (Chopin's pupils reported that he disliked this style.)

The development sets out in the harmonically remote key of F sharp minor, but ends by reintroducing the tonic minor with an augmentation of the basic motif in a texture of extreme calm and with the *tremolo* of the opening bars transferred from the piano to the cello:

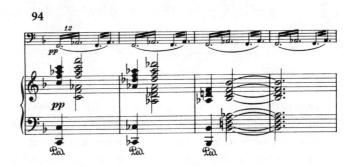

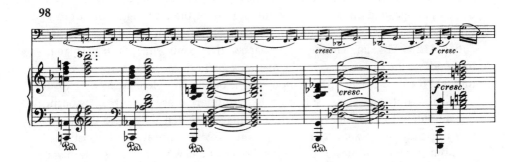

105

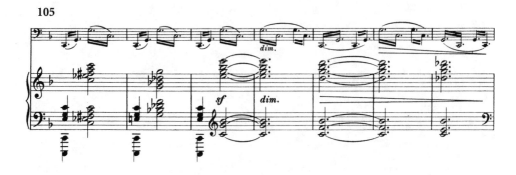

112

Preparing the return to the tonic major and to the main theme through the tonic minor is traditional, used occasionally by Mozart and most frequently by Beethoven, and Brahms could have taken the sense of extreme calm at the end of a development from Mendelssohn,[5] or even, as is most likely here, from the mysterious close of the development section of the Sonata for Piano and Cello in A Major, opus 69, by Beethoven. None of these precedents, however, have the scale of this passage, and augmenting the initial note of the motif eightfold from a thirty-second note to a quarter in bar 94 gives a new significance to the process.

Bars 112 to 118 augment the entire shape of the opening melody in a way that foreshadows the similar place in the first movement of the Symphony no. 4 in E minor. When played in strict tempo, and avoiding the pleonastic effect of a ritardando, both passages result in an extraordinary sense that time has been, not slowed, but momentarily suspended. This is heightened by the twenty-four bars of steady *tremolo*, most of it *pianissimo* and very awkward for the cellist to play. But this awkwardness is put in the service of a new view of classical sonata form. What is novel is the alteration of the large-scale rhythm, the suspension of movement and drama at a crucial structural point of form.

5. See my *Sonata Forms* (W. W. Norton, 1980), p. 272, and *The Romantic Generation* (Harvard University Press, 1995), pp. 583–584.

There is an analogous suspension toward the end of the movement, created by entirely different means. The dominant/tonic cadence of bar 195, which seems to lead to an imminent close to the movement, is reharmonized in a gesture of sudden lyricism by the subdominant preceded by the subdominant of the sub-dominant. This enlarges and sustains the two-bar phrase of the piano into seven bars, which finally return to the original dominant/tonic cadence and to a brief recall of the end of the development.

Brahms's attempt to master the techniques of a past tradition entailed certain limits. The musical language had changed too far since Mozart and even since Beethoven for the range of these composers to be possible. Beethoven had a hundred ways of constructing a sonata movement; Brahms had only three or four. In Beethoven's sonata in E Major, op. 109, for example, the establishment of the tonic, the presentation of the opening theme, and the modulation to the dominant take about seven seconds. There is no way that Brahms could achieve this brevity and rapidity: the harmonic and rhythmic systems had lost too much of their subtle precision. Yet Beethoven could also construct an opening group in the tonic with the Mozartean breadth of the Prague Symphony or the Viola Quintet in C Major when he composed the *Eroica* Symphony or the Quartet in F major, op. 59 no. 1. Structures of an equivalent expanse in Brahms carry a sense of strain and tension that is, of course, part of their compelling effect.

The old forms were a challenge to Brahms, not an opportunity nor an easy solution. He made them new not simply by pouring new material into earlier molds, but by transforming the nature of the forms.[6] This demanded, however, the most thorough study and understanding of the past, and Brahms acquired an immense knowledge of music from Palestrina to Schubert. This is why he edited so much music from Handel to Chopin, why he collected examples of forbidden fifths in the work of the composers he admired, and why he continued to do counterpoint exercises late in life. It is rare that an important effect in a large work by Brahms is absolutely without precedent in the work of an earlier composer. It is also rare, however, to find a case in which he has not profoundly altered his model. Brahms never borrowed, even for ideological purposes, without rethinking. The study of Brahms's relation to the past should not be the identification of sources, but an inquiry into the transformation of what he had learned through study and meditation on history.

III

The standard opinion that Brahms began as a Romantic and only later turned to a revival of the classical approach does not work. In addition to falsifying the inherent classicism of the earliest work, this view hides the continued force of the Romantic tradition throughout Brahms's life. One example of this survival is the set of variations on a theme of Paganini for piano. They are called studies because they are simple, short finger-exercises, and they sound like basic finger-exercises more than do the etudes of Chopin or Liszt. An essential characteristic of Romanticism was to take a marginal and despised genre and elevate it to the grand style, as Blake transformed little moral poems for children in doggerel verse into the *Songs of Innocence and Experience,* John Constable and Caspar David Friedrich made simple landscape with no narrative content a substitute for

---

6. He was one of the few composers to be able to recreate Beethoven's balance of mediant relations: in his F major cello sonata, the exposition closes in A minor, not in C major, and Brahms ends the recapitulation in D minor, not in the tonic. Beethoven always resolves these mediant relations at least partially within the recapitulation. Brahms, however, unprecedentedly places the entire resolution in an elaborate coda.

religious and historical painting, Schumann transfigured popular dance music in *Papillons* and *Carnaval,* and Chopin turned the mazurka and the etude into creations of extraordinary profundity. The transcendence of the finger-exercises in Brahms's Paganini Variations is one of the last and most daring projects of the Romantic movement in music.

If new life was to be breathed into a moribund classical tradition against the school of Liszt and Wagner that Brahms found basically so repellent, this could not be accomplished simply by continuing to employ the old forms. The reference to the choral finale of Beethoven's Ninth in the finale of Brahms's C minor symphony is a polemical answer to Wagner's claim that after Beethoven's last symphony the future no longer lay in pure instrumental music but in music drama. In a sensitive book with excellent analyses of the orchestral work, *Brahms: The Four Symphonies,* Walter Frisch points out how early Brahms's intentions were recognized. The great scholar Friedrich Chrysander, who edited Handel with some minor help from Brahms, wrote ten years after the premiere of the Brahms C minor symphony: "What is involved here [the reference to Beethoven] is the problem of how to create an antitype [*Gegenbild*] to the last portions of the Ninth Symphony, an antitype that can, without the aid of the human voice, match the manner and strength of the Ninth. And insofar as this attempt has succeeded, it signifies an attempt to lead back from the symphony that comprises instruments and voice to the purely instrumental symphony. At the same time it signifies an expansion of those effects that can be created through purely instrumental means."[7] For Brahms it meant returning not only to Beethoven but to the purely instrumental works of Bach, Haydn, and Mozart. At the same time, the procedures of these composers could not be simply reproduced, but they had to be given a contemporary power. Most neoclassical composers have taken only that part of the past which they found congenial, adding a few personal touches, and dropped the rest. The extraordinary project of Brahms was to incorporate almost the entire classical tradition in his work while expanding it with the techniques that he had both developed himself and learned from his knowledge of Chopin, Schumann, and even Wagner.[8] It was, paradoxically, his success that helped to destroy the classical tradition as much as Wagner did, and that inspired Arnold Schoenberg's claim to derive his innovations from Brahms.

Brahms's relation to the past is therefore subtle and complex. Many scholars try to find quotations from earlier composers in his works. Along with this goes

7. Frisch, *Brahms: The Four Symphonies,* p. 146.

8. The finest recent treatment of Brahms's relation to the classical tradition is Reinhold Brinkmann's book on the second symphony, *Late Idyll* (Harvard University Press, 1995).

a small musicological sub-industry identifying "Clara" allusions in Brahms and Schumann: that is, melodies that spell out the notes CAA, or transposed variants like FDD, or upside-down forms like ACC, as well as transpositions, or backward forms like AAC. These are easy enough to find in whatever tonal pieces one looks at—or even in atonal music. Proving that a passage of Brahms signifies Clara, or Beethoven, or whatever is like proving that Shakespeare was written by Bacon or by the Earl of Oxford or by Queen Elizabeth: if one accepts the decoding procedures, it is easy enough to find evidence for any of these figures. One can find a "Clara" motif untransposed and right side up at the beginning of the finale of Mozart's Sonata in A minor, K. 310, and backwards in the theme of Bach's fugue in A minor from the first book of the *Well-Tempered Keyboard.* Since the portrait of Clara in Schumann's *Carnaval* is composed with the letters of Asch,[9] the town where his fiancée of the time, Ernestine von Fricken, was born, I do not find many of the occurrences of the "Clara" motif in Schumann very impressive, and most of the examples winkled out of Brahms are even less cogent.

As for Brahms's reminiscences of other composers' melodies, it should be noted that although there are twelve notes of the chromatic scale, and one might think that the permutation of twelve elements will give a large variety of forms, nevertheless almost all tonal melodies outline in some way the three notes of the tonic triad, and the permutation of three elements provides only a very small number of basic forms. Each tonal melody is therefore structurally identical with thousands of others, and most of the resemblances that one finds are consequently trivial. The second theme of the slow movement of Haydn's Drumroll Symphony is remarkably like the folksong that opens the last of Bach's Goldberg Variations,

and the principal motif of the coda to the first movement of Beethoven's Sonata in D Major, opus 10 no. 3 (which opens with the same four notes as the above examples), is exactly the same as the beginning of the song "How dry I am," and

9. ASCH in German musical notes is A-E♭-C-B♮.

is also the exact inversion of the opening of the D♭ major second theme in the finale of Brahms's Sonata for piano, opus 5.

However, Haydn probably did not know the Bach set of variations, and the passage in Brahms is not an upside-down souvenir of Beethoven's opus 10 no. 3 (nor a forecasting of a later popular tune), but an adaptation of Beethoven's use of a chorale tune in the rondo of the Sonata in C Major, opus 2 no. 3:

The pitches of these two hymn-like melodies, however, are entirely different, but the rhythm and the texture are the same, and the function of the tune is also identical: Brahms learned from Beethoven that a lyrical chorale placed at this point in a brilliant and agitated finale was a good idea. He studied Beethoven not to steal tunes, but to learn how to compose. Borrowed melodies are mostly inadvertent and rarely important: the first two bars of the main theme of Mozart's overture to *The Magic Flute* are the same as the beginning of a sonata by Clementi, but this was interesting largely to Clementi, who pointed it out to everyone for years ("Mozart heard me play this piece").

IV

Yet Brahms's adaptation of classical models was essential to his style, and his use was exceedingly refined. To see how his mind worked from the beginning of his career, we might consider his variations for piano on a theme of Schumann, opus 9. These were composed a year after Schumann's voluntary incarceration in an insane asylum. A year earlier Clara had written a set of variations on the same theme, which is one of Schumann's most expressive:

Thema
Ziemlich langsam

One of the variations was immediately recognized as a literal quotation of another piece by Schumann: that is, Brahms took a piece by Schumann in B minor:

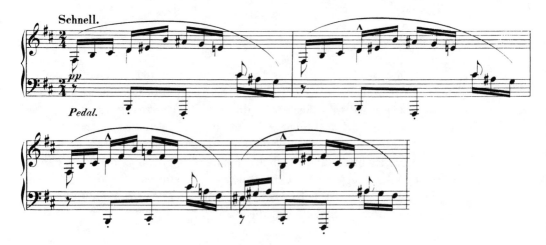

and turned it into a variation of the theme in F sharp minor:

which, in fact, just preceded the B minor piece in Schumann's collection, so Brahms expected everyone to notice the adaptation.

When the variations were published in 1857, this gave rise to a strange incident when a journalist wrote an article praising Brahms, who liked the attention. In a letter to Clara, however, he claimed that there were "some downright stupidities, as when, e.g. he is of the opinion that the B minor variation was not intentionally written to imitate the corresponding piece in your husband's work." The imitation, Brahms thought, should have been obvious.

The other references to Schumann in this set of variations are more complex. At the end of the tenth variation, a theme by Clara that Robert used as the basis for his *Impromptus on a theme of Clara Wieck* is literally quoted by Brahms in an inner voice; the melody of the opening of this variation, Jan Swafford writes in his biography of Brahms, is derived from the bass of the F sharp minor theme. This is not quite right; the melody has been recognized by many scholars as a quotation from the slow movement of a string quartet by Schumann:

Brahms cleverly remarked the identity of the string quartet melody with the bass of the F sharp minor theme, and built his variation on that, and he produced a very learned inverted canon with it.

Other allusions to Schumann's works may have escaped notice. The last variation is clearly a reworking of the second of Schumann's Impromptus on Clara's theme:

There is also a variation based on the scherzo from another string quartet, opus 41 no. 3, and one on the Toccata for piano.

The 22-year-old Brahms must have spent his months in the Schumann household studying Robert's complete works until he knew them perhaps better than the composer. I can identify about eight of the models, and I am convinced the other variations are based similarly on works of Schumann that I do not know or do not understand as Brahms did. In a sense, the variations are a young composer's homage to the whole of Schumann's life.

The most instructive adaptation is the second variation, which comes from the last piece of the *Kreisleriana*. In that work a theme in ⁶⁄₈ time and steady dotted rhythm is played by the right hand, while the left almost always comes in on what sounds like the wrong beat:

In Brahms's variation, it is the left hand that plays the same dotted rhythm, and the right hand that always comes in on an off-beat:

The two pieces do not sound at all alike, but Brahms has been taught something about composition by Schumann.

This second variation is a guide to a study of Brahms's use of models. When he is quoting an earlier composer, it should be obvious to any jackass. When he is learning a way to write, the original is so transformed that the two works do not resemble each other in performance. "There is no song of Schubert from which one cannot learn something," Brahms once claimed, but that does not mean that he ever tried to sound exactly like Schubert. The opening of Schubert's Quintet for strings in C Major begins with a tonic chord, a diminished seventh on the tonic, and a return of the tonic harmony. That is the way Brahms's Third Symphony begins, but the effect is transformed beyond recognition, from a quiet phrase in the middle register to a rising fortissimo motif with the brass. I can only assume that if I have noticed the identical harmonic progression, then Brahms, who knew much more music than I do, must have observed it, too; and since the next bars heroically employ the typical Schubertian procedure of alternating major and minor, I think he was intentionally expanding what he had been able to glean from studying Schubert into massive effects that the earlier master could not have imagined.

The distance from model to imitation in Brahms is often so large that all resemblance seems to disappear. One of the variations from Beethoven's "Eroica" set is the only case that Brahms could have known in which the theme is hidden in the grace notes. It is the bass theme that is so represented. In the Handel variations, Brahms was inspired to try the device. The Beethoven is harsh, brilliant, and satirical; the reworking of the idea by Brahms is fluid, delicate, and lyrical.

V

Other composers have used models for composing. Most young composers do until they find their own voice: Mozart imitated Haydn's quartets closely when he was sixteen, but later, when he dedicated six quartets to Haydn "who taught me how to write," his forms are his own. Beethoven imitated a Mozart quartet closely once (with opus 18 no. 5) because, I think, he needed to prove that he could write a Mozart quartet if he wanted to as well as his more original inspirations. Schubert closely modeled a few works on Mozart and on Beethoven. Later composers were more systematic. Strauss has references to *The Magic Flute* throughout *Der Rosenkavalier* in order to create a proper Viennese atmosphere: the comic entrance of Baron Ochs, for example, is absurdly modeled on the trial by fire and water of Pamina and Tamino. The last movement of Samuel Barber's piano sonata is an almost servile imitation of Brahms's fugue from the Handel

Variations. Stravinsky once told Elliott Carter that he always used models when composing. Nevertheless, there is a great difference between Stravinsky's procedures and Brahms's method. Stravinsky had no intention of reviving a style of the past: as he himself said, he used classical formulas in his neoclassical period the way he used folk material in his earlier ballets. For Brahms, it was only possible to write large-scale works—symphonies, string quartets, and chamber sonatas—by mastering the techniques that originally brought these forms into being.

The study of the way Brahms exploited his knowledge of the musical past is generally marred by an exclusive concentration on thematic resemblance. That is not how Brahms worked. As I have said, when there is a thematic allusion in Brahms, he expected it to be immediately evident. He did not like talking about it. When someone commented on the obvious dependence of his Scherzo in E flat minor for piano, opus 4, on Chopin's scherzos, he replied acidly that he had never heard or seen a piece by Chopin in his life. (See p. 137 above.) I would not have thought that anyone could believe that the young Brahms in 1852 with his already extensive knowledge and devouring curiosity for all kinds of music had never come into contact with the works of Chopin, but some musicologists have taken his claim seriously: one can only marvel at their credulity. Brahms's awareness of the second and third scherzos of Chopin is shamelessly demonstrated on almost every page of his opus 4.

Thematic relationships in his music are vitally important, but they are almost always easily recognizable. Everyone hears that the opening themes of the first and last movements of his G Major Violin Sonata begin with the identical motif. If the relation was not easily identifiable, Brahms claimed that it was uninteresting or fortuitous—or even implied a lack of inspiration. In a letter to Adolf Schubring on February 16, 1869, he wrote:[10]

> I dispute that the themes of the various sections of No. 3 [of the *German Requiem*] are *meant* to have something in common with each other. (Except for the small motif . . .). *Should this be so, however,* (I purposely summon nothing to my memory): I want no praise for it, but admit that when I work my ideas don't fly far enough, hence unintentionally often return with the same thing.
>
> However, if I want to hold on to a single idea, it should be clearly recognizable in every transformation, augmentation, inversion. Anything else would be the worst kind of playing around and always a sign of the most barren invention. Unfortunately the fugue in No. 6 is evidence that (for the sake of "momentum"?) I am not exactly strict.

10. Styra Avins, *Johannes Brahms: Life and Letters* (Oxford University Press, 1998), p. 383.

Given Brahms's reluctance to discuss thematic relationships—or, indeed, to discuss his musical technique seriously—we need not take this literally, but it ought not to be dismissed. Unifying a work of music by building it around a single motif and its transformations is an integral part of Western musical technique since Bach—or, indeed, since the late fifteenth century with Josquin des Pres. This motivic work holds the piece together, but the successive transformations of the motif do not always raise the ghosts of all the earlier ones. It is clear that for Brahms, however, if some kind of significance is to be attached to any thematic resemblance, if it is the bearer of a message, it must be clearly recognizable. The same must be said of Brahms's rare direct allusions to the works of another composer (as opposed to his adaptation of devices he discovered through his study of the past). The allusions had a meaning for Brahms's contemporaries: they were not esoteric, to be discovered only a century later.

In *Brahms Studies 2*, David Brodbeck demonstrates Mendelssohn's importance for Brahms by uncovering allusions to Mendelssohn's works. I do not think they are allusions, but reminiscences (which is what Brahms's contemporaries called them): they may even have been unconscious in origin, although Brahms probably recognized their source more quickly than his critics. In a letter of 1878, quoted by Brodbeck,[11] to a composer, Otto Dessoff (who noticed with consternation that he had unconsciously stolen something from Brahms), Brahms dismisses the whole subject with contempt: "I beg you, do nothing stupid. One of the stupidest topics of stupid people is that of reminiscences . . . Don't spoil it, leave it alone . . . After all, you know that I too have stolen on occasion, and much worse than you have done." Brahms's debt to Mendelssohn is not an occasional tune. He learned to use a Mendelssohnian texture as early as a short passage in the slow movement of the first piano concerto, and it was Mendelssohn, rather than Beethoven or Schubert, who taught him the most subtle ways of bringing back an earlier movement in a finale: the G Major Violin Sonata uses a Schubert trio as a model for this effect, but in the Third Symphony, where the finale in the end dissolves back into the first movement, Brahms clearly learned from Mendelssohn's works, above all, the E flat string quartet and the E major piano sonata. In Brodbeck's volume, Kenneth Hull claims to find an allusion to bars 31–34 of the slow movement of Beethoven's fifth symphony in bars 106–110 of the slow movement of Brahms's fourth. The two passages are similar in rhythm and partially similar in melodic contour, but they are so different in harmony, dynamics, and dramatic function that the allusion is not easily recognizable. The resemblance could be entirely fortuitous, and cannot be con-

11. David Brodbeck, *Brahms Studies 2* (University of Nebraska Press, 1994), p. 228.

strued as carrying a message. Hull interprets the difference as ironic, but this game seems to have no rules: if the two passages are alike, that proves the allusion; if they are different, then the change proves that Brahms is being ironic.

In his biography, Swafford observes that the main theme of Brahms's third symphony of 1884 is rather like the opening of Wagner's *Rheingold* played upside down:

Both themes, of course, consist entirely of the simple tonic triad, the least convincing basis for a resemblance. In any case, the opening of Brahms's String Quartet in C Minor of 1873 starts with a theme that resembles Wagner's even more closely and is right side up:

I think it more likely that Brahms remembered and inverted his own theme than Wagner's, but I cannot imagine why he would have thought it a good idea to do either.

In short, Brahms's intentional or unintentional borrowing of melodies is no greater than that of most composers from Bach to Stravinsky. Where Brahms differed from his predecessors and his successors was in the adaptation of structural devices learned from the past and transformed into a modern idiom. The disadvantage of all the industrious hunting and decoding of thematic allusions is that it deflects attention away from his formidable achievement.

VI

When Brahms adapts new material to a procedure he had learned from his study of the past, he generally appears most original, sounds most like himself. As we have seen, his melodies often outline spiky, dissonant shapes that resemble Stravinsky's, and his motifs leap into forbidding intervals like sevenths; he uses odd rhythmic periods, and loves strange groups of five bars, or even five-beat rhythms. Wagner also uses dissonant melodic forms on rare occasions for sinister figures like Hagen, and even five-beat rhythms, but only when he wants to represent hysteria, as when Tristan tears the bandages from his wound in the third act of *Tristan und Isolde*. Brahms's five-beat rhythms, however, are integrated seamlessly into the musical texture and made to seem almost normal, as in the wonderfully expressive and melancholy double stops opening the C minor section of the development of the Violin Concerto, where the beats are really 5, 5, 5, 5 and 4 (the last two groups unified by the indications of phrasing):

This five-beat grouping can probably be ascribed to Brahms's close study of Baroque technique. Five-beat sequences can never, as far as I know, be found in late eighteenth-century music. (Chopin has an experimental ⅝ slow movement in his first sonata, written when he was sixteen and which he never published.) However, there are rare examples of five-beat sequences earlier in the eighteenth century. The Courante of the Partita in D Major from Bach's *Clavier-Übung* has an interesting hidden sequence passed from soprano to alto to tenor: in ⁶⁄₄ time, the sequence begins one beat earlier in each bar. In Handel's Suite no. III in D minor, the fugue develops a five-beat sequence toward the end. These sequences are possible in the first half of the eighteenth century, as Baroque rhythm has a fluidity impossible later in the more clearly defined classical system, and I think that Brahms was attempting to recapture some of that fluid movement and to magnify it. In the examples from Bach and Handel, the basic rhythm in six or four is loosened by these groupings in five, and Brahms's violin concerto similarly attacks the strictness of a ¾ beat throughout its first movement by occasional groups of five.

Brahms's music is easy to listen to, but, because of its reticence, difficult to assess and to appreciate. He was still, for most of the twentieth century, a composer who excited no little controversy. Immensely popular with audiences and performers, he was condemned as the embodiment of bourgeois cultural values by many critics. Virgil Thomson despised him: he was the symbol of the Teutonic musical tradition that Thomson hoped would be supplanted by Gallic elegance. Arnold Schoenberg adored him, but he was not interesting to many other composers, including Pierre Boulez and Stravinsky—although the latter suddenly changed his mind very late in life when he became fascinated by the rhythmic experiments he found in Brahms.

His instrumentation is extraordinary in its resolute elimination of facile effect. Tovey remarked on the astonishing use of the triangle in the scherzo of the last symphony, astonishing above all because Brahms introduces it at once while the rest of the orchestra is making a loud noise: a few pages later when it plays a delicate solo part, we are no longer aware of the strangeness of its timbre. The early Piano Trio in B Major begins with a beautiful cello melody clearly designed for that instrument—except that the cello does not get to play until the fifth bar, while the opening is given to the piano. The Horn Trio, as well, opens with a melody obviously intended for the horn but first played by the violin. Brahms would not openly exploit tone-color at the expense of form.

He had a weakness for themes that another composer would have thrown out (the scherzo of his A Major Piano Trio used to be called the "wastebasket scherzo," because that is where any other composer would have tossed it). Such melodies were a challenge to him. He once remarked that it would have been wonderful to be a composer at the time of Mozart, when it was easy to write music. That is the key to his triumph. He always chose the hard solution. He knew that the great forms and traditions of eighteenth- and early nineteenth-century music could be revived and continued only with difficulty. The nostalgia for the past that informs so much of his work was neither facile nor self-indulgent. He was ruthlessly self-critical and apparently modest, unsure of himself only because he knew that the kind of work he produced and the nature of its style could only survive if it measured up to the greatest achievements of the past.

PART FOUR

Musical Studies: Contrasting Views

CHAPTER TWELVE

The Benefits of Authenticity

To take a harpsichord concerto by Johann Sebastian Bach and arrange it for a four-part chorus, organ, and orchestra would not, for most music lovers today, be considered the proper way to realize the composer's intentions or even to show decent respect for the score. Yet this is what Bach himself did to his own harpsichord concerto in D minor—which was, incidentally, in its original version a violin concerto of a somewhat simpler cast. The ideal of performing a work as it would have been done during the composer's lifetime or even by the composer himself gives rise to unexpected considerations, of which this is an extreme case, but by no means a rare one.

The effort to revive ancient instruments and early performance practice is not strictly modern: it can already be found in the first half of the nineteenth century. Early in our own century Arnold Dolmetsch and Wanda Landowska became major public figures with their championship of the harpsichord. It is, however, during the past two decades that the "Early Music" movement has taken on the character of a crusade, above all as it has moved beyond the sphere of medieval and baroque music and into the late eighteenth and the nineteenth centuries. Early Music is still a good name for the movement even now that it has reached Mozart, Beethoven, and Chopin and is looking to Brahms and Debussy: the goal is to make these composers sound more ancient than we had imagined.

The success of the crusading spirit is undeniable: it can be measured by the extent to which it has imposed a new orthodoxy. In the days of our innocence,

Originally written in 1990 as a review of Nicholas Kenyon, ed., *Authenticity and Early Music: A Symposium.*

what we wanted was a performance that was technically perfect, effective, beautiful, moving, and even, for the most idealistic, faithful to the work or to the intentions of the composer. Fidelity is no longer enough: a performance must be authentic.

The new rallying cry, authenticity, represents a goal simpler and grander than fidelity: it is aptly modern in that it transcends the composer's intentions, or at least circumvents them. The old ideal of fidelity demanded that the performer try to infer the composer's intentions, and realize them with the least possible distortion. In a faithful interpretation, the performer's own personality and his need for expression come into play essentially as a medium through which the work can be made public; the performer's style would be capricious, willful, lyric, or dramatic as the work demanded it. Fidelity has its dangers, as the performer identifies himself only too easily with the composer, convinces himself without difficulty that the composer would have approved such-and-such a cut, been delighted with this accent, made an expressive relaxation of tempo in just that place. Nevertheless, fidelity demanded of performers a genuine sympathy with the composer's style.

Authenticity dispenses with all this guesswork and uncertainty. It does not ask what the composer wanted, but only what he got. Intentions are irrelevant. (Some performers of Early Music now claim to return to the study of intentions, but the concentration is still on what was actually heard.) We no longer try to infer what Bach would have liked; instead, we ascertain how he was played during his lifetime, in what style, with which instruments, and how many of them there were in his orchestra. This substitutes genuine research for sympathy, and it makes a study of the conditions of old performance more urgent than a study of the text.

The success of the battle for authenticity is well merited, above all when one considers the contempt with which most professional musicians and critics only a generation ago greeted the efforts to revive old instruments and old ways of playing—the present intolerance of modern instruments is a natural reaction. Nevertheless, a new orthodoxy inevitably provokes doubts, inspires heresies. The hostility to Early Music is no longer as significant as the dissension within the ranks. Things are not as simple as they seemed in the earlier days of the movement, and the certainties of some decades ago have evaporated. We are no longer so sure that Scarlatti wrote his five-hundred-odd sonatas for the harpsichord and not for the pianoforte; there is no agreement on whether Bach's rhythms are to be executed in French style, with an irregular swing to it. There is fierce controversy about tempo in Mozart and Beethoven and about improvised ornamentation in opera and instrumental music. Above all, as our knowledge has increased of the wide variations in performance practice that coexisted throughout the eighteenth and nineteenth centuries, it has become less and less evident what it means to return to the style of playing current during a composer's lifetime—what, in short, an authentic interpretation would be.

A collection of essays called *Authenticity and Early Music*, skillfully put together and edited by Nicholas Kenyon, confronts some of the issues raised by Early Music and glances at others. All of the contributions are intelligent and stimulating. Will Crutchfield of *The New York Times* writes of the role of the performer, and of the necessity to substitute personal conviction and freedom for the arid realization of simple rules of historical performance. Philip Brett of the University of California at Berkeley discusses the problems of editing, and what it means to prepare an authentic text. He describes persuasively how even the most neutral and apparently inoffensive modernization of old forms of musical notation can alter our conceptions of the music and influence the performance. Even the simple reproduction of the old notation will not lead directly to authenticity; just the act of printing a score may lead to misunderstanding when the work as we have it was intended to be executed only a few times by a special group of singers and musicians and only under special circumstances.

Such circumstances are dealt with by Gary Tomlinson of the University of Pennsylvania, in an essay on Angelo Poliziano's mythological play *Orfeo*, written at Mantua probably in 1480. Tomlinson claims that the "authentic meaning" of the music depends on a reconstruction of the historical circumstances and background of the work. He confesses to "some polemical mischief" in his choice of example, since the music to *Orfeo* has not survived, and may not have been written down in the first place, but only improvised by the singer, Ugolini, who portrayed Orpheus. Tomlinson gives a brilliant exposition of the probable influence of contemporary Platonism on Ugolini, with its idiosyncratic views of music, magic, and poetry frenzy. He does not speculate on the ways in which these ideas might have affected either the music that Ugolini may have improvised or the manner in which he performed, and perhaps Tomlinson is right not to attempt such speculations.

This makes his argument, however, an evasion of everything of major importance to music lovers, to musicians, and even to most historians of music. No one denies the interest of an initial study of the historical conditions in which a musical work was created; the point of difficulty, however, has always been to apply this knowledge to the music itself and how it was once, and might be again, performed. There is some point to a savage remark by Richard Taruskin of the University of California at Berkeley (in a later essay in the same book) that by

Tomlinson's "lights an 'authentic' performance would seem to be a performance accompanied by a good set of program notes."

Taruskin writes brilliantly and at the top of his voice, and his most crushing arguments are often reserved for opinions that no one really holds. He asserts: "To presume that the use of historical instruments guarantees a historical result is simply preposterous." No doubt. Still, Taruskin beats his dead horses with infectious enthusiasm, and some of them have occasional twitches of life.

His main thesis, repeated here from earlier articles, is that the Early Music movement is not a genuinely historical crusade at all but a variety of modernism, an attempt to make the music of the past conform to the austere aesthetic that we associate with Stravinsky and his successors, and to make it sound astonishingly different in order to achieve that shock of originality demanded by the modernist ideal. This does, indeed, describe and clarify certain aspects of Early Music with great precision, and Taruskin demonstrates his thesis with easy conviction. As he says: "Changes in performing styles in the twentieth century, no less than in past centuries, have been allied with changes in composing style, and with more general changes in the aesthetic and philosophical outlook of the time." When he adds, however, that "a multiplicity of styles is always available in any present, of which some are allied more with the past and others with the future," this seems true but is only too pat. To group styles into reactionary and progressive as he tends to do is not helpful either: they all reach backward and forward. Taruskin's view of modernism is too narrow, and is fueled by his hostility to many aspects of contemporary art. Modernism in music is not confined to the hard-edged neoclassicism of Stravinsky, but has its neo-Romantic side in Schoenberg and Berg which reaches into the work of Elliot Carter and Karl-Heinz Stockhausen and even into much of Pierre Boulez. In many ways, Furtwängler, classified by Taruskin as a ghost from the past, was as "allied with the future" as Toscanini was and John Eliot Gardiner is today. In addition, Taruskin is curiously grudging; he does not want to admit that our greater knowledge of performance practice and instruments of the past can have a beneficial effect, and can do more than give an unwarranted sense of superiority.

The relation of Early Music to the past is seen in a more sophisticated light by Robert Morgan of Yale University. The successive revolutions of style imposed by modernism in the twentieth century from Schoenberg and Stravinsky to Stockhausen and Boulez have made not only the general public, but many professional musicians, feel that the apparent continuity of tradition from Bach to the present has now been interrupted. Even the most unequivocal successes of modernism have not yet taken deep root in our musical consciousness: only fifteen years ago I still saw Philharmonic subscribers stalk out noisily in protest during Alban Berg's delicate and enchanting "Post-card" songs. Those who accept Stockhausen or Philip Glass do not generally think of them as sharing a common language with Mozart. The works of the eighteenth and nineteenth centuries have become museum pieces that we continue to love but no longer think of as playing an active part in the creation of new music. As Morgan observes: "All this suggests that the past is slowly slipping away from us. It is no longer ours to interpret as we wish, but ours only to reconstruct as faithfully as possible." Historical accuracy for Morgan as for Taruskin is both a product of modernism and a reaction to it: a way of making the past different, both old and new at the same time.

Historical accuracy in performance matters a great deal to Howard Mayer Brown of the University of Chicago, and he sketches the history of attempts to achieve it. His style may be all velvet paws, careful to offend no one, but he approaches his subject with considerable sophistication and sharpness. The nature of his skepticism is sufficiently shown by the title of his contribution: "Pedantry or Liberation?" He holds the balance amusingly between these two tendencies of the Early Music movement.

Brown is the only contributor who sees the fundamental distinction between music that demands a reconstitution of the original style of performance with the original instruments and music that is susceptible to reinterpretation by different styles and sounds.

> The truth—although it may seem controversial to say so now—is that it is more acceptable to play Bach's music on modern instruments than Rameau's, for it can be argued that authentic sonorities and old playing techniques are less important in the one than the other, and that therefore the essential nature of Bach's music can emerge in a performance that translates the original into modern terms. In short, it is possible to defend what might be described as a woolly-headed liberal approach to the question of repertory.

It is refreshing to get away from a monolithic view of music, to be reminded that the "essential nature" of one composer's music is not the same as another's, and that the possibilities of realization in sound will be more varied in one case, more restricted in others. This flexibility of approach, however, makes life difficult for musicians: it is much more convenient to assume that there is only one ideal sound for each work of music—either the sound the composer imagined in his head as he wrote, or the one he knew he was going to get from current instruments and contemporary practice—and that the goal of the responsible performer should be to renounce the delights of imagination and realize this ideal sound as closely as possible.

II

What goes largely unrecognized or unstated in these essays is that the basis of the Early Music movement—aesthetic as well as commercial—is recording. Only Nicholas Kenyon in a parenthetical comment in his introduction seems to notice that there is something interesting about this:

> It is of course ironic, and a comment on the whole "authenticity" business, that most of its artefacts are in the extremely inauthentic form of recordings without audience which sound the same every time one plays them.

("Most of its artefacts"? An odd phrase.) Indeed, the recent success of Early Music was originally stimulated by recordings, and it is still today largely sustained by the recording industry.

The expansion of Early Music came when it invaded the symphonic repertoire of Mozart and Beethoven to play it with the original instruments, as they were before the violins had had their necks lengthened to give the strings extra tension, before wind instruments were made considerably more powerful. The trouble was that twenty years ago few musicians knew how to handle these old instruments, which tend to go out of tune much more quickly than modern ones and to emit strange grunts, squeaks, and quacks in inexperienced hands. The only solution was magnetic tape, which could be pieced together in 30-second segments so that the orchestra could retune every half-minute or so and the more objectionable noises could be edited out.

By now there are many performers who have become expert enough with these ancient instruments, and even learned to keep them better in tune, although not, of course, quite as well in tune as modern ones. Tuning had always been a problem, and we must not imagine that no one was troubled by it in the eighteenth century and earlier. "At the beginning of the concerts," wrote Saint-Evremond in 1684, "we observe the accuracy of the chords; nothing escapes of all the different variety that unites to form the sweetness of harmony; some time after the instruments make a din; the music is for our ears no longer anything but a confused noise, which allows us to distinguish nothing." Nevertheless, in spite of the more convincing sounds now made in public by orchestras made up of ancient instruments (or replicas of them), the commercial interest of Early Music is largely confined to records.

The reason for this is partly acoustics, partly economics. Eighteenth-century instruments (except, of course, for organs) were largely meant for halls with a capacity of a few hundred people. In typical modern halls seating fifteen hundred to three thousand they sound thin and puny, and their more delicate nuances are lost in space. They can of course be amplified, but that radically alters and, in fact, homogenizes their tone colors. With an amplified harpsichord, for example, nuances of registration are obscured, and different sonorities begin to sound alike. The modernization of instrumental construction was inspired largely by the growth of public concerts and the gradually increasing use of larger halls.

Recording takes almost no account of volume of sound: maximum levels (and minimum as well) remain approximately the same for all records, whether of an orchestra and chorus of a thousand or of a solo flute. I have always found, when a radio station follows the playing of a recorded symphony with a record of a single harpsichord, that I must rush to adjust the dials, because the blast of sound from the harpsichord is not only as loud as the symphony but much louder. The range between the softest and loudest points is much smaller with a harpsichord than with an orchestra, and sound engineers generally set their levels as high as is compatible with the system of reproduction, since this gives the greatest possible fidelity. Good microphone placement can make three violins sound like a dozen, and the recording industry allows Early Music to rival the power and volume of more conventional orchestras.

In public, "historical" orchestras can compete with the standard bands only if they can afford to muster the necessary forces. It is well known that Handel called upon forty oboes and as many bassoons with the other instruments in proportion, but this of course was on a special occasion and outdoors. Nevertheless, Mozart enjoyed doing his C major Symphony, K. 338, at one indoor concert with forty violins, eight oboes, eight bassoons, twelve double basses, and the rest to match. This would unmercifully stretch the purse of any Early Music society.

The other solution—playing in smaller halls—is also not economically workable, not at least without a heavy subsidy. Half a century ago a pianist or a string quartet could make a living playing to audiences of five hundred people: those days are long gone. Travel and advertising expenses have risen disproportionately to any acceptable increase in the price of tickets. It costs more than eight hundred dollars in New York just to move a concert piano across Fifty-Seventh Street from Steinway to Carnegie Hall. Established symphony orchestras and opera houses have their regular sources of fund raising, and often their traditional access to government subsidies. Early Music societies are still somewhat in the position of outlaw raiders: they depend on the aid of the record companies to force their way into the mainstream of the classical music business.

With the success of their recordings, Early Music has come to seem less radically different—objectively so, indeed, since the greater expertise at handling old instruments in recent years, coupled with the ability of the sound engineers to make a chamber group sound like a large symphony orchestra, has brought Early Music performance much closer to conventional sound. In fact, the more professional an Early Music orchestra becomes, the more it sounds like a conventional one; in addition, the most successful conductors of Early Music— Nikolaus Harnoncourt, Christopher Hogwood, Roger Norrington, and John Eliot Gardner—have turned increasingly toward engagements with established orchestral groups. One has to listen carefully now to a recording of a Handel concerto grosso or a Mozart symphony to decide whether it is an execution on old instruments or a regular symphony orchestra that has picked up some of the new ideas on old performance practice from Early Music. (Of the fruitful influence of the authenticity crusade on general performance there can be no doubt.) In large halls, however, the public (resembling, in this respect, the audience at rock concerts) is often forced to rely on its memory of what the record sounded like.

We generally listen to records with the hope of hearing the acoustical effect of a large concert hall; at Early Music concerts we hope to hear what we remember from playing the record in our own living room. This is particularly true when we are dealing with late eighteenth- and early nineteenth-century pianos. In a recent article in the *New York Review of Books* (May 18, 1989) on the Mozart piano concertos, Joseph Kerman wrote at length on Malcom Bilson's recordings on an eighteenth-century piano, but said not a word about what these performances are like in public. Bilson's musical qualities remain the same in a public performance as on disc; but when one is using late eighteenth-century instruments (or replicas thereof), it is much easier on disc than in a live performance to make the piano stand out clearly from the orchestra, and to avoid its being overshadowed by the other instruments.

The problem of balance between piano and orchestra already existed in the eighteenth century. The violins and other string instruments were reduced to one on a part whenever they accompanied the piano, a traditional practice deriving from the Baroque concerto grosso, where a small group of solo instruments were contrasted with an orchestra.[1] The real solution to the problem of balancing piano and orchestra was to build bigger and louder pianos.

No other instrument changed so radically between 1780 and 1850, and from 1790 on a wide variety of instruments were produced, all called pianoforte, fortepiano, or *Hammerflügel*. They all had a lighter bass and a faster decay of sound than modern instruments, but the difference between a Viennese piano and an English piano in the 1790s was far greater than that between a Steinway and a Bösendorfer, to take the two most commonly called upon today for public use. Piano construction changed constantly during Mozart's, Beethoven's, and Liszt's lifetimes in response to the use of larger concert halls, and above all to meet the demands of the music. Not only did pianos become bigger and louder, but they also had enlarged keyboards with higher and lower pitches.

It is a familiar mistake to think that a composer writes only for the instruments available to him, a mistake basic to the hard-line Early Music dogma. In a sense, composers already used the extra high and low notes before they had them. The existence of these notes is implied in the music. There is an irritating or piquant wrong note in the first movement of Beethoven's first piano concerto, a high F-natural where the melody obviously calls for an F-sharp. Pianos did not yet have that F-sharp when Beethoven composed the concerto, although they did some years later when he wrote the most interesting of his cadenzas for the work and employed the new high register. We know that Beethoven himself would have played the F-sharp, as he once announced his intention of revising his early works in order to make use of the extended range. To the new aesthetic of authenticity, his intentions count for very little: to employ an instrument contemporary with the work would mean not only playing a note evidently wrong but even renouncing the best cadenza.

The heavy, thick-sounding bass of modern concert pianos makes it very difficult if not impossible to achieve the light, detached sonority demanded by many passages of Mozart and Beethoven. On the other hand, the rapid decay of sound of the old pianos would not have allowed them to sustain the longer melodic notes in Beethoven and Schubert, as even modern instruments are barely

---

1. This was a much more standard procedure than Kerman believes. There are even a few places where Mozart takes advantage of the convention of accompaniment by only one instrument to each part to write a duet for the concertmaster and the pianist, making a virtue of necessity, notably in the wonderful canon for first violin and piano alone toward the end of the slow movement of K. 271 in E-flat (it is absurd to do this with half a dozen violins). An equally exquisite moment occurs in the last slow movement of the last piano concerto where all the instruments of the orchestra drop out, leaving only flute and first violin to double the melody in octaves with the piano.

adequate here.[2] And where Beethoven, in opus 90, asks for a successive *crescendo* and *diminuendo* on a single sustained note, the instrument that can realize this has not yet been invented.

From a common-sense viewpoint, the most nearly adequate instruments, although still imperfect, might be those whose construction was inspired by the music rather than those that the composer was forced to use. The desire for authenticity, however, is driven by idealism rather than just common sense. I have even heard a pianist on a modern Steinway play the clearly wrong F-natural because that is what Beethoven wrote. An authentic wrong note is evidently better than an inauthentic right one. With a piano of the time, Beethoven's public could easily see that the F-natural was the last note on the keyboard, and sympathetically supply the necessary sharp in imagination. The wrong note has a pathos in this case, but only if one can see it—and of course this pathos is not available on a recording. One of the chief advantages of using an early piano is that the public can appreciate the way Haydn, Mozart, and Beethoven used the upper and lower limits of the keyboards for the most powerful climaxes. The visual aspect of the performance on old instruments may seem a trivial point, but the dramatic effect of striking the highest or lowest note on the keyboard was an essential part of the musical structure—an effect that can be realized neither on a modern instrument nor by the recording of an ancient one.

The forced alliance of Early Music and the recording industry is more than odd: they have a natural affinity for each other. Recording fixes the sound of a single performance and enables one to reproduce it. Early Music seeks to ascertain the original sound of a work of music and to reproduce it. Both are admirable endeavors with what may seem like minor flaws. Combined, these flaws have a pernicious effect, doubly dangerous because largely unconscious. Both of them reduce a work of music to its sound, and tend to abstract it from all of its social functions, from any interaction with the rest of culture—all this with the innocent conviction that nothing essential is lost in this process of abstraction, and without the slightest suspicion of how profoundly the nature of music is altered.

III

To try to figure out as well as one can how a composer thought his music would sound and do one's best to realize this in performance—what a simple and reasonable program! Its attraction needs no explanation. What is astonishing is that almost no one ever thought of it before.

2. See, for example, bars 28–29 of the slow movement of Schubert's last sonata.

Of course, people were interested in how a composer played his own works: both Czerny and Schindler described, accurately or not, the way that Beethoven played, and conveyed his ideas of style and execution. Neither of them ever suggested, however, that we return to the instruments available to Beethoven when he originally wrote his works—just as Beethoven in later life would have found incomprehensible a recommendation to return to the pianos of the 1790s for his early sonatas instead of using the more powerful instruments at hand after 1815. Not just the volume but the tone quality of the pianos had changed.

Czerny described not only how Beethoven played his own works but how he played Bach's *Well-Tempered Keyboard* as well. He did not consider Beethoven's way of playing his own sonatas and concertos more authentic but more authoritative—most of all because it was better, just as he thought Beethoven's way of playing Bach was better.

This apparent indifference to the actual sound of an old piece when first performed (or at least to certain aspects of the original sound) went along with a dedication to selected details of the original style, and this coupling has been an integral part of Western music since the eighteenth century. It has even deeper roots within that tradition than Robert Morgan suggests when claiming that the old sense of a living and unbroken musical language from past to present has enabled us to translate the sound of the past into the new sounds of contemporary instruments. It came also from the fundamental idea that musical composition is partly divorced from the actual realization in sound.

When Bach transcribed his D minor harpsichord concerto for organ and chorus, he made no attempt either to preserve some of the qualities of the original sonorities or to give the work a more choral or organ-like character. He just rescored an abstract set of pitches and rhythms for a different sound. He did remove the keyboard-style ornaments from the melodic line of the slow movement—but ornamentation was considered precisely as belonging not to composition but to the realization of the sound of the notes, and it was often left entirely to the performer. (If Bach's choruses were performed with only one singer on a part, as Joshua Rifkin has insisted, then some ornamentation might have been restored.) Bach in fact irritated his contemporaries by writing out the embellishments and so constraining the imagination of the performers.

When Mozart arranged his wind serenade in C minor, K. 384a, as a string quintet (K. 516b), he was only interested in making it possible for five string instruments to execute the notes originally given to eight winds. Considerations of the actual sound played little part in the arrangement. Similarly, when Beethoven arranged his violin concerto for piano and orchestra (a task which had a financial interest for Beethoven and, except for the cadenza, no musical interest for anyone), he gave the violin part to the pianist's right hand, allowing the left to strum the harmonies. No thought of making the work pianistic entered the composer's head. Nor, on the other hand, did he think of finding a way for the piano to create a violinistic sonority.

This does not mean that composers did not care how the music sounded, but that composition and realization were not identical, and that while composition was more or less fixed, realization was more or less open. Mozart's Symphony in G minor, K. 550, exists in two versions, one without clarinets, but it is the same composition. Mozart no doubt preferred the version with clarinets, since he used them elsewhere when he could get them. The clarinet concerto was originally sketched for basset horn, with the structure and details of the solo part fully worked out; reconceiving it for clarinet did not involve any process of recomposition. It is clear that for Mozart as for Bach, composition did not entail fixing all aspects of the sound in advance.

Things changed radically in the middle of the nineteenth century. In 1838, when Liszt arranged the Paganini caprices for the piano, he not only rethought the music to make it sound spectacularly pianistic, he also rewrote the caprices to allow the piano to sound like a violin, and to reproduce effects like spiccato and pizzicato on the keyboard. Other composers (Scarlatti, Handel, and J. S. Bach, for example) had imitated horns, trumpets, tympani, and guitars with the keyboard, but only with original works: their transcriptions from other instruments never bother to evoke the original sound. Liszt, however, in his transcriptions of the Beethoven symphonies was unbelievably ingenious in imitating the original instrumentation on the piano. Liszt also rewrote his own music all his life: if the two versions of Mozart's G minor Symphony are the same piece with two different sonorities, that is no longer true of Liszt's multiple versions. There is almost as much difference between his two piano versions of Sonetto 104 of Petrarch as there is between works with different titles. For Liszt, realization—actual sound, in short—was becoming a more essential and intimate part of composition.

From the eighteenth century to the present, many of those aspects of realization left to the decision of performers (guided by the relatively loose, but never completely free, performance practice of their time) were gradually incorporated into composition. With Beethoven's work, for example, the traditional forms of embellishment—trills, grace notes—have become part of the basic musical structure; they now figure among the work's motifs, and nothing more can be added by the performer—Beethoven was known to make a disagreeable scene when a performer dared to add a few trills.

Even what might seem like trivial aspects of realization could become essential to a musical conception later in the nineteenth century. When Brahms made a transcription for piano of Bach's Chaconne for solo violin, he scored it for the left hand alone, partly as a finger exercise, and partly, as he confessed, because it made him feel like a violinist as he played it, determining all the pitches with his left hand. Not only the sound of an instrument became an essential element of composition, but even the physical experience of playing. Liszt's transcription of Paganini's Caprice in G minor also begins the principal melody with the left hand alone for a similar effect. Like the promoters of Early Music, Brahms and Liszt were trying to preserve a part of the original experience of the work that would once have been considered marginal. Brahms, in fact, is the real precursor of Early Music: when he edited the works of Couperin, he insisted on using all the old clefs, by then extremely difficult to read for contemporary musicians, and was only prevented by the refusal of his coeditor, Chrysander. Brahms wanted the text to look archaic: it is only a step from wanting it to sound archaic as well.

Early Music's narrow concentration on the sound the composer would most probably have heard rather than on the sound that he explicitly said he would like to hear represents a giant step forward and an almost equal step backward. It is an immense progress because every composer writes to a great extent with the performance he is likely to get in mind, even if he is deeply dissatisfied with the performance practice of his day and with the actual forces and instruments that are available. The notation of music can only be understood in terms of how people really played; and the body of knowledge gained about old music in the past two decades and the experience of playing the obsolete instruments for which it was written have been an inestimable boon to musicians and scholars alike.

The authenticity movement is also a regression because many composers write partly with the hope of an ideal performance which transcends the pitiable means and degenerate practice they have to compromise with. New ways of writing create new ways of playing, and composers are often unaware that the music they have just set down on paper demands a new style of performance. If one could resurrect both Mozart's performance of his own Concerto in D minor, K. 466, and Beethoven's performance of the same concerto (which he is known to have played, and for which he wrote a set of startlingly innovative cadenzas), which one would seem to us to reveal more adequately the character and originality of the work?

Yet some of the most distinguished practitioners of Early Music have openly professed a policy of forgetting everything that happened to performance after Bach or Haydn or whomever they happen to be playing. Walter Benjamin was right to characterize the origin of this kind of historical outlook as melancholy and bitterness of heart. It springs from a rejection of the contemporary world. For many Early Music enthusiasts, the alienation was triple: a rejection of avant-garde music, of the standard performance of the classics, and of the conditions of professional musical life.[3] A large number of the most radical seekers after authenticity as late as the 1950s were amateur musicians, for whom Early Music was part of a style of life that included playing the recorder, eating brown rice and whole wheat bread, and making their own clothes. The movement has now developed into a genuinely professional and profitable one, but some of the prejudice against the modern world remains with it.

Much of the prejudice was, and is, justifiable. The conventional aspects of all standard performances of music from Bach to Debussy—the customary insistence on producing a "beautiful" or "expressive" sound, for example, even when that kind of expression or beauty may be unsuited to the music being played—can become repulsive, doubly offensive when the performers are truly accomplished. When we realize how much of even the finest music making is mechanical rather than spontaneous, it needs only a moderately refined or jaded sensibility to find little to choose between artists as opposed as Toscanini and Furtwängler. The original impulse behind Early Music was a desire for a thoroughgoing renewal. Nevertheless, to refuse to come to terms with the way Bach, for example, has been interpreted and misinterpreted through time, to see how his work carried the seeds of its own future, is to shut oneself off sadly from the real life of music. The search for "authenticity" is often forced to remain content with the ways the composer's contemporaries understood his music, and this can amount to perpetuating misconceptions rendered obsolete by two centuries.

IV

The true sadness of "authenticity" is that its scholarly and idealistic interest in the sound of music *as it once was* divorces music and realization (or performance) from the life of which they were, and are, a part. Even the way many practitioners of Early Music conceive the original sound of a work is flawed. The discovery that Haydn's and Mozart's symphonies were conducted during the composer's lifetime by a pianist who played the harmonies to keep the orchestra together gave rise to a series of recordings in which a piano or harpsichord could be heard obtrusively in the foreground, even at times messing up Haydn's delicately austere, dry moments of two-part counterpoint. (All the evidence points to the orchestral piano or harpsichord being heard in the late eighteenth century largely by the orchestra alone; it was almost inaudible to the public, and it was dropped as musically unnecessary as soon as one had found a better way to beat time.)

On the other hand, no one as far as I know has revived the French eighteenth-

---

3. See the brilliant article by Laurence Dreyfus, "Early Music Defended Against Its Devotees," in *Musical Quarterly* 64 (1983).

century operatic practice of keeping orchestra and singers together by a loud banging on the floor with a big stick. Of course, the practice was deplored even at the time as distracting in soft passages, and it was not strictly part of the music, but surely it was a part of the auditory experience less incidental than the underground rumbling of the subway in Carnegie Hall, or the whine of an overhead plane at open-air concerts. A good thump at the beginning of every bar must have added definition and even induced a little rhythmic excitement.

Much more serious is the refusal to take into account how styles of playing and even instruments are dependent upon social circumstances—not the size of the hall, but the character of the audience and its interests and reasons for being present. Let us start with the zero degree of the question, with no audience at all: music not intended for any form of public or semi-public performance. This includes two of the supreme masterpieces of the eighteenth century: Bach's *Well-Tempered Keyboard* and his *Art of Fugue*, both educational works.

A fundamental distinction must be made in Bach's output between public and private works—or, better, between music to be played for oneself and one or two pupils or friends and music to be played for others. The organ toccatas and fugues are public, meant to be played in church—the closest that we have to works by Bach for the modern concert hall, since their liturgical function is not an important aspect. Performing them in public has never been a problem. The *Art of Fugue* and the *Well-Tempered Keyboard* are a different matter: both were intended for completely private performance, by two hands on a keyboard—any keyboard that one had at home, harpsichord, clavichord, small portable organ, early piano. (Bach was interested in early pianos and even sold them.)

Mozart, who arranged fugues from these two educational works for string trio and string quartet to make them available for semi-public performance in the 1780s, once asserted that fugues must always be played slowly or only moderately fast—otherwise one would not hear the entrances of the theme in the different voices. This is not a consideration that would have occurred to Bach, and it shows to what extent the change from private to public music entailed radical changes in performance only thirty years after the composer's death. The entrances of the theme in Bach's public fugues for organ are easily heard and appear with dramatic effect. In the private works, however, the theme is often hidden, disguised, its opening note tied to the last note of the previous phrase. There was no need for the performer of these educational fugues to set the theme in relief: he could hear it himself as he knew where it was, and, even more, he could feel its presence in his fingers. If he allowed a pupil or friend to hear him play the work, both of them would be reading the score. The different appearances of the theme needed no illustration or emphasis from the performer.

When the *Well-Tempered Keyboard* was played for a small or large group of

people, this easy intelligibility disappeared. The first public or semi-public performances of the *Well-Tempered Keyboard* that I know about took place after
1780 either for string ensemble or on the piano. It now became imperative to allow the listeners to perceive what went on in the fugue, to give them an idea of
how the individual voices moved, where the theme was. Here the Early Music
aesthetic cannot help us. What the composer wanted or what he expected to get
is no guide unless we are content to leave the public in the dark.

The proper question now is: which instrument will deliver Bach's original conception to the public most adequately? The piano is clearly more capable of setting details in low relief than either the harpsichord or organ (we must remember that a performance of these private fugues would in Bach's lifetime rarely
have used any change of registration or employed more than one keyboard); and
the clavichord, which can make dynamic nuances, is too soft for effective rendition of the larger fugues even on records (unless we turn up the dial to produce
an "inauthentic" volume of sound).

It is true that harpsichordists today in performing these once private fugues
have exercised their ingenuity to bring out the entrances of the theme. Taruskin,
attacking Edward Cone for claiming that neither harpsichord nor organ was capable of "applied accentuation," observes that "harpsichordists and organists . . .
have invested gallons of sweat and tears learning successfully to belie [this]." The
sweat and tears are indeed necessary: in all the performances I have heard of the
Well-Tempered Keyboard on the harpsichord, the performer has executed a set of
stylistic shenanigans in order to make this music truly public. Is there any evidence, or any reason to believe, that anyone ever played a fugue that way in the
first half of the eighteenth century? Nevertheless, to perform this music in public
as if it were still private is not only self-defeating but psychologically impossible.
(Professional musical training today is directed toward the format of public presentation in large halls.)

On the other hand, most of us have heard pianists produce the egregious style
of fugue playing in which the melody is brought out to the detriment of everything else—the standard way of playing Bach on the piano, and still encouraged
in all conservatories. In a fugue, however, it is not the theme that is fascinating,
but the way it combines with the other voices, into a homogeneous sonority. The
ideal is still to play these fugues on the harpsichord for oneself, to see the voices
as separate in the score and to hear them come together in a harmonious whole.
In public, however, the most satisfying performance in my experience was one,
on a piano, by Solomon of the C minor Prelude and Fugue from Book II of the
Well-Tempered Keyboard: it was in the immense barn of the Salle Pleyel in Paris;
the effect of transparence made one think that Solomon was setting nothing into

relief, but in fact he delicately shifted our attention from voice to voice throughout, and it was profoundly moving.

Playing this private music as it would have been played during the composer's lifetime is not only never done even by the most fanatical seeker after authenticity; it is also neither a practical nor a desirable ideal. When we reach the semi-private music of Mozart, Beethoven, and Schubert, written to be played to small gatherings, often in private houses, the ideal of authenticity is even more treacherous, as we are less conscious of how we are deforming the music. We shall also find that Tomlinson's view of authenticity as a reconstruction of the historical moment when the work of music came into being produces results of insoluble ambiguity both for performing and for understanding the music.

Perhaps more than any other city, Vienna had a very active tradition of semi-private music making, regular gatherings of twenty or thirty friends and guests: it was in this way that the majority of chamber works, piano sonatas, and songs were made known. Beethoven's piano sonatas are not fully public works: only two of the thirty-two were performed at a public concert in Vienna during his lifetime, while all of his string quartets were presented in public. In spite of the current mythology of the intimacy of the string quartet, written for the delectation of the players and a handful of connoisseurs, the piano sonatas of Beethoven and Schubert were even more clearly designed for a semi-private setting.

The force of this tradition is largely neglected today, and we fail to recognize how it influenced the works that were created for it. This matters least for Beethoven: he was a brilliant and famous concert pianist; he had considerable experience of public performance with his symphonies and concertos; and several of his sonatas (the "Waldstein" for piano, the "Kreutzer" for violin and piano) are clearly concert pieces. Most of his sonatas transfer without difficulty to the modern concert hall, but many of them nevertheless show that they were not intended for a large public: the sudden soft return to a strict tempo in the last few seconds of Opus 90, for example, is genuinely poetic, but can seem almost offhand in public, and pianists rarely resist the temptation to lengthen the very short final note to make it more impressive.

Schubert, on the other hand, was only an indifferent pianist, and few of his works were performed in public during his lifetime: his real element was the small gathering of friends at which his songs and chamber music were performed. At relatively informal occasions, attention may be as keen as at the public concert, but it is caught and held in different ways: delicate nuances are more telling, an almost hypnotic uniformity of texture is more effective, and large climaxes do not have to be prepared so long in advance, but can spring out as a surprise. The aspects of Schubert's style that are singularly well adapted to this semi-private occasion came out in an interesting recent article in the *New York Review of Books* by the distinguished pianist Alfred Brendel, and a subsequent controversy with Walter Frisch of Columbia University on Schubert's indications for repeating the long expositions of his sonatas.[4]

Brendel, whose viewpoint is partly determined by his project of playing Schubert's last three sonatas in one program, quotes Antonin Dvořák's remark about the length of Schubert's symphonies: "If the repeats are omitted, a course of which I thoroughly approve, and which indeed is not generally adopted, they are not too long." Brendel also adds that Brahms omitted the repeat of the exposition of the Second Symphony at one concert; the composer explained: "Formerly when the piece was new to the audience, the repeat was necessary: today, the work is so well known that I can go on without it."

In sonatas, symphonies, and quartets from Haydn to Beethoven, the expositions were repeated not in order to let the audience familiarize itself with the material, but for reasons of proportion and harmonic equilibrium—the exposition set up the basic harmonic tension of the work, and it was generally much less complex and chromatic than the succeeding development. At the end of his life, Haydn had experimented with leaving out the repeat, and Beethoven early on had continued these experiments, but Schubert was resolutely conservative: not once is the indication omitted.

The remarks of Brahms and Dvořák were made a half century after Schubert's death when this sense of proportion had largely disappeared, and had become an old-fashioned convention; this was a process that had only begun during Schubert's lifetime. More interesting for us here is that Brahms and Dvořák were both speaking of the public genre of the symphony, and they were considering the question of repeats with regard to the reactions of the audience. However, the tolerance of a small intimate group of listeners is much greater than that of a large crowd. A small intimate group will bear a long work with greater stoicism and courtesy. Moriz Rosenthal related that once in Vienna after dinner Ferruccio Busoni was persuaded to play, and he sat down and played the last five sonatas of Beethoven without getting up from the keyboard. ("It had been a very heavy dinner," was Rosenthal's comment.)

Walter Frisch wrote in to protest that the indications of repeats in the last two sonatas contain material not otherwise present in the exposition, and to observe that Brendel's public would be happy to spend the extra half hour that the repeats would add to the program. Brendel replied with a condemnation of the new material in the first ending of the exposition of the B-flat major Sonata: he

---

4. Alfred Brendel, "Schubert's Last Sonatas," *The New York Review of Books,* February 2, 1989; exchange with Walter Frisch, March 16, 1989.

objected to "the new syncopated, jerky rhythm," as well as the fortissimo trill, which remains "elsewhere in the movement . . . remote and mysterious," and he feels that "its irate dynamic outburst rob[s] the development's grand dynamic climax of its singularity." These bars are indeed violent, and contain the most brutal dynamic indications of the entire work. They explode without warning, and for this reason a convincing realization is not easily achieved in a modern recital hall.

Brendel's point of view can only be appreciated in relation to his ideas on the *molto moderato* tempo mark of the opening movement. He interprets this as corresponding "to a none-too-dragging allegretto," and attacks the recent fashion of conceiving the *molto moderato* as very slow: "While some older pianists played the first movement of the B-flat Sonata in an almost nervous *alla breve*, two beats to a bar, it is nowadays, in extreme cases, played in eight, with the repeated exposition thrown in for good measure." Most of the musicians I have spoken to have taken, rightly or wrongly, Brendel's target here as Sviatoslav Richter. His is indeed an extreme case: Richter's interpretation is notorious for a first-movement tempo that makes it last almost half an hour. As his recording shows, the tempo may be perversely slow, but the performance is a tour de force, never ceasing for a single instant to hold our attention.

The recording tells only part of the story: on occasion, when playing this work in a large hall, Richter has closed the piano—not just half closed, as if to accompany a singer, but with the lid down over the strings and sounding board, damping most of the brilliance and removing much of the volume. It is clear that Richter's idea of music has been conditioned as much as Brendel's by the concert stage, but that he has also been infected to some extent with the ideology of Early Music, although he has not remained within its narrow boundaries and tried to reproduce an antique sound in a modern hall: he essays a large-scale illusion of the intimate setting for which Schubert's sonata was designed and tries further to dramatize this intimacy for a public of two thousand or more.

The Sonata in B-flat major is often considered Schubert's greatest work for the piano. The first movement has, nevertheless, posed difficult problems. Donald Francis Tovey, who loved most of it, described the exposition as descending from "the sublime to the picturesque and then drifting from the picturesque through prettiness to a garrulous frivolity." The difficulty lies in an attempt to adapt the work for the exigencies of modern concert life, to make it "go." Most pianists opt for a reasonably brisk tempo, which does indeed make the latter part of the exposition sound pretty and garrulous, and they abridge the first movement either by cutting the repetitive phrases, as Harold Bauer did, or by omitting, like Brendel, the repeat of the exposition.

Yet it is the unequaled breadth, tranquil and even leisurely, that gives the work its supreme lyricism. It is the only sonata movement ever written to sustain such intense lyricism at such length, and it is the intensity as well as the length that makes the work difficult for a large audience. Unlike the opening movements of the other two late sonatas, this one has no technical display, no apparent virtuosity. The only technical difficulties lie in sustaining the line and balancing the delicate nuances demanded by the texture: astonishingly, more than half the exposition must be played within the range defined by pianissimo. At the end of the exposition, the music breaks into fragments, and erupts without warning into forte and fortissimo; the most dramatic of these fierce explosions is reserved for the disputed first ending.

These bars were originally not a first ending at all but an integral part of the exposition to be played twice according to the first draft. It is the second playing that Schubert revised, and he substituted a magical pianissimo transition into the development, with a harmonic change of the utmost daring, the kind of liberty for which he had been reproached by critics all his life. The dynamic explosion of the first ending and the harmonic outrage of the second complement each other, and the wonderfully poetic effect of the return of the inspired opening theme after the thunderous roar of the trill in the first ending is a counterpart to the opening theme's return after the end of the development with the long trill now heard twice pianissimo.

This sonata's creation may have been shaped by the intimate setting for which it was intended, and its tranquil breadth, lack of display, and sudden violence are more easily realized in such a format, but the sonata is not contained by it. I do not know if it was ever played in Vienna before being published a decade after Schubert's death, but it would have destroyed the *gemütlich,* Biedermeier intimacy of the semi-private musical evening, just as the songs of *Winterreise* made Schubert's friends ill at ease and uncomfortable. An "authentic" performance today is an absurdity. A recording on a "Schubert" pianoforte would add little to our appreciation of the work. It is also possible to maintain that Brendel's practical, modern concert approach distorts the music less than Richter's theatrical illusion of intimacy in a large space. Just as the sonata would have burst beyond the frame of the semi-private concert, so today in the modern concert hall, even though it must be played in a way that Schubert would never have imagined, it makes the traditional brilliance and dramatic effect that the recital demands seem irrelevant. Every performance today is a translation; a reconstruction of the original sound is the most misleading translation because it pretends to be the original, while the significance of the old sounds have irrevocably changed.

Style of performance may be affected by aspects of presentation that seem irrelevant at first glance. Sir Charles Mackerras pointed out to me that a great deal of evidence tells us that in the early nineteenth century, the first three movements of a symphony of Mozart or Beethoven were most often played faster, and the last movement slightly slower, than in performances today. This is easy to understand if we reflect that at the time, the public clapped and cheered after each movement (often forcing a repeat of the slow movement), and not just at the end of the symphony, so that the musicians were not forced into extra brilliance in the finale in order to get their meed of applause. To make sense of an authentic restoration of the original tempi, we should have to encourage applause between the movements (by holding up a sign, perhaps?); yet the modern tradition of keeping back the applause until the end is a justified tribute to the unity and integrity we now perceive in (or attribute to) the symphony as a whole. An unthinking restoration of the original tempi is not a wholly rational project—and if recordings ever become not just a mimesis of public performance but the normal musical experience, our concepts of musical excitement and intensity will have changed and will alter our ideas of tempo once again.

It is clear that I think that the basic philosophy of Early Music is indefensible, above all in its abstraction of original sound from everything that gave it meaning: authentic sound is not only insufficient, as most people would grant, and not only often an illusion, as many now realize, but sometimes positively disastrous. Sound is dependent on function: Bach's harpsichord concerto became a concerto for organ, chorus, and orchestra when it was used for a church service.

It remains to acknowledge that Early Music has been and is a remarkably beneficial movement. It has made us realize how contrasting are the demands of concert life, which force us to play Bach, Mozart, Beethoven, Chopin, Brahms, Debussy, and Boulez with the same instruments, the same kind of sound—looked at rationally, an insane result, even if the facile solutions of Early Music are equally odd and even more constricting. Early Music has laid bare the deadening uniformity of today's conventional concert world, where we find the same phrasing for Mozart and Beethoven, the same vibrato for Mendelssohn and Tchaikovsky, the same pedaling for Beethoven and Chopin. It has also had extraordinary successes, from Roger Norrington's work with Beethoven and Sir Charles Mackerras's performances of Mozart and Schubert symphonies to John Eliot Gardiner's reconception of Monteverdi.

One could say that the successes have been achieved in spite of the philosophy. This would not be true: it has been by taking the indefensible ideal of authenticity seriously that our knowledge has been increased and our musical life enriched.

CHAPTER THIRTEEN

Dictionaries: the Old Harvard

I have always been fascinated by dictionaries and the special problems of lexicographers and encyclopedists. This is the first piece I wrote for The New York Review of Books, *in 1970, and Harvard University Press has very graciously agreed to reprint it. The dictionary's successor,* The New Harvard Dictionary of Music, *was magnificently edited by Don Randel and is a model for all enterprises of its kind. As computers little by little replace graduate students and take away the possibility of paid research to earn the expenses of an advanced degree, future dictionaries will have neither the personal virtues nor the quirky faults of the old monuments, which will be recalled with nostalgia.*

THE conventions of a dictionary are as formal as those of a sestina, a minuet, or the architectural orders. In a preface, Dr. Willi Apel ominously compares the use of his volume to a visit to the dentist, but that, too, has its formalities and its ritual. In his dictionary, revised and enlarged after twenty-five years, the useful is evidently intended to outweigh the sweet. Nevertheless, no literary genre can so easily combine instruction with delight as the dictionary. The majesty of the *OED*, the intimate charm of the *Petit Larousse*, depend on the classical sense of propriety that they exemplify, works of art never read as wholes, but whose unity radiates and reveals itself in all their parts. In a dictionary, lack of grace entails a loss of utility.

The *Harvard Dictionary of Music* offends against decorum on the first column of its first page. It explains *con abbandono* only as "unrestrained, free" and not as "passionately"; under *Abbreviations* it gives *con 8va* (i.e., with octave doubling), but not *8va* itself (transpose an octave upward or downward), which is more often used; and it implies that there is only one way to interpret on the piano, when there are two clearly distinct meanings to that notation (the *Harvard Dictionary*'s interpretation would simplify a lot of wrist-breaking music, including Schubert's *Erlkönig*). Even the initial entry, *A,* betrays its innocence of the properties of lexicography by listing *a 2* as an example without explanation, apparently because it needs none. Yet if there were a cross-reference to *A due,* which comes up thirteen pages later, the less wary would learn that the meaning of *a 2* is very ambiguous indeed.

In many cases, of course, if not in all, the uninstructed will be able to figure out what is intended (just as most anglophones will assume correctly that *con abbandono* means "with abandon"), but if this is to be the plea, why bother printing anything at all about *A due* beyond an identification of "due" as the Italian for "two"?—and this could safely be left to Italian-English glossaries. The *Harvard Dictionary* is cavalier about cross-reference, and even that first article, *A,* is miserly with the asterisk that indicates a separate entry under the word lucky enough to be starred: *partbook* and *a piacere* are among the elect, but *antiphon* must hope for the enterprise of the individual reader.

Now in none of these opening articles is the information given absolutely false: they contain errors of method rather than of fact. True howlers and misinformation of course abound in all dictionaries, and the *Harvard Dictionary of Music* is no exception, but they are to be expected and even welcomed; they complement the more serious parts of a work of reference as the satyr-play sets off the tragedy. I am as delighted as the next reader to find Ravel's *Jeux d'eau* defined as *Water-games,* as if it were not the play of fountains but a form of water-polo. To read again that Beethoven introduced the trombone into symphonic music (to say nothing of the triangle and the big drum) should excite more sympathy than censure, and the idea that Schoenberg actually intended his *Music for a film sequence* as part of the repertoire for silent films, like the pieces labeled "Help, Help," is too ludicrous to mislead, and too engaging to wish corrected.

The biggest howler of the first edition is left unaltered: on page 4, perhaps the most famous phrase that Mozart ever wrote, the opening of the G Minor Symphony, is quoted to exemplify a combination of agogic accent with an irregular dynamic accent:

—only that is not what Mozart really wrote. His phrase, of course, has neither a dynamic accent (even the editors sense this as they put it in parentheses) nor an agogic accent: the B flat is short and followed by a rest. The reviser must have left this error because of its grandeur.

Methodical errors, however, are more damaging than comic mistakes; *8va* can only be omitted by a slapdish approach to listing musical abbreviations; and *con abbandono* can be translated as "unconstrained" in a musical dictionary by someone who has before him only an Italian dictionary and not a single instance of the use of the term in a musical work—one, say, by Liszt. That is why the opening page of this dictionary is disquieting; it seems to be the work of a committee that never asked itself why anybody would look up a given entry. In the rest of the dictionary, the separate entries are largely composed as if specific musical considerations did not exist. They are brilliantly crammed with information, and often dangerously misleading.

How a correct and informative article can deceive the ingenuous may be seen from *Swell:*

> In organs, mechanism for obtaining a gradation of sound, crescendo and diminuendo. It consists of a large room (swell box) built around one or more divisions of the pipes and provided with shutters similar to Venetian blinds, whence comes the name Venetian swell (G. *Jalousieschweller*). The chief enclosed division is called *swell organ,* a name that also applies to the manual from which it is played. The swell box is opened and closed by a swell pedal, operated by the feet. The first practical swell mechanism, invented in 1769 by Shudi, was used in harpsichords before it was adopted for the organ.

Leaving aside the minor irritant of a "pedal operated by the feet," let us affirm at once that the information is absolutely accurate. The article, however, implies that the swell was little used before 1769; yet Burney, when he visited Europe in the early 1770s, was astonished to find only one swell mechanism in all the organs in Germany because, as he said, they had had them in England already for half a century. No doubt the English mechanism was not a "practical" one, but it existed and this may have its importance for Handel's organ concertos. Most students and music lovers will look up *swell* to find out when and where they were used, and the *Harvard Dictionary* will only fool them; the entry is useful chiefly for people who want to settle a bet about Shudi and the date of his invention.

This kind of lexicography is corrupting in an odd way; it gives the reader who happens to know better and can avoid the traps innocently set for him the pleasant sense of knowing more than the team of musicologists, many of them distinguished, who compiled the dictionary. This agreeable glow of self-satisfaction is unwarranted. The *Harvard Dictionary* knows perfectly well that English organs had swell mechanisms early in the eighteenth century. It does not relay Burney's comment, nor is there any reason why it should, but it does inform the reader in the entry under *Organ* about the English swell. It does not, however, add a cross-reference to the entry under *Swell* because it is content to get things abstractly right without thinking of the reader or indeed of the musical reasons for consulting its pages.

For this reason, the praise that must be accorded the *Harvard Dictionary* with one hand must often be withdrawn with the other. The article on *Swell* is not an isolated instance, but the reflection of a fundamental irresponsibility. A *Positive organ*, for example, is indeed "a medium-sized *medieval* organ," but the "very small positive" mentioned two sentences later existed during the eighteenth century. Under *Rückpositif* we are referred to *Positif* but not to *Positive organ*, and the complete entry for *Positif* reads "choir organ" with an asterisk referring the reader there. Why *Rückpositif* sends one only indirectly to *Choir organ*, and not at all to *Positive organ*, is not easily explained, at least not charitably, and one must add that *Choir organ* sends one to *Organ* part III, and *Rückpositif* to *Organ* parts II, VII, and XII, II being here evidently an unchecked error.

Digging information out of this dictionary can therefore be a major excavation problem, and at the end one might still be forgiven for assuming that a small positive was exclusively medieval. *Mit Andacht* is thoughtfully and ridiculously indexed under both M and A, but I cannot see that the definition "with devotion" will enlighten anyone who does not already know that a religious context is meant. *Luftpause* is defined only as "breathing rest," but not as a slight pause that is not indicated except by a comma, and that forms no part of the regular rhythmic structure.

If one wants to know why the finale of Mozart's *Entführung* is called a *vaudeville*, he will not find here a definition of the form: a song for which the whole cast lines up, while each one separately sings a verse (this is sometimes called a *vaudeville finale*, but more often simply a *vaudeville*). Anyone puzzled by the eighteenth-century use of the term *modulation* will not be told that it meant voice-leading. The examples of typical rhythms of *ars nova* and *ars antiqua* are oddly chosen: the purpose of *ars nova* notation was to accommodate easily a wider and more complex range of rhythm, and the *ars nova* example is both simpler and more limited than the one of *ars antiqua*. This is another case where a correct presentation can misrepresent the essential musical point.

The failure to observe the fundamental courtesies of a dictionary makes a hash of the simplest musical concepts. Are the words and phrases, following Samuel Johnson, to be interpreted "with brevity, fulness and perspicuity"? Let us take as elementary an article as *Answer*, with its definition at once verbose, incomplete, and obscure (I quote the entire entry):

In fugal writing, the answer is the second (or fourth) statement of the subject, so called because of its relationship to the first (or third) statement. Hence, the succession of statements is subject-answer-subject-answer. See M. Zulauf, in *ZMW* vi. See Fugue; Tonal and real; Antecedent and consequent.

What is this mysterious relationship from which the veil is not to be torn? Simply that the answer is on the dominant or, more rarely after 1700, on the subdominant, or in the case of counterfugues inverted on the tonic. The further references will not help much: in *Fugue,* one must plow through a page of turgid, badly organized prose before finding that an answer is on the dominant and the matter is left at that. *Tonal and real* makes no further advance on this, and *Antecedent and consequent* is even more reticent, and contains, besides, a misprint in the musical example doubly unfortunate because it is just plausible. In any case, why is there no reference to *Dux, comes,* which would at least give students a chance to display some unnecessary erudition? The editors of the *Harvard Dictionary* know all about answers at the subdominant (see *Imitation*) and at the inversion (see *Counterfugue*), but they do not know how to tell anyone that they know.

These omissions are not isolated, but systematic. No work, even of almost a thousand double-column pages, can embrace the whole of music, and it is an unfair game to play with dictionaries and encyclopedias—particularly revised editions—to see what is in and what is out. But it is an instructive game to play with the *Harvard Dictionary,* because it reveals the principles with which the revision was undertaken. Composers do not get separate entries, so the amusement of seeing that one's friends have been left out is barred. But individual works are listed. *La Cosa Rara* is in, but *Le Devin du Village,* one of the most influential works of the eighteenth century, is out. *Oberon* and *Euryanthe* are also out, although *L'Africaine* is in. *Theodora,* which Handel said contained his greatest music, is out, as is *Samson, Semele, Esther,* and *Susanna,* but *Susannah* by C. Floyd and even *Il Segreto di Susanna* are in.

The twentieth century is heavily represented by Hindemith and Honegger, with comically disproportionate results. I am unmoved by Dr. Apel's loyalty to his youthful idols. *Jeux* by Debussy is out, but *Rugby* by Honegger is in; *Le Martyr de St. Sebastien* is omitted, but room is made for *Jeanne d'Arc au Bûcher. Le Marteau sans Maître, Gruppen,* the *Gesang der Jünglinge,* and the *Improvisations sur Mallarmé* are unlisted, while *Pacific 231* and the *Schwanendreher* keep their place although they have long since disappeared from the musical scene. *La Fanciulla del West* is there, but not *Fancy Free,* to say nothing of *West Side Story.*

The principle on which the dictionary was revised and brought up to date seems to have been that the research assistants jotted down a few items which occurred to them. And they live in a small, tight, closed world. There are newly written articles on jazz and even on bop, but there is nothing at all on rock, not even a brief definition of the term.

If this haphazard revision merely applied to contemporary musical life, while the musicological side had been done with care, there would be no excuse for niggling. There have certainly been considerable additions to bibliographical lists, and many articles have been entirely rewritten. New terms have been defined, and there is a considerable expansion of material and discussion. Some, but not enough, of the silliness in the first edition has been removed: we are no longer told that the "solemn dignity [of *Parsifal*] . . . does not always escape the danger of monotony." Dr. Apel's stern admonition that even the greatest piano virtuosos need to practice finger exercises every day has unfortunately been blue-penciled: in compensation, we may still read the splendid alliteration that some wiseacre slipped into the first edition: "Among later composers Tchaikovsky showed a particular predilection for pedal points."

But why has Leo Schrade's interesting and brief discussion of the sixteenth-century use of the term *maniera* been excised? The one sentence that replaces it now does not even tell us what *maniera* is. Schrade died since the first edition, but that is surely not sufficient reason for the change. His article was a serious attempt to relate music theory to the other arts, which makes the articles that have been retained (e.g., *Expressionism* and *Impressionism*) childish by comparison.

The improvements are naturally many: the new article on *Development* is considerably better than the old one. The entry on *Krakowiak* is more informative. There are excellent entries on *Descant* (written by the late Sylvia Kenney), *Parody Mass, Glass harmonica, Fauxbourdon,* and numerous others. The second part of the article on *Sonata form*, the historical section (revised by Leonard Ratner), is now intelligent and sophisticated, but the first part is little changed, and the quality of thought and writing is still so flat here that the student will receive more illumination from the new *Britannica* article by Donington, or even the old one by Tovey. *Melody* is as nonsensical as ever, and cannot even be summarized: Part IV must be read to be disbelieved.

Articles on individual countries are much expanded. I read the one on *Java* with great interest. Czechoslovakia has now, it seems, the longest article of any country, longer than France or Germany—or even Harmony. There are many more works represented, although Schumann's *Carnaval* has disappeared by mistake, I presume, as many much less famous works of Schumann are there. Someone must have confused it with the *Carnaval des animaux,* which has been added in the new edition, ousting the Schumann to avoid duplication. In addition, there seems to be no editorial policy at all on the admission of expressive terminology: *mit Wärme* has been added, *aufgeregt* has been left in, and *mächtig* has been taken out. There is only whimsy in all of this.

The updating is seriously defective in many places; it is also contradictory. *Pitch* lists the recent and well-known articles by Mendel in its bibliography (he is called R. Mendel—R. for Arthur), but the text itself takes almost no account of his researches, and is largely a slightly reworded repetition of its twenty-five-year-old predecessor. *Chiavette,* however, does take account of these same articles, but renders the discussion totally unintelligible by misprinting the first F clef on the fourth instead of the third line—the point at issue being exactly the unusual position of the clef.

Until now I have dealt largely with errors that could easily have been avoided by a respect for the nature of a dictionary—its necessary clarity, elegance, and order. But there are graver charges to be preferred against the *Harvard Dictionary:* it is often tendentious, its approach is too frequently unhistorical, and it is consistently stuffy in outlook.

It is unsportsmanlike to have an entry on a controversial subject written by a fanatical partisan of one side. An argument has been raging for some years on *notes inégales,* and while the article on the subject takes a position that seems to me judicious and even unexceptionable, it does not fairly represent the present conflict of opinion. *Serial music* is an example of a different kind: written by Henri Pousseur, its opening is interesting and lucid. Its last section, however, is a long, apocalyptic vision of the future, of what serialism will become (with the obligatory structural linguistics thrown in). At the end, the heavens open: "A vast system is now beginning to emerge, able to assimilate all the earlier systems that have contributed to its development (including, e.g., the tonal system)." I congratulate myself on not being able to understand this.

The tendentiousness gets its comeuppance. One of the most egregious lapses in the first edition is rendered even more ludicrous in the second. In the article on *Musica ficta* (the problem of adding, or not adding, sharps and flats to medieval and Renaissance music), the first edition remarked with justice that no answer could be found that "would apply equally to music of the 13th and of the 16th century." Then, with a straight face, examples of "unusual but entirely legitimate formations" were appended—all undated and unidentified.

The examples of *ficta* in the second edition have been dated—1955, 1939, 1959, 1947, etc. They are the dates when various editors have inserted, or have not inserted, accidentals. The article makes it clear that it is not the musical text which is at stake, but musicological fashion. The brief reference to Lowinsky's theories in the first edition has been excised, and the article in the second edition, without naming him except in the bibliography, is conceived largely as a covert attack upon his position. Lowinsky may be right or wrong (and my own opinion on the matter carries no weight even with myself), but the article represents the general state of musicological opinion only in the most biased fashion. It is, therefore, a pleasure to note once again the foolishness of giving examples that span almost two centuries of revolutionary developments without dating any of them, and to remark that no account is taken of the evidence of lute arrangements (although organ tablatures are mentioned), and that no hint is dropped that the use of *ficta* probably varied from country to country as well as from age to age.

The lack of dating is endemic in this book. Modulation is treated as if the process remained relatively unchanged from 1450 to 1900 and only its application to different formal schemes was altered. How change of key can mean the same thing in fifteenth- and eighteenth-century harmony is difficult to comprehend. In any case, a discussion of modulation that does not once mention the preparation of a modulation declares itself out of court to start with, and the bibliography omits the most famous of all books on modulation, Reger's little treatise.

Examples in *Counterpoint* are not dated, either, and they span four centuries: identifying the composers does not help in a book where composers have no separate entries. The kind of reader who knows the dates of Perotinus and Dunstable will probably not read the article *Counterpoint* unless he is reviewing the book. If it is noted that it is by these examples *alone* that contrapuntal practice between 1200 and 1620 is covered, that they are presented with the barest minimum of commentary, in captions, and that contrapuntal theory is treated cursorily and is largely a list of theorists, it will be seen that the approach is not historical but taxonomic.

This is at the root of many of the deficiencies in the book: the role of *Thoroughbass* after 1750, for example, has occasioned a good deal of research, not a word of which seeps into the article on the subject. Only the lack of historical sense could characterize Bach's music as without "a definite emotional character" (p. 2) and say that "baroque instrumental music tends to appeal to present-day listeners because of its detached, non-expressive character" (p. 301), and at the same time, print an excellent article on the *Affections, doctrine of* in which a Baroque theorist is quoted as describing "the affections (characteristic emotions) of numerous dances, saying that the gigue expresses 'heat and eagerness,' the courante 'sweet hope and courage.'" The relation of theory to practice is never simple, but the conception of a single *Affekt* as the basis of every piece of music is fundamental to the period 1700–1740, and an allemande by Bach is as "expressive" as a nocturne by Chopin.

The same unhistorical turn of mind makes a terrible confusion of the article on *consonance* and *dissonance,* combined with an inability to define a musical term in a musical sense. *Chambers's Twentieth Century Dictionary* defines a *dissonance* as "a combination of musical sounds that calls for resolution or produces beats," but you can read all the many hundreds of words in the *Harvard Dictionary* article without finding resolution mentioned once. Dissonance is defined only as "a disagreeable effect," as if music had neither significance nor structure.

This produces the historically incredible statement that the intervals of the fourth and the fifth, "from the point of view of musical composition of all eras . . . must be regarded as consonances," although (p. 329) the most important of late fifteenth-century theorists, Tinctoris, is quoted as saying that the fourth "was considered by the ancients the foremost of all consonances, but actually, taken by itself, it is not a consonance but an intolerable dissonance." Back in *Consonance, dissonance,* the dictionary becomes uneasy and adds that "the fourth has a decidedly unpleasant effect for an unbiased listener." Contemplating this, we peer into an abyss of naïveté.

In harmonic theory, the *Harvard Dictionary* has not progressed beyond Riemann. *Fingering* at the piano stops with Clementi (what happened to the Liszt fingering of the scale, and Chopin's use of the 3rd, 4th, and 5th fingers for chromatic passages, etc.?). The list of theoretical works stops at 1900, with a few more added pell-mell in a final short paragraph. *Performance practice* is called "the study of how early music, from the Middle Ages to Bach, was performed," and the article concludes, "in the period after Bach the problems of performance practice largely disappear, owing to the more specific directions of composers for clearly indicating their intentions." This breathtaking provinciality makes it possible to claim (p. 731) that "after 1750, metric developments are relatively uninteresting until Beethoven" because the editors have not heard of Haydn's and Mozart's revolutionary treatment of rhythm, and to write (p. 120) that "the cadences of the classical and romantic period are of little historical interest since they usually conform to the standard types outlined"—and Beethoven's minute-long hammering at the tonic and Schumann's poetically unresolved cadences were as if they had never been.

It is an analogous provinciality of style that makes the often pontifical and patronizing tone of the *Harvard Dictionary* offensive, whether one agrees or disagrees with the judgments gratuitously offered. We read (p. 7) that Tchaikovsky "rarely went beyond a chordal accompaniment in lush harmonies of rather ephemeral interest"; that Tovey's point of view in analysis was one-sided (p. 36); that Hugo Wolf's songs are better than Schumann's—and this in a long article on *Lied* which omits even a mention of Loewe. The *Harvard Dictionary* thinks that late fourteenth-century French music is decadent (p. 58), but, in compensation (p. 350), Italian music of the fourteenth century "is perhaps too 'earthy' and 'lively' (too 'proto-Renaissance') to be termed Gothic"—it must be many years since a major university press allowed itself to print so grotesque a statement on the visual arts.

The *Harvard Dictionary* does not, of course, adequately represent the viewpoint or the achievements of American musicology. The real glory of the volume is its two immense lists of *Libraries* and *Editions, historical.* The bibliographical notes, if unsystematic, will be very useful to graduate students. It is the only musical dictionary in one volume of such pretensions and range, taking in terms like *Echegiatta, Echiquier,* and *Ecphonetic notation.* The learning and labor behind such an enterprise are formidable, and it is a tragedy that it has been marred by poverty of thought, inconsistent editing, and a rebarbative style of writing.

I feel myself competent in only a small part of the range of this book, but it is difficult to take on trust a dictionary that defines the scheme of the medieval *ballade* incoherently (the last two lines appear to rhyme with nothing at all), and that is both embarrassing and inaccurate about Chopin's ballades. It is, perhaps, merely bad luck that (p. 94) of the two examples of ternary form given, one (the slow movement of Beethoven's op. 10 no. 3) should be binary according to the dictionary's own discussion of an often-confused term (first paragraph of p. 95), and in any case is not ternary. Even simple terms like *Waldhorn* and *Arabesque* are improperly defined. "Waldhorn" is only used today to mean a French horn *without* valves (and that is, in fact, the way the dictionary itself uses it on p. 392), and the unmentioned analogy with a curved, unbroken ornamental line is essential to any musical use of the word "arabesque."

The dangers of this pedestrian, unreliable, and often useful book may be illustrated from within its own covers. The *Harvard Dictionary* (p. 517) thinks that Schoenberg's *Erwartung* consists of spoken dialogue with a musical background. Not even *Sprechstimme*—real, genuine, honest-to-goodness spoken dialogue. How can this be? Even if we admit Apel's ill-mannered remarks elsewhere (p. 482) about Schoenberg's "unvocal line," the soprano in *Erwartung* sounds at least as if she is *trying* to sing. How did anyone get the idea there was any spoken dialogue?

It is possible to reconstruct what happened. The correct term for spoken dialogue against a musical background is *melodrama,* and the article so named remarks that "if only one or two actors are involved, the terms 'monodrama' or 'duodrama' may be used." *Monodrama* reads "See under Melodrama." Schoenberg called *Erwartung* a monodrama because there is only one singer. Somebody working on the dictionary had a sudden twinge of conscience and did some rare but this time unfortunate cross-referencing.

It remains to be added that the book is handsomely presented, the paper is splendidly white, the print agreeably black and legible. The text has been admirably proofread (a difficult task for such a long work), but the musical examples swarm unprecedentedly with errors. In *Arioso*, to quote only a single instance out of a hundred, one mistake from the first edition has been corrected and three new ones have been added. Many of the notes are printed so that they are neither quite on nor off a line. The volume is sturdily bound, and sports its crimson colors bravely.

CHAPTER FOURTEEN

Dictionaries: the New Grove's

The New Grove's *gave a relatively good reflection of the world of musicology in 1980, and* The New York Review of Books *wanted an article which would be an assessment of that world. At that time, there was bitter opposition between historians and analysts. For the analysts, music existed in an atemporal sphere, and a work could be understood equally well outside of any cultural context, if one would only spend the time understanding its deep structure and its surface intricacies. For the historians, elaborate analysis was a waste of time: recognizing the themes and motifs and knowing what key the music is in was all the analysis that was needed, and one could go on to more piquant matters like social function and biography. The result was, on the one hand, a natural reaction against the abstract and absurd constraints of strict analysis, the best-known example being Professor Joseph Kerman's, arising no doubt from feelings of guilt at having practiced analysis himself so skillfully. Historians, on the other hand, were often reduced to the crudest generalizations about the history of style, could not distinguish between significant and trivial motivic relations, and did not always recognize that merely identifying the tonality is not always a simple matter.*

It was as a demonstration of this rift, only imperfectly healed today, that my account of Andrew Porter's attempt at tonal analysis is so harsh and so lengthy (I have very slightly abridged it here, but have left in a mistake that I myself made that was caught by Edward T. Cone and Walter Frisch). Andrew Porter was too distinguished a critic for a simple affirmation of these errors to be believed, and a lengthy presentation was necessary. It is only fair to Porter to note here that his Grove's *article does not represent him at his best or even properly display the invaluable research he has done on Verdi. And it should be added that his mistakes in analysis are made by other historians, including (see Chapter 4 above) the great H. C. Robbins Landon. At the root of several of these errors is the unfounded belief that a chord attacked by its dominant is enough to define a key. This makes nonsense of the relation between*

*a key area and local harmonic movement, a relation essential to all tonal music
from 1700 to 1900. Graduate students in musicology continue to misunderstand the
question, although the late Donald Francis Tovey wrote some eloquent pages about
it. The problem in theory today, as Alexander Goehr has wisely observed, is that students are trained in very advanced and sophisticated forms of analysis, and the simpler principles, which Schenker and others took for granted and even dismissed because they seemed so obvious then, have been forgotten.*

*Dr. Stanley Sadie's point, made in a letter, that they could find no one person
who could have written on "Music" and the changing significance of the term
through the ages was disingenuous. The article on the "Mass" through the ages has
seven authors, and even then, none of them seems to think it worth mentioning that
the musical representation and expression of the words of the mass changed radically from the fifteenth to the twentieth century.*

*This review turned out to be useful. When the Schubert article was reissued as a
book, the gaps I complained of were very substantially filled. The publishers of* The
New Grove*'s used a quotation from the review in almost all their publicity for two
decades, so they must in the end have been pleased.*

THE makers of dictionaries and encyclopedists in general have mixed, impure
motives. The simple alphabetical order of the articles disguises other orders,
more complex, less explicit. The editors of *Webster's Third New International
Dictionary,* for example, wished to transform our notions of what was correct
speech and to legitimize a whole series of popular American usages. Pierre
Bayle's great *Dictionnaire historique et critique* of 1695–1720 was a covert attack
on religious intolerance. His spiritual descendants, the editors of the famous
French *Encyclopédie,* hoped to transform society and all the traditional institutions of Europe. The first edition of Grove's *Dictionary of Music and Musicians* of
1877 was an extension of George Grove's activity as a promoter of concerts at the
Crystal Palace in London. It was intended to educate and widen the potential
audience, and to confirm its taste for what Grove considered the best classical
music.

Grove was, in fact, one of the most important forces in the establishment of
Schubert's reputation in nineteenth-century England. Grove's *Dictionary* was
meant primarily for the educated layman, for those who hoped to set their appreciation of concert music on a firmer foundation, to correct their taste by
knowledge. It went successfully through five editions, each one brought more or
less unsuccessfully up to date. In the later editions, of course, what was left of the
original stock of articles had often been cut, slashed, and generally disfigured by
rewriting.

The arrival in the 1950s of a German rival in fourteen volumes, *Musik in*

Geschichte und Gegenwart (familiarly called MGG), put the preeminence of *Grove's* into question. Musicology had meanwhile become an important and moderately thriving academic discipline, and until the 1930s the Germans had been the leaders in the field. A transition into English of MGG was proposed and, fortunately, rejected. It was decided to redo *Grove's* almost from scratch, using practically nothing from previous editions. This was a courageous and a sound decision. Stanley Sadie, critic of the London *Times,* was appointed editor-in-chief, and turned the *New Grove* from the start into an Anglo-American enterprise. Partly because of the influx of exiles from Hitler's Europe and partly because of the academic explosion of the 1950s and 1960s, during which even musicology became a growth industry, the United States had outstripped Germany in the production of valuable musicological research. The music departments of British universities are few in number, and ill-endowed; against what they considered the high-powered, jargon-ridden, and German-influenced work of American musicologists, the British gloried in the native tradition of the gentleman-amateur in music, with his superior taste and his mastery of belle-lettristic style. Nevertheless the *New Grove,* although still parochially British to some extent, is largely dominated by the Americans, with a good deal of aid from the most distinguished European scholars.

The layman, to whom Sir George Grove addressed his work, has not been completely forgotten in the *New Grove,* but he takes second place (and a distant second, at that) to the professional. Not the professional musician, mind, but the professional musicologist. The performer and the composer will find a great deal to interest them in these pages, but not often much help—less, in a few instances, than they could find in some shorter musical dictionaries. The *New Grove* is a monument to present-day musicology, considered as a science or a humanistic discipline, a *summa* of musicological knowledge, a mirror of the profession.

The priorities may be seen in the listing of performers and musicologists. There are far too many unimportant entries for both, but whereas every minor musicologist receives a relatively full bibliography of his articles and books, only occasional mention is made of the recordings of a performing musician, and no discography is attempted. In the case of jazz musicians, whose work as composer-performers was rarely written down but often recorded, the omission of even a selective discography shows a lack of common sense, not compensated by a list of books that enables one to guess where a discography might be found.

The entries on individual musicologists generally repeat in large print what can be more exactly deduced from the appended bibliography. The breath of criticism is rarely allowed to ruffle the placid surface of these bland entries, and the *New Grove* reads like a musical encyclopedia into which a computer has alphabetically intercalated a union directory. One ought not to complain about the wasted space, since it is precisely this sense of the dignity of a profession that is responsible for the triumphs of the *New Grove.*

And there are many triumphs. Foremost among them should come Harold S. Powers's article on Mode,[1] which reads like the brilliant, extensive, and elegant summing up of a life's work. I am, of course, incompetent to deal with many sections of this article, which occupies more than 150 columns, and I take much of it on trust, but the pages on modal theory of the fifteenth and sixteenth centuries have an unsurpassed clarity and cogency. Powers not only outlines the way the old Gregorian modes were conceived at the time but also discusses the extent to which the theories did or did not play a role in the composition of music. Carl Dahlhaus's article on Counterpoint after 1600 has a similar brilliance without as much fullness: Dahlhaus, with full justification, mounts an extraordinary polemical attack on the most common views of the relations of harmony and counterpoint.

Both these articles require from the reader a considerable background in musicological literature, and in music as well. The layman will find them impenetrable, the amateur and professional musician difficult. I doubt that many doctoral candidates in musicology will get through them with ease. The average student has almost disappeared as a possible audience here: Powers and Dahlhaus are writing for colleagues. No doubt we must say (along with the admirers of Symbolist poetry): so much the worse for the common reader if one can produce writing of such excellence.

There are many articles in the *New Grove* of similar quality, and from many of these the common reader can benefit. But he is never present for long in the writers' and editors' view of their public. For example, about nineteenth- and twentieth-century gavottes M. E. Little writes: "While all these share the duple metre of the old dance, none seems to have more than a vague neoclassical association with older music, nor exhibits any of the rhythms characteristic of the Baroque Gavotte." No doubt the old gavotte was very different from the one Prokofiev wrote in the "Classical" Symphony, but in that case what did Prokofiev—and everybody else in the twentieth century—think a gavotte was? Modern gavottes do have certain rhythmic characteristics in common—at least, the modern gavotte is no more inconsistent than the seventeenth-century one was. The readers who expect to find out what most musicians today think a ga-

1. The best definition of a modal system that does not go into technical detail would be "a means of classifying the ranges and types of melody."

votte is are not going to find out from the *New Grove*. (They could find out quite clearly from Don Randel's *Harvard Concise Dictionary of Music*.)

Other examples of this neglect are only too easy to find. Here are two more: In "Donizetti," we are told about *"pertichini,"* and the reader who thinks they are a little-known form of pasta will not be enlightened anywhere in the *New Grove*. In "Gossec," we learn that this composer used "rocket themes." If the reader looks under R, he will be wasting his time. (I know where "rocket themes" are defined in the *New Grove*, but I am not going to tell.)

II

The heart of *Grove's Dictionary* was always in the long biographical entries on composers, and the *New Grove* is no different. It has, in fact, considerably improved on its predecessors and provides perhaps the finest body of articles on composers to be found in any reference work. Many are models of their kind, but before coming to them, I must record two exemplary and instructive misadventures: Maurice Brown's "Schubert" and Andrew Porter's "Verdi."

Porter is brilliant and satisfying on Verdi's relations with his librettists, and good on Verdi's life. It is in the section labeled "Composition, Style," where he comes to the music, that his problems begin. He astonishingly groups all the middle-period operas from *Ernani* to *The Sicilian Vespers* together in this section, making a kind of monstrous amalgam about which he produces scattered observations, so that no sense of musical or dramatic growth comes forth. Even the late operas are stirred into the mixture. Verdi's progress was not all upward in a straight line, of course, but those middle years from 1843 to 1855 were ones of great and interesting development.

An even graver defect is that Porter is able to convey no sense of how Verdi organizes an act. He mentions harmonic organization, and toys with it briefly and helplessly, finding too many contradictions. About the integration of aria, dialogue, scene painting, and action, which is at the center of Verdi's musical achievement, he has not a word to say. Perhaps for this reason, when he arrives at the late operas, he does not mention the third act of *Aida*, which has generally been considered the *locus classicus* of such integration. On such matters, as well as on Verdi's development of dramatic effect, the reader will learn more from Frank Walker's jolly and superficial article on Verdi in the previous edition of *Grove's*.

Finally, the whole section on Verdi's music is filled with mistakes of analysis. These mistakes are of so elementary a nature that it is astonishing to find them in a musical encyclopedia of such high standards. I am afraid that I must detail some of them here if I am to be believed, and I hope that readers with no taste for these matters will skip the next few paragraphs.

Porter begins by discussing harmonic movement in Verdi, and writes:

> Ex. 1 demonstrates one characteristic way of reaching D-flat major, a key much favoured by Verdi; *Il trovatore* can provide three others. The Act I trio, the baritone's scena in Act 2, and the tenor's aria (not its cabaletta) all end in D flat, though none begins in it. In the trio, Di Luna strikes into the key from its relative minor, by attaching a high F natural, *tutta forza* after a series of phrases starting with an emphatic F flat. The aria of his scena begins in B flat ("Il balen"); from a cadence in that key, a chromatic sequence settles on E flat, treated as dominant of a little A flat chorus, whose final notes are then reiterated as a dominant to the D flat cabaletta ("Per me l'ora fatale"). Manrico's "Ah si, ben mio" begins in F minor and then makes 3rd moves to A flat, F flat, then A flat again as dominant to the D flat final section.

Even if the three examples from *Il Trovatore* were correct, they would be of no interest. Why would anyone want to know how Verdi gets to D flat major, unless it was as an illustration of some larger point about Verdi's harmony?[2] As Porter himself writes later: "Verdi's predecessors all made notable departures from the standard form. So did he. It need only be remarked what is particularly individual about his practices." None of Porter's observations reveals anything about Verdi's technique that could not be duplicated earlier in Rossini, Meyerbeer, or Donizetti. In any case, Porter's analysis of each one of the three examples contains a vital error.

The first one is the most foolish: the Act I trio does not go from the relative minor (i.e., B flat minor) to D flat major, but is in D flat all the time. It goes from *D flat minor* to D flat major, and there is no change of key, but only a change of mode.

In the second example, the baritone scena "Il balen," the crucial step in the harmonic movement which makes the structure intelligible has been omitted. After the end of the aria in B flat, there is a jump from that key into F minor. This key is the relative minor of A flat major, and Verdi has already modulated to A flat major by the time the chromatic sequence on E flat has begun. It is the leap

---

2. The context suggests that Porter is talking about the use of mediant relationships, but I cannot believe that he thinks that the movement from relative minor to major, although a minor third away, can be classified as a mediant relationship.

into F minor which therefore provides the fundamental preparation for the move to D flat major through its dominant A flat. (The chromatic sequence mentioned by Porter is subsidiary, and confirms an action which is largely accomplished.)

It is the third example which reveals the most misleading confusion. The series F minor, A flat, F flat, A flat, and D flat is a set of objects of different orders of magnitude rather like "Afghanistan, Schenectady, and Times Square." F minor, the first A flat, and the D flat are keys, the second established as a secondary related tonality. The second A flat is only a chord, and F flat is the prolongation of a chord into a phrase. Neither has been established as a key. Here, once again, Porter has left out a crucial step, one which explains the F flat. There is a change of mode from A flat major to A flat minor, and the F flat is merely a harmony in the minor mode prolonged through several measures. Unless this hierarchy is understood, no account of tonal relations makes any sense: it would seem as if the great D. F. Tovey had written in vain.

Perhaps I should say at once that I do not consider this form of analysis (by tonal area and harmonic roots) particularly interesting or of much value in itself until it is combined with other considerations; I would agree with many schools of analysis (like that of Schenker) that it touches only the surface of the music. However, if it is to be done at all, it should be done with professional competence.

In the paragraph that follows the examples from *Il Trovatore*, we find the following analysis of the duet "Sì, pel ciel," for Othello and Iago, from the end of the second act of *Otello:*

> Othello begins this duet in A; his line descends to a low mediant, which is treated as a C sharp tonic, and three bars later to a high mediant in the new key, to which the orchestra supplies F major harmony. Othello ends his strophe in F, but with his voice on the mediant, A, which Iago and the orchestra at once take up in an A major cadence, completing the chain of 3rd moves. Iago then sings the bass line that had accompanied Othello, but harmonized now with an effect of 6-4 on its recurrent A.

This does not make pleasant reading even if one has the score or knows the passage by heart. The only point of such writing is a display of technical expertise—an expertise gravely compromised by the final observation "but harmonized now with an effect of 6-4 on its recurrent A." Porter has not noticed that the duet starts with a 6-4 chord, and that every important harmonic change is in the 6-4 position. We can therefore make Porter's two points about mediant relationships and 6-4 chords more clearly and more accurately, and replace all of his clotted prose with the following simple sentence: "The melody is conceived on a large scale as a series of rising mediants (A, C sharp, F natural, A), each step emphasized by a 6-4 chord." This would be understandable even without a score.

To lay bare such errors is harsh. After all, conductors give false cues, oboists crack at expressive moments, and pianists hit wrong notes. In an opera catalogue, I once listed a cello as a trombone, a mistake more comic than anything in Porter. But Porter's mistakes are systematic, and they concern the elementary principles of harmonic relations. And all of these mistakes occur in a single column of the entry.

The later operas from *Simon Boccanegra* on are treated chronologically and individually. Porter's treatment of the revisions of several of the operas and Verdi's work with the librettists is informative and enlightening. His account of these late years is well done, in an entertaining journalistic style that sets it apart from the other contributions to the *New Grove*.

There is, finally, in this exceptionally long article on Verdi no convincing assessment of Verdi's relation to his contemporaries. An instance of this failure is the treatment of the "patriotic" element in Verdi's music. Porter speaks eloquently of the "power of Verdi's melodies and strong, slow-surging rhythms to generate mass emotion." Nowhere does he mention that this power to generate mass emotion is a characteristic of nineteenth-century grand opera from the Napoleonic period on. Influenced by the cantatas composed for the *fêtes* of the French Revolution, opera became the chief vehicle for the stirring march rhythms that are presumed to incite jingoism. Auber's *La Muette de Portici* is even said to have caused a revolution in Belgium. Rossini (with *William Tell*) and Meyerbeer were the composers from whom Verdi learned most for this aspect of his musical technique. The political significance of operas like *Un Ballo in Maschera* and *Simon Boccanegra* does not interest Porter. The ferocious anticlericalism expressed in *Aida* (by musical as well as verbal means) is only relevant for him as revealing Verdi's personal belief. We learn more about the politics of Verdi's career from earlier editions of *Grove's*.

Other contributors to the *New Grove* were either less adventurous or more expert. Many of them prudently offer no technical information at all. The entry on Prokofiev goes into enormous detail about the life but barely mentions the works beyond giving titles and dates; you would never know from *Grove* that Prokofiev had ever changed his style, or even that he had one. Some composers were divided up between two contributors: it would perhaps have been wiser to treat Verdi like Beethoven, for whom Alan Tyson wrote the biographical, Joseph

Kerman the musical, sections—but it must be added that Tyson is incapable of the kind of mistake that one finds in Porter.

"Donizetti" was divided up, with Julian Budden taking the purely musical section: he enables us to trace his composer's progress with great clarity, and his technical comments are always judicious, unpretentious, and illuminating. Friedrich Lippman wrote "Bellini": there are unfortunately no musical examples, but many specific references to the music, all of which I found to be exact on consulting the score, as one would naturally expect from Lippman.

The disaster of the late Maurice Brown's "Schubert" is a much graver matter: it arises not from imperfect competence or ambition but from a perversity in no way individual but professional. After recounting the life in much detail, Brown reaches the music. Amazingly and absurdly, there is no discussion of the significance of Schubert's song cycles. I went over the article several times before believing that this could be so. *Die Schöne Müllerin* is not mentioned at all except for its date in the biographical section—and the new tragic tone of the individual songs of *Die Winterreise* is briefly discussed under "Mature Instrumental Music"!

Nowhere does the entry tell us what a Schubert song cycle is, and how it differs from Beethoven's (and you are not going to find out from the inadequate article on "Song Cycles" either). Nowhere is the nature of what might be considered Schubert's greatest achievement set out for the curious reader. The choral music gets even shorter shrift: in the section on the music, the beautiful series of works for male chorus and the masterpiece that is the A flat major Mass are wholly ignored. The famous problem of Schubert's omission of part of the text of the "Credo" did not catch Brown's attention.

On the other hand, we find two and a half columns on Schubert's operas, which are of little interest to anyone except to a writer seeking to attract attention by exploring a wasteland where few have ventured before—and with good reason. (Not that there are not some good pages in some of the operas—how could there not be somewhere in a five-act opera by Schubert?) These columns are preceded by revealing sentences: "Nowadays the last of the sonatas in B flat (D. 960) is frequently played and has taken its place with foremost examples of the classical sonata. His operas still await discovery, and thus need to be discussed in more detail."

III

The editorial standard of the *New Grove* is very high. A certain amount of foolishness is bound to creep into an enormous undertaking, but there are no other such major blunders in the articles on composers. (I have read all the longer biographical entries, and hundreds of the shorter ones as well.) Before turning again to celebrate the triumphs of the *New Grove,* it may be asked how "Schubert" and "Verdi" could have been printed in their present state. There were numerous subeditors; much busy checking of facts and theories went on during the long gestation period. Some articles indeed were almost withdrawn by their authors because of subeditorial rewriting. To see how these mistakes could slip by is to realize how the *New Grove* is in many ways the mirror of contemporary musicology. The extreme case often reveals what is hidden at the center.

The preference for the unknown and the imperfectly appreciated is natural in a profession devoted to the production of doctoral theses and research papers. No other biographical article in the *New Grove* throws overboard the most important works to make room for the author's narrow specialty as "Schubert" does, but many give disproportionate emphasis to the little-known. This is, in fact, not at all something to be deplored, but a good thing—provided that what is most important is given at least adequate treatment.

No one could object to the lengthy paragraphs on Mendelssohn's *Singspiel* if the *Songs Without Words*—perhaps his most influential works for many decades—had been accorded more than two sentences (and not very interesting ones). The generous space given to Gesualdo's religious works or to Rossini's piano music are welcome because the madrigals of the former and the operas of the latter are so satisfyingly presented. Given the professional bias, it is surprising but not really incomprehensible that after Brown's death in 1975 his article was not given to someone else for a necessary expansion. (The article is, in fact, a revision of the one in the previous edition of *Grove's.* Brown never discussed the song cycles, but he did treat the choral music—could this section have been dropped by accident in the revision?)

The errors in musical analysis in "Verdi" probably went uncorrected for a different reason. Scholars of Western music are divided by and large into two groups: historians and analysts. They do not much like or trust each other. Historians who have mastered analytical techniques are rare (although there are more than there used to be); analysts with a sense of history are perhaps even rarer. I should imagine that the subeditors of the biographical entries were historians even less equipped to deal with music theory than the authors they were checking. At any rate, such matters evidently did not lie close to their hearts.

This rift in musicological ranks is detectable throughout the *New Grove.* In many of the theoretical articles there is a lack of historical perspective. In most of the historical and biographical entries the theory is fairly primitive, and does not provide considerations of much interest, even where no gross errors have crept in. There are some grand exceptions to this opposition, however, and they provide the glories of the new edition. And it must be further admitted that there are cases where the mastery of one part of the musicological discipline is so fine that it would be ungracious to complain about what is missing.

Many of the biographical articles cannot be too highly praised. The "Haydn" of Jens Peter Larsen repeats what he has been saying for years, but it is good to have it in English at last. The "Beethoven" of Tyson and Kerman is now the best available summary of recent thought and research on his life and work, and contains much that is original as well. Everything of importance is covered, and it is all readable. The summary of Beethoven's place in history could not be bettered.

Kerman's "Byrd" is equally fine and even more beautifully written. The "Handel," "Bizet," and last sections of "Gluck" are by Winton Dean. They are informative, provocative, and entertaining.[3] If there is an article in the *New Grove* about one of the contributors, it generally lists the major articles that he wrote for the dictionary—a form of self-reference which is very useful. The article on Dean, however, suppresses this information. And while we are on this subject, why does the list of contributors in the final volume not tell us what they contributed? What is the use of knowing that Robert L. Marshall contributed to the dictionary if you cannot find out without a page-to-page search that he wrote the splendid series of articles on the chorale?

The "Rossini" of Philip Gossett is a dazzling model of its genre: the relation of Rossini to his time, the nature of his originality, his contributions to new formal structures, the details of his career—all this is set out with clarity and wit. A good deal of the history of the nineteenth-century Italian opera is illuminated in this one entry. The "Frescobaldi" of Antony Newcomb is also very fine and continuously interesting. Lewis Lockwood did the "Palestrina" with great elegance (as well as the excellent articles on "Renaissance" and on "Ferrara"): one wishes only that it were longer. His contribution to "Musica Ficta" and his "Cantus Firmus" are so good that one would like them expanded to twice their length as well.

The "Mozart" by Stanley Sadie, editor-in-chief, is clear, readable, judicious, and embodies much of the latest research. The biographical section of "Wagner" is by someone called Curt von Westernhagen (he was not distinguished enough to get an entry in the *New Grove*, so I do not know where they found him, although the bibliography indicates that he has been working on Wagner since the 1950s). It is enlivened by a spirited defense of Wagner's anti-Semitism which I

---

3. In the article on "Berenstadt, Gaetano," Dean opines that castrati rarely had a sense of humor: how does he know? And he unfortunately makes no distinction in "Handel" between the keyboard suites that are completely written out and those that are left bare for improvisation.

do not much appreciate; the sections on Wagner's music by Carl Dahlhaus are brilliant and original, as one would expect from this great scholar. He dismisses *Rienzi* with two sentences of no comment (I was amused to note that he, too, cannot bring himself to look at that score again—"the *worst* opera that Meyerbeer ever wrote" is how I think it should be known), but the pages on *Tristan* and *Die Meistersinger* are remarkable (particularly the insistence on the implicit chromatic background to the diatonicism of the latter work).

Nicholas Temperley's essay on the music of Chopin is a great improvement over earlier efforts in *Grove's* and over other reference works as well, but the article as a whole is an ill-sewn crazy quilt. The biography is the old one by Arthur Hedley tinkered with by Maurice Brown and a subeditor (only a subeditor desperate to justify his existence would have made the kind of niggling stylistic changes which neither improve nor worsen the original). They have left standing Hedley's foolish denial of George Sand's claim that Chopin revised and then went back to the original version, although an examination of the manuscripts will show that this was indeed sometimes the case; and they have added: "For Schumann, to whom Chopin owed the doubtful honor of being placed with Pantaloon and Columbine in the musical charade of *Carnaval,* he had little respect." Chopin's place in *Carnaval* is not with Pantaloon and Columbine, but between "Chiarina" and "Estrella," that is, between the musical portraits of Clara Wieck and Ernestine von Fricken, the two women that Schumann loved.

Temperley claims the *Préludes* of Chopin represent "the art of 'preluding'... used in the type of salon concert that Chopin occasionally gave." That type of preluding, however, was modulatory—to get pianists from a piece in B, say, to one in F. I used to hear elderly pianists (like Moritz Rosenthal and Josef Hoffmann) do that when I was a child, and it has little to do with Chopin's *Préludes.*

Temperley has many fine things to say about Chopin, but his understanding of Chopin's polyphony is not very profound. Chopin's transformation of what he learned from Bach was complex, and the relation of inner voices to melody is extraordinary. Temperley also misinterprets Chopin's phrase structure.[4] Never-

---

4. He cites a rare exception from the conventional four- and eight-bar phrase: "What some consider his greatest melody, that of the Study, op. 10, no. 3, . . . is built in units five, three, five and seven and a half bars long." Five and three make eight, and the seven and a half is clearly divided by Chopin into three and four and a half. The four and a half is a five, as it ends on the fifth measure and the new phrase begins on an upbeat. The structure is

$$\overbrace{5 + 3}^{8} + \underbrace{\overbrace{5 + 3}^{8} + 5}_{8}$$

theless, his discussion is on a high level, it dispels most of the more banal misapprehensions of Chopin's work, and it treats Chopin's historical position excellently and succinctly.[5]

Contemporary composers have been bravely tackled. The "Berg" of George Perle and the "Bartók" of Vera Lampert and Laszlö Somfai are both outstanding (although the latter unfortunately does not mention Bartók's experiments with quarter tones or discuss the extraordinary rhythmic experiment of the third piano etude); and Bayan Northcott's article on Elliott Carter is excellent. The article on Roger Sessions is absurdly inadequate—indeed, incredibly so, and it took two authors to produce this mouse; except for the part that comes from *Who's Who,* there are only a couple of columns of text (and two examples). The entry on Leonard Bernstein is equally unsatisfactory, with no real assessment of his achievement as composer, conductor, and educator. The article on George Antheil does not say anything much about the music, but at least it tells us that he collaborated with Hedy Lamarr in inventing a torpedo.

Most important living composers have found satisfactory advocates in the *New Grove,* and you would hardly guess from their defenders that any of them had ever provoked hostile criticism. Admiration is the order of the day, and the articles on twentieth-century music turn out somewhat bland. I suppose this was inevitable, and it is better than having a series of hostile entries, like the ones on Schoenberg and Stravinsky that were such a disgrace in the earlier editions of *Grove's.*

The only modern composer who gets the knife in the new edition is Carl Orff. Since I have always detested the music of Orff, I have no personal objection, but it does abstractly seem a little unfair when others of equally low merits receive their meed of praise. Hanspeter Krellman writes: "Having discovered his technique in *Carmina Burana* Orff has continued to use the same means, though his later works are distinguished by a diminishing musical content and increasing metaphysical pretensions." A little later he ends by giving his subject the coup de grâce: "Orff's success has been in proving the potency of barbarism, and its limitations." The editors add a long assessment of Orff's educational work and print a big picture of a stage set for *Carmina Burana,* but I cannot think this will appease admirers of Orff. A great deal more of this kind of writing would have made the *New Grove* a livelier and even a better dictionary, but that would have

---

In other words, there is an overlapping grid of eight measures. This is very typical of Chopin, who often groups phrases by 7 + 9, and gives a wonderful surface suppleness to a slow, eight-measure beat with an almost hypnotic effect.

5. But when he says that "Bach and Mozart were his favorite masters," we must add Hummel to the list, since his influence extends at least until 1844.

meant the editors' sticking their necks out, and no one likes to fear that he will look a fool in a couple of decades.

There seems to have been no consistent policy about musical examples. Why should there be several for Domenico Scarlatti (in an excellent entry by Joel Sheveloff) and none for Clément Jannequin, the greatest French composer of the first half of the sixteenth century, too briefly treated by Howard Mayer Brown? Bibliographical policy was equally erratic. Modern editions of Wagenseil are not mentioned (at least for the concertos), while for other composers we can find out what has recently been made available.

I have certainly forgotten to cite some of the finest articles on composers, as well as a very large number that are merely completely satisfactory (that "merely" seems churlish, but what else is there to say about good entries printed alongside those which are incomparably better?). However, when we are faced with a monument like the *New Grove*, some problems of editorial policy should be mentioned. The difficulty of their solution is instructive about the state of musicology today.

IV

Contributors were, to a certain extent, given their head—by and large, a good thing. Some treated life and works together, some separated them, some alternated them decade by decade or period by period. In general, this worked well. Yet there are certain aspects of every composer's work that need to be taken up in a work of reference such as *Grove*: the influences on his work, his relation to his contemporaries, and, finally, *Rezeptionsgeschichte*—that is, the history of a composer after his death, the publication of his works (including the state of the text), his influence on posterity, his reputation and his place in concert life including the performances of the present day. Some contributors cover all of these, most leave out something or other.

The most influential composer in the history of music is J. S. Bach. The article on "Bach," started by Walter Emery and finished by Christoph Wolff, is one of the finest in the *New Grove*. It stops short with Bach's death in 1750. This is not Professor Wolff's fault. He was evidently told that someone else was to cover the history of Bach's music after his death. There is, indeed, an article called "The Bach Revival" by Nicholas Temperley. It does not fill the gap, or rather the yawning gulf, in the *New Grove*. The treatment of Bach's reputation in the latter half of the eighteenth century is deeply inadequate. Temperley does not think it interesting enough to mention that the thirteen-year-old Beethoven knew the *Well-Tempered Clavier* by heart. (And why does Temperley think that with the works of the last years Bach "turned his back on what remained of his public" when his final work, *The Art of Fugue,* was prepared for publication almost at once by the composer?) "The Bach Revival" has only two sections: (1) Germany and Austria; and (2) England. I can see that Italy was not interested in Bach, but what happened to France?

Nor does the article treat the influence of Bach's music on composers of the first half of the nineteenth century—Mendelssohn, Chopin, and so forth. This information is scattered elsewhere (and sometimes even simply forgotten)—but there are no cross-references and no index. Temperley's history of English performances of Bach before 1850 is interesting. After 1850, however, all is silence. The Bach Revival had been accomplished. The role of Bach's music as the most important in music education that we have known; the extraordinary changes in the performance of Bach's music in the past century; the totally unfounded theories of the early twentieth century that *The Art of Fugue* was for some unspecified ensemble instead of for two hands at the keyboard as everyone had known until then; the gradual entry of the Goldberg Variations into the public consciousness largely through recordings—all this does not, for the *New Grove,* belong to the history of music.

One might almost infer something shameful about the history of Bach performance. The article on Busoni hurriedly dismisses his arrangement of Bach's organ works in two sentences, and stays mum about his extraordinary and influential edition of Bach. When one reaches "Liszt," Humphrey Searle writes only that "Liszt's arrangements [of Bach's organ preludes and fugues] are simple and straightforward and quite in keeping with the spirit of the music." Six of them are, but the seventh is not. And why is a simple and straightforward arrangement in keeping with the spirit of Bach's music? His own arrangements were sufficiently extravagant.

Wolff's completion of the little that Emery had been able to write on Bach is so grandly satisfying and so clear that another lack goes almost unperceived: a discussion of recent theories on symbolism or numerology in Bach. (You will not find anything about symbolism in the music of Bach if you look at the article on Albert Schweitzer either.) I presume that Wolff considers most of these theories silly, and so do I, but the nonsense inspired by a composer's music is often an important part of history. In a dictionary of this scope, the nonsense should have been sympathetically presented and then refuted. There should at least have been a cross-reference to "Cryptography," which lists the studies of numerology in its bibliography.

The problems of editing music do not in general seem to interest most of the contributors to the *New Grove,* perhaps because the day when you could get a Ph.D. in music history just by making an edition of an unpublished piece of ancient music is fast disappearing. (Some of those doctoral editions were more useful and a lot more interesting than the theses that have replaced them.) In any case, the article on Brahms does not bother to tell us that he edited Couperin, the Chopin mazurkas, the Schubert symphonies, and the Mozart Requiem, and realized the figured bass for some of the volumes of Handel (and the bibliography lists none of his editorial work). The article "Editing" by Howard Mayer Brown becomes very perfunctory in the last section, entitled "Music from 1750 to the Present Day": most composers after Beethoven, he tells us, "followed his example by preparing their scores in so detailed a way that virtually every decision about performance was set down in writing, leaving performers merely to follow their instructions." The naïveté of this is particularly staggering in so sophisticated a writer as Professor Brown. It actually represents, however, a considerable progress in musicological thought. In the 1969 edition of the *Harvard Dictionary of Music*, under "Performance Practice," we read, "In the period after Bach the problems of performance practice largely disappear, owing to the more specific directions of composers for clearly indicating their intentions." The awareness of the subject has now been pushed up a half century from Bach to Beethoven. With a little effort we can get it up to Boulez.

The state of the text for each composer is sometimes dealt with well: by Dean for Handel, and by Karela Johnson Snyder for Buxtehude, for example. By others, it is brushed aside without comment. In his revision of his old article on Schumann, Gerald Abrahams passes over in silence the grave problems of all editions of Schumann's music, including the most recent.

V

There is no article on "Music" in the *New Grove*. No doubt the editors think that they and everybody else know what music is and what "music" means. From a purely modern point of view they are quite right, and such historical innocence is disarming. The word music and its earlier equivalents (μουσική, *musica*) have signified very different things from the Greeks to our time: present-day readers would not even suspect some of these meanings. What has been accepted as music by different cultures at different times has varied widely.

Would Mozart have considered Stockhausen, or even Harold Arlen, music? (Which reminds me, the article on Arlen, whom many consider to be the finest writer of popular songs along with Gershwin, is grossly inadequate.) Schumann thought the last movement of Chopin's B-flat minor sonata was not music, and Chopin felt the same of Schumann's *Carnaval*. Surely an article that made us understand what they could have meant would have been a credit to the *New Grove*.

A little more skepticism would help our study of music in every way. A little less confidence that scholars know what music is, or even what a piece of music is, a little more uncertainty about what the history of music is and how it is to be approached, a larger suspicion that the way to arrive at an adequate idea of performance is never simple and absolutely never straightforward—this is what we all, musicologists, critics, and performers, need to acquire. In other arts and sciences the most common and fundamental axioms of the different disciplines are being questioned, but not in musicology—at least not in the *New Grove*. The self-confidence is sometimes appalling: we are told in "Word Painting" that the art of expressing an individual word by music ceased after the Renaissance and the Baroque, except for the rare composer like Haydn and Brahms! "History is what you remember" may have a certain subjective grandeur, but "history is what belongs to my narrow specialty" is only comically petty.

The blinkered sense of history that one finds in such a large body of the profession—I am not of course speaking of the dozens that transcend those limitations, but of the thousands who are happily unaware of them—made the article "Historiography" a kind of complacent bibliographical survey which raises few of the problems of writing felt so keenly in other fields—and for more than a century. *"Wie es eigentlich gewesen war"*—to reconstruct the past "the way it really was"—often seems to be the naïve ambition of the average music scholar. Those who stand a little aside are treated discourteously. The summary of the musicologist Leo Treitler's historiographical views is mistaken, and the article on Theodore Wiesengrund Adorno, about a quarter of the length it ought to be, is a travesty of his thought. I deeply dislike the work of Adorno, but he is the most important and influential writer of our time on the sociology of music, and no responsible historiographer would have treated him as the *New Grove* does.

Theory, with some great and honorable exceptions, seems to exist way above the sublunar, historical sphere. Else how could Roger Bullivant, in an otherwise mediocre article on "Fugue," write that Hindemith's *Ludus Tonalis* "is in fact intended, like Bach's *Art of Fugue*, for complete performance"? Except for this, Bullivant pays no attention to Bach's system of classifying fugues in the *Art of Fugue*, but why does he think Bach intended a complete performance? Under what circumstances? For what audience?

Roger Scruton's articles on "Expression" and on "Program Music" are among the best written in the *New Grove*. Although for Scruton the concept of "expression" has a history, the "nature of musical expression" has been platonically withdrawn from the reach of the hand of time. The possibilities of "expression" seem absurdly to be the same for all ages, for Gregorian chant as for the Italian madrigal. Program music, although it has a history, is not related to the history of musical style and to the way music is embedded in the cultures that produced it. This suggests that Scruton, like the editors of the *New Grove*, thinks there is something eternally fixed and absolutely independent of culture called Music (although revealed in different forms to different peoples)—which is why we do not need an article to tell us what musics are.

In "Absolute Music," Scruton never suspects for a moment the way the creation of this concept coincides with the rise of public performances of pure instrumental music. It would have been better for Scruton to have considered the purpose for which the idea was invented before examining its coherence or its tenability. A similar isolation from reality characterizes Winton Dean's graceful and charming revision of his earlier article on "Criticism." For him, in an elegant, old-fashioned way, criticism is judgment: it concerns only values. The role of the critic in musical life as a whole occurs to him only peripherally.

The critic disseminates information: he conveys professional opinion (advanced or reactionary, depending on his taste) to the lay public. He is necessary to the economy of music. If the article had been called something less highfalutin than "Criticism," like "Journalism," perhaps it would have been more cogent. However, when Dean says that critics should be gentle with performers who may be playing below their best, he warms my heart. He must be a very kind man. Nevertheless, *Grove* could use a whole new set of articles on aesthetics that relates it to the development of musical style, and to the realities of musical life.

Even for some of the historical articles, the static conception dilutes their usefulness. George J. Buelow's articles on rhetoric and music (a now very fashionable subject) represent a great advance in the study of Baroque music; they are interesting, beautifully documented, and solid—indeed, too solid. There is a very long list of rhetorical tropes with references and several musical examples; the references come from books written between 1601 and 1745. The impression given by the article that the use of rhetorical figures was a consistent practice from 1600 to 1750 supported by an unchanging body of doctrine is an illusion. History is much more jumbled than that. Buelow never asks to what extent rhetorical doctrine guided composers and to what extent it was a post-facto justification of things done for quite other reasons, and he never considers whether some of his tropes (like *antitheton,* a musical contrast) are so general that they could be found in practically any music anywhere any time.

The lack of historical perspective in musicology as reflected by the *New Grove* arises largely from the naïve but rooted belief that a piece of music is what a composer heard in his head as he wrote it down—or, since this is too speculative and unverifiable an approach, what his contemporaries thought the piece should sound like when they played it. This old-fashioned attitude is beginning to crumble, and there are many musicologists who understand the peculiar metaphysical and ontological assumptions on which it rests, but it appears solid in many quarters.

Both the erosion of the old philosophy and the resistance to change are revealed in one of the most useful and enlightened articles in the *New Grove*, Robert Donington's "Ornaments." At the end of the section on trills, he distinguishes brilliantly between the expressive trill of the Baroque (which is both a harmonic and melodic dissonance) and the modern trill, which is a prolongation and coloring device: "The modern trill, which is lower-note and unterminated . . ., is neither a harmonic ornament nor scarcely a melodic one, rather an ornament of emphasis or a coloration of the texture." Exactly. Then why does Donington a page earlier write: "Neither is it any more correct . . . to apply the modern trill to Beethoven than to J. S. Bach. . . . Hence Beethoven's trills should begin with the upper note"? It is clear that some of Beethoven's trills already reveal the modern emphatic and coloristic function while others retain the old expressive one.

Even if Beethoven played all his trills in the old-fashioned way as he was brought up to do, that by no means implies that he was right, but only that he did not see the significance of his own innovations. As a matter of fact, Beethoven vacillated: he began writing the trill at the end of the *Waldstein* sonata in the modern fashion and then crossed it out and shifted to the old. Was he right? My own practice would be to play Beethoven's trills inconsistently—bringing out the new functions the modern way, the old ones in Baroque fashion according to the passage and the context. (Perhaps there was no time at the last minute for the editors to enter the lengthy controversy between Robert Winters and W. S. Newman on this matter into Donington's bibliography.)

"Ornaments" is comically restricted to the Baroque era, leaving the Renaissance and the nineteenth century to "Improvisation," although not all of Renaissance and modern ornamentation is improvised and much is written down. That gives eighty columns for Baroque ornamentation, and six (in "Improvisation") for everything after 1800 (excluding jazz), a grotesque proportion. No details about Rossini's or Chopin's ornamentation are given, for example. But then in "Fingering," pianistic advance seems to stop with Czerny: none of the innovations of Chopin, Liszt, Ravel, or Stockhausen rates a mention.

Even more astonishing is Donington's omission of "Rubato" from his article on ornaments, although it was classified as an ornamental technique by eighteenth-century theorists. In his separate, brief, and drastically inadequate article under this heading, he does not quote Mozart's or Chopin's definition, or Türk's (in his *Klavierschule*, published in 1800, but written years before). Donington's description would not fit Mozart's practice (which was to play the melodic notes in the right hand late, after the left, the way Harold Bauer and Paderewski, among many others, used to do). He gives no examples. At least Liszt's strange system of signs for indicating rubato, invented in the first edition of the Paganini etudes, should be cited (they are also ignored in "Liszt," "Notation," and "Tempo and Expression Marks"); and an example of Mozart's written-out rubato should be printed (the slow movements of the C minor piano sonata, or the late A major violin sonata would provide good ones).

This would have provided some sense of historical continuity between the late eighteenth and the nineteenth century. A feeling for this would have helped the two contributors to the *New Grove* who say that E. T. A. Hoffmann considered Beethoven the typical Romantic composer, without adding that Haydn and Mozart were Romantic for him, too. And Bach as well. "Romanticism" by John Warrack goes no further than the platitudes of the 1930s and 1940s on this subject. There has been considerable revision of the prevailing ideas on Romanticism in literature and art recently. The platitudes of the 1970s may be no better than the earlier ones, but musicians do not need to be protected from them.

A noble exception to this isolation from non-musical culture is Daniel Heartz, whose articles "Rococo," "Classicism," "*Sturm und Drang*," and others show a wide and impressive grasp of recent developments. In my opinion, these articles are also wrong-headed, but I take no particular stock in my own opinion, so why should anybody else? Arguments would be necessary, and I have no more space to argue—only to urge everyone to read Professor Heartz.

The rigid historicism of orthodox musicological thought does not prevent some astounding anachronisms. The greatest composer in England at the end of the fifteenth century was John Browne, about whom nothing is known—understandably, with a name like that, no one can decide which of the possible John Brownes was a composer. The *New Grove* clearly knows how important he is, since it gives a full page of quotations of his music, an honor accorded to few others. Comments on these quotations are absolutely minimal, nor did the contributor, John Caldwell, think it necessary to list Frank Harrison's *Music in Medieval Britain* in the bibliography (he lists nothing at all except the music), although Harrison's pages on Browne are the only substantial thing written about him.

All that Caldwell finds to say on the third quotation is: "In the penultimate bar a particularly harsh form of false relation between [*sic*] the first, third and fourth voices is notated quite explicitly and insisted upon in a way which is most unusual in this period (ex. 3). Although the word is 'gaudia,' the use of this device perhaps suggests that the joy is not to be easily won." The "perhaps" of the last clause is an ineffective lightning-conductor: an ironic relation between text and music of this kind was just not possible around 1500. Even a sophisticated madrigalist a century later could not pull off a stunt like that: the appearance of such irony in the eighteenth century was a landmark in music and rare even then. But the comment rests on another anachronistic assumption: that an Englishman of the sixteenth century found false relations "harsh." "False relations" are a dissonant use of major and minor either simultaneously or one right after the other, and there is good reason to think that the English, in their eccentric way, enjoyed the effect. They certainly seem to have used it more than any other nation and may have thought it expressive but not in the least disagreeable.

Some articles transcend a narrow historicism: Barry Brook places the *"Symphonie Concertante"* in a large social and historical context and relates its development with great clarity. Howard Mayer Brown's "Chanson" is equally illuminating, but "Concerto" was written by a committee in a sort of parody of dictionary style—finding out details of the developing form or social function of the concerto is like trying to coax live snails out of their shells.

In "Modulation," history has wholly deserted theory, leaving it stranded high and dry. The eighteenth-century meaning is nowhere acknowledged (the term used to mean "voice-leading" or even "counterpoint"). The authors (there are two) have not heard that a modulation must be prepared, and that the new tonality should be confirmed. There is no bibliography, not even to mention Max Reger's famous book on the subject (Alfred Einstein once told me that when he was a student, he and his friends tried to find a modulation that Reger had not thought of: they invented one and sent it to him as a joke, and he printed it). There is no history of modulation. All the authors talk about is pivot chords (i.e., the chord between the old key and the new one). But history has her revenge: their first example of a pivot chord is not a pivot chord, and it does not occur in a modulation.

"Characteristic [character-] piece" provides our final bit of evidence to show how the absence of historical imagination can mislead one to the polar opposite of the original meaning:

> An early use of the term occurs in Beethoven, who called his *Leonora* Overture no. 1 a "Characteristic Overture," by which he must have implied that it was characteristic of operatic overtures and dramatic in style. The two marches by Schubert published posthumously as op. 121 (D968*b*) were called "Characteristic Marches" by the publisher Diabelli, no doubt to suggest that they were characteristic of Schubert's marches, many of which had already been published; this was in 1830, when the term was still unusual.

The *New Grove* thinks that "characteristic," like "music," is defined for all time, past and future, by our present use. A characteristic-piece is actually uncharacteristic, untypical—it has an individual character of its own. (The central importance for the nineteenth century of this kind of writing is very briefly but revealingly alluded to by Carl Dahlhaus in "Wagner.") Far from being still rare in 1830, the term "characteristic" was used frequently in this sense (related to character-actor, *caratteristico* in Italian) around 1800 with the many "characteristic" sonatas of Vanhal (one of his title pages is illustrated in the *New Grove,* not with "Vanhal," but with "Printing").

Criticisms such as these must be justified, and consequently take a misleading and disproportionate amount of space. I have an enormous ragbag of niggling criticisms left (whatever happened to B. H. Haggin, Doda Conrad, Carlo Gozzi, etc., etc.?) and many major ones (the articles on Vienna, New York, Paris seem to have been written by Chambers of Commerce), but what are they when compared to the virtues of the work? Praise is too quickly achieved: there is little to say about the best articles (like Eric Sams's "Hanslick") except "Read them." An honest estimate of the *New Grove* must end with banal praise.

In its new professional form, the *New Grove* is the greatest musical dictionary ever published. Stanley Sadie and his colleagues have rendered a service to the world of music. Their dictionary far surpasses not only the earlier editions, but the German MGG: it is more readable, more informative, easier to use. The work lists, once you get the hang of them, are wonderfully useful, the bibliographies inconsistent but far-ranging. The *New Grove* is a magnificent achievement—so good, in fact, that it should be revised without delay.

Postscript: People who write about music are divided into three classes: those who contributed to the *New Grove;* those whose contributions were rejected; and those who were never asked. It is therefore hard to find an unbiased reviewer, the resentment of the members of the third class being sometimes the greatest of all. I belong to the second: my article on "Sonata Forms" was rejected, mainly as too speculative, and I rewrote it, quadrupled its size, added all the jokes and examples I had been leaving out, and turned it into a book—which, in fact, beat the *New Grove* to the press because the editors had a computer which filed articles with foreign accents (like Dvořák) and refused to disgorge them.

When the *New Grove* arrived, I was delighted to find that I admired the article by James Webster that replaced mine on "Sonata Form"; it is a brilliant, solid, and concise exposition of orthodox doctrine with many original touches of Webster's own. I was of course secretly pleased to discover a tiny error toward the end. Webster seems to think that Beethoven wrote thirty-four Diabelli variations and brought the theme back at the end. There are only thirty-three and he didn't. However, Webster is right to think that Beethoven would have brought the theme back if it had only been good enough. Instead, he transformed Diabelli's waltz into a minuet.

CHAPTER FIFTEEN

The New Musicology

A LMOST everyone agrees that performing and listening to music are primary activities; writing about music is secondary, parasitical. Ideally, musicologists ought to write for listeners and performers. In real life, they write for other musicologists. Because they have to.

The profession of musicology is changing. European music from 1700 to the present is still at the center of music studies, even in Asian countries, but it has become less isolated. The canon of works to be studied is no longer sacrosanct: serious attempts to widen it are being made, above all to find a place for female and non-white composers, and for pop music. University music departments are understandably anxious to hire ethnomusicologists to salve their bad consciences about their years of neglect of other cultures rather than to strengthen the traditional teaching of Western art music.

There is a general, and not unfounded, sense nowadays that the historian of so-called classical music is being forced to rescue himself and his subject as well. If there were not a real intellectual crisis, then one would have to be invented, and the demands for an overhaul of musicology that have been advanced recently are only natural in this climate.

Despair, however, is the mother of invention. The "new musicologists" (they themselves use the term ironically and with a certain graceful embarrassment)

Originally written in 1994 as a review of: Lewis Lockwood, *Beethoven: Studies in the Creative Process;* Elaine R. Sisman, *Haydn and the Classical Variation;* James Webster, *Haydn's "Farewell" Symphony and the Idea of the Classical Style;* Susan McClary, *Georges Bizet: "Carmen,"* and *Feminine Endings: Music, Gender and Sexuality;* Richard Leppert and Susan McClary, eds., *Music and Society: The Politics of Composition, Performance, and Reception;* Ruth A. Solie, ed., *Musicology and Difference: Gender and Sexuality in Music Scholarship;* Steven Paul Scher, ed., *Music and Text: Critical Inquiries;* and Philip Brett, Elizabeth Wood, and Gary C. Thomas, eds., *Queering the Pitch: The New Gay and Lesbian Musicology.*

deplore the pretended autonomy of traditional musicological studies and present an explicit program of bringing the subject into contact with social science, political history, gay studies, and feminism, to achieve a genuine intellectual prestige, and to transform musicology into a field as up-to-date as recent literary criticism. In fact, the borrowings today from figures outside music like Derrida, Bakhtin, and Lacan are very heavy. This openness to new ideas from other fields has infused a sense of excitement into musicology, a recklessness missing before and badly needed.

I do not want to imply that more traditional musicology is not thriving and producing original and stimulating studies. Lewis Lockwood's recent *Beethoven: Studies in the Creative Process* goes farther than any other work I know to show how Beethoven mapped out and controlled a large-scale form: the pages on the *Eroica* Symphony, above all, are definitive and persuasive. Elaine Sisman's *Haydn and the Classical Variation* is the first satisfactory study of one of the most neglected aspects of Haydn's art. After reading it, I am astonished that no one had considered at length so important a subject, but in any case it has now been done brilliantly. A new book by James Webster, *Haydn's "Farewell" Symphony and the Idea of the Classical Style*, discusses the works of Haydn's middle period in great depth. I should perhaps say here that Professor Webster treats me at length but with great courtesy as the enemy, since I was concerned to set off Haydn's late period from all of the earlier work and to show what he had in common with the much younger Mozart, while Webster demonstrates convincingly how much of the late style was already implicit in the preceding decades. There is not really much contradiction between us except that Webster is right to maintain that I insufficiently appreciated the earlier Haydn; he too, however, knows that Haydn changed in the 1780s and could tell us more about it. In any case, Webster has written easily the best book I know about Haydn's middle period. All three of these books, however, treat music in isolation, with little relation to other arts or to contemporary history.

The attempt to drag musicology out of its isolation into—well, not the real world, exactly, but the other worlds of literature, history, and politics is marked above all by studies of the way music can take on, or appear to take on, a nonmusical meaning, and the movement is well illustrated by several collections of essays that have appeared in the last few years. In two of these, *Music and Text: Critical Inquiries*, edited by Steven Paul Scher, and *Musicology and Difference*, edited by Ruth A. Solie, there are essays by Laurence Kramer, who is often referred to by the other contributors and who is also co-editor of *19th Century Music*, the most influential of the professional reviews that are attempting to give musicology some of the glamour of literary criticism. Professor Gary Tomlinson of the University of Pennsylvania has called him "one of the shrewdest and most theoretically savvy of a younger generation of musical scholars." Kramer is the author of two books, *Music and Poetry* and *Music as Cultural Practice, 1800–1900;* the titles give a good idea of the direction of his thought.

The strength of Kramer's work lies in his passion for new ideas and the facility with which he can juxtapose music and contemporary developments in other fields. He has a remarkable range of reference to literature, is aware of the most recent developments in theory and criticism, and keeps abreast of the most innovative aspects of current thought. For many musicologists less gifted in this way, he provides their principal point of contact with critical theory outside their own fields of specialization.

The limitations of Kramer's writing become apparent when he tries to submit these multiple layers of cultural history to "close reading," to a scrutiny of the musical text. He has a weak grasp of the experience of music. He seems, indeed, to make a specialty of concentrating on a trivial point and reading an exaggerated significance into it; his favorite strategy is a kind of homemade adaptation of deconstructive criticism, a claim that some hitherto unnoticed aspect of a well-known piece is unintelligible within the aesthetic system of the work.

Both strength and weakness are apparent in his essay, which is printed in *Music and Text,* on the opening "Chaos" of Haydn's *Creation.* In the first six pages of his essay he cites, among others, Plato, Boethius, Pythagoras, the seventh-century encyclopedist Isidore of Seville, the second-century theologian Clement of Alexandria, the musicologists Donald Francis Tovey, Edward T. Cone, Carl Dahlhaus, Anthony Newcomb, and himself, the early nineteenth-century poet Gabriela Batsanyi, the astronomer Kepler, Milton, Dryden, Mikhail Bakhtin, and the twentieth-century philosophers J. L. Austin and Nelson Goodman. Some of this, of course, is academic window-dressing, but much of it is genuinely instructive, and all of it is exhilarating, with the effect of watching a grand and motley parade.

With Haydn's musical representation of chaos, Kramer is less convincing, although he has taken some good points from Tovey, A. Peter Brown, and, above all, Heinrich Schenker and H. C. Robbins Landon. His own contribution consists largely of a demonstration that there is an inherent paradox in Haydn's structure. Haydn calls his opening an "Introduction," and Kramer observes that an introduction in the late eighteenth century traditionally moves to finish on a dominant chord[1] (Kramer can point to seven of the slow introductions to Haydn's "London" symphonies), while the "Chaos" movement, on the contrary,

---

1. A dominant chord is the next-to-last chord in the traditional final cadence of a tonal work.

ends on a tonic after a kind of sonata recapitulation (the latter point has been made by almost everyone who has ever written about the *Creation*).

Kramer then claims that this entails a profound contradiction with sonata form, as Haydn has placed a "dominant pedal" in his recapitulation.[2] He comments:

> In Classical practice, a dominant pedal often leads to a recapitulation, but the pedal is supposed to stop where the recapitulation starts. To displace a pedal into the recapitulation itself, as Beethoven made a point of showing in the "Appassionata" Sonata, is profoundly destabilizing. To do such a thing during a slow introduction, where no recapitulation belongs in the first place, is to form precisely what Haydn's contemporaries would have understood as chaos: a crazy mixture, a *Mischmasch*. A sonata-style recapitulation discharges tension, recalls the past, precipitates a definite end; an introductory dominant pedal accumulates tension, delineates the present, precipitates a definite beginning. Superimposed, the two processes create a temporal snarl.

"Delineates the present" is a fine phrase, and even if it is distantly derived from Bakhtinian criticism, it admirably characterizes the effect of a dominant pedal in a Classical work.

Nevertheless, Kramer's reasoning rests on two elementary fallacies. The first is his absurd assumption that an introduction to an oratorio that lasts two hours will have the same form as a short introduction to a single symphonic movement. Whatever Haydn meant by calling "Chaos" *Introduzione,* he certainly did not think that we would expect an opening like the one to his last symphony.

Kramer's second error is his belief that a dominant pedal after the beginning of a recapitulation is essentially contrary to Haydn's style. The wonderful Sonata for Piano in C minor (H. 20), for example, has two dramatic dominant pedals in the recapitulation, and the emphasis on the dominant here takes up more than half the recapitulation. The Sonata for Piano in G minor (H. 44), as well, has a significant pause in the dominant in the middle of the recapitulation, with a long and expressive cadenza. In any case, a recapitulation is supposed to resolve the material of an exposition, and the dominant pedal in "Chaos" only transposes an almost identical earlier passage which appeared in the exposition in the

---

2. Pedal in this sense has nothing to do with the pedal on a piano, but means here a long-held note in the bass. Sustaining the dominant harmony creates tension by making the listener wait for the expected resolution into the tonic. It is often used for a dramatic effect.

harmonically very remote key of D flat major.[3] Astonishingly, Kramer does not comment on the fact that all this material for the dominant pedal has occurred before. (A transposition to the dominant is, in fact, the only way that Haydn could have resolved the earlier passage and prepared his dominant/tonic cadence.)

Kramer's assumption that Haydn's contemporaries would have found the emphasis on the dominant "destabilizing" and "a crazy mixture" is gratuitous: as far as I know, Kramer is the only one who has ever worried about this detail of "Chaos," although other listeners have been impressed and even shocked by the chromaticism and the way the music refuses to complete most of its cadences until the recapitulation (which may, indeed, be described as two simple dominant/tonic cadences, the first almost complete and the second complete and deeply satisfying). I do not for a moment wish to challenge Kramer's contention that Haydn's "Chaos" is a genuine representation of its subject and not a piece of absolute or abstract music, but Kramer's method of decoding does not correspond to Haydn's sense of musical imagery. This is principally because Kramer's grasp of cultural history, and his evident love of music and delight in its manifestations, are not matched by a sensitivity to the ways in which music can be perceived rather than analyzed on paper.

His treatment of Schumann's *Carnaval* brings out these contradictions even more clearly.[4] Perhaps it would only be fair to declare an interest here, since Kramer has characterized my sleeve notes for an old 1963 recording of *Carnaval* as "phallocentric." He includes the most distinguished of recent German musicologists, Carl Dahlhaus, in his attack. This is rather flattering, and the word "phallocentric" in these days of gender studies has become a picturesque catchphrase like the expressions "running dogs of the capitalist press," "Fascist hyenas," or "tax-and-spend liberals." In any case, Kramer's belief that my six-hundred-word sleeve note "set[s] aside Schumann's claim to be engaged on significant terms with the social and psychological dimensions of carnival festivity" is unfounded: I should have thought that my emphasis on rhythmic vitality, about which he complains, would have given more than a suggestion of carnival festivity, and the only thing I set aside as of little interest for present-day record buyers was simply the question of which of Schumann's acquaintances were supposed to be portrayed by Schumann's character sketches and by the meaning of his anagrams. If Kramer were really concerned about this biographical aspect of

---

3. Extra emphasis on the dominant is very frequent in recapitulations, in fact, including dominant pedals when the composer wishes to add suspense (see, for example, the first movement of Mozart's "Hunt" Quartet and the slow movement of the "Dissonant" Quartet).

4. His discussion is summarized in *Music as Cultural Practice*, but a more detailed account appears in the collective *Musicology and Difference*.

Carnaval, he might have asked why young Clara Schumann was portrayed in a piece based on the musical notes corresponding to the letters in the name of the town in which Ernestine von Fricken, Schumann's fiancée at that time, was born. Perhaps he would take more seriously Schumann's contention about his music that first he wrote the pieces and then gave the titles to them.

Kramer's ambition to explain the poetic meaning of Schumann's fragmentary character sketches requires more good sense and less ingenuity than he is generally willing to offer. His remarks about Schumann's "Pantalon et Columbine" are a typical misreading:

> *Pantalon et Columbine* evokes the lecher's pursuit with a frenetic, exaggerated *staccato,* and his prey's escape with a slower, exaggerated *legato.* The piece ends with Columbine's articulation gradually overtaking and retarding Pantaloon's, as if, in a fulfillment of standard male anxieties, she were appropriating his phallus for uses of her own.

Kramer assumes that the staccato portrays the masculine Pantalon, and the lyrical legato Columbine, but listening to the piece will tell us that this is quite wrong: we begin with a dancing staccato motif that places the melody in the right hand or soprano part; the phrase is then repeated with the melody in the bass or left hand with loud accents added and an indication to use the pedal. A simple interpretation of this would hear Columbine as the soprano and Pantalon as the bass, or a *pas de deux,* with both dancers in a sprightly and jerky dance, and this would also be the assumption of anyone who had ever seen Pantalon and Columbine in a performance of the *commedia dell' arte.* The legato section would confirm this, as it starts as an imitative duet between right and left hand, and its amorous tone suggests flirting and at least a pretense of yielding. I interpret the surprise ending as Columbine's final pretense of yielding and then—with a pause and two soft offhand staccato chords—a last-minute escape. Kramer obviously wants a more provocative scenario in which Columbine is appropriating Pantalon's phallus, and I do not envy him.

When Kramer deals more closely with the details of Schumann's score, the results are even more disconcerting. He would like to demonstrate the way male and female aspects mirror each other in a succession of four pieces of *Carnaval:* the two successive self-portraits of Schumann's introvert and extrovert nature, "Eusebius" and "Florestan," followed by "Coquette" and a short "Réplique." "Eusebius" finishes with a chord that traditionally is resolved to a B flat major triad, while "Florestan" ends on an even more dissonant harmony. The next piece, "Coquette," begins with a B flat major cadence, which Kramer calls the deferred resolution to "Eusebius." After "Coquette" comes "Réplique," and Kramer writes:

> *Réplique* begins by mirroring in the upper voice a short figure first heard as an inner voice at the opening of *Coquette*. A reprise of that opening follows immediately, remirroring the figure in its original position.

All this is technically correct, but the way it is described betrays the fact that Kramer has looked at the score and not heard the music.

Listeners who want a resolution for the final chord of "Eusebius" (I am not one of these: see note 5) will not have to wait for the opening of "Coquette," because there have been several resolutions on to a B flat triad in the course of the intervening piece, "Florestan." Any desire for a resolution will have been by then fully satisfied.

It is also true that the beginning of "Réplique" mirrors the opening of "Coquette," but that is not how one perceives it, because the last phrase of "Coquette" is the same as its first phrase. A listener will hear that the opening of "Réplique" repeats the *end* of "Coquette," and any sense of mirroring with the opening will be radically undercut and can occur only on reflection or when one examines the score. Kramer's way of describing the music works on paper, but it neglects the most elementary facts of the experience of hearing or playing *Carnaval*.[5]

The inability to distinguish insignificant details from more important ones has characterized Kramer's work from the beginning, and frustrated his ambition to unite formal analysis and cultural history. Nevertheless, he is an intelligent critic with a great power of imagination and an intuitive grasp of what is interesting and fashionable in criticism today. The distinguished theorist now at Yale, Robert Morgan, wrote a review of Kramer's first book which was as harsh as this one, and considerably more detailed; he concluded by saying: "What is perhaps most discouraging about this book is that it has apparently impressed at least some members of the academic community who should know better and who should have been able to read it more critically."[6] I think Morgan was wrong to be discouraged: the continued favorable reception of Kramer's work is a hopeful sign. It shows that there is a desire for a change in the air so urgent that

5. The final chord of "Eusebius" is theoretically a dissonant form of the tonic E flat major triad, but it is placed in a way to make it seem stable, creating an open-ended final sonority which does not demand resolution, and this satisfies the Romantic taste for a form at once fragmentary and complete.

6. In *Modern Philology*, vol. 84, no. 3 (February 1987).

it is worth overlooking or forgiving Kramer's pretentious expansion of triviality; his defective perception of musical significance matters less than his attempts to go beyond the purely formal analysis of music and his ability to suggest what is new and interesting in the world of criticism inside and outside of musicology. If I may be forgiven a phallic image, he is a valuable weathercock to show us which way the wind is blowing.

II

Perhaps the greatest stimulus for change, at least for the moment, comes from gender studies (and Kramer's writings are a witness to the popularity of this relatively recent field). Work in this field, as in every other, is uneven, ranging from the enlightening to the loony, but musicologists—like artists—must be judged by their finest work, just as criminals will be remembered for their greatest crimes (as Lord Acton remarked about the history of the papacy). The acknowledged leader of these studies, the figure most in view, is Professor Susan McClary of McGill University.

McClary writes with a racy, vigorous, and consistently entertaining style. Her forceful, colloquial manner tends to frighten British musicologists. I should think that she enjoys frightening her colleagues. With McClary, we find a very different level of competence from Kramer. What she has to say specifically about the music and the text is sharp, accurate, and telling; she hears what takes place musically with unusual sensitivity. When she inflates her ideas, her purpose seems to be not so much to dazzle, or to attract admiration, as to shock. The initial form of one of her lectures can indeed cause a certain amount of consternation; the final published version may sometimes seem rather bland, as she has refined out and expurgated the more sensational points. Her critics unfairly—or, perhaps, fairly—tend to quote the original versions. They do, in fact, make better reading.

McClary's account of *Carmen* is consistently interesting and often original. It is preceded, as its first chapter, by an unfortunate analysis by Peter Robinson of Prosper Mérimée's original story, or rather the revised version to which Mérimée added a long disquisition of the Gypsy language. With the kind of exaggerated metaphor now rampant in the best circles, Robinson describes this as an attempt of the male writer to appropriate the language of the heroine, making her destruction complete, and writes: "Sealing every possible orifice, the sexual and the verbal, he brings the story to its end—silence. In this way he hopes forever to bury and deny the terrifying reality of Woman's inalterable and unutterable superiority." One can only admire Robinson's humility, and his success at uttering the unutterable, but we may feel, nevertheless, that sealing orifices is an insensitive way to characterize the fate of a heroine who has been stabbed to death. I quote this only because McClary herself succumbs to the same rhetoric when she writes a very goofy metaphor about male attempts to suppress a figure like Carmen: "Not even José's knife suffices to contain her." With or without the knife, containment is not a happy description of what Don José wants from Carmen: he needs, in fact, to be owned by her, to be, as he says, her "thing," and she is tired of being possessed by her possession.

McClary deals better than anyone else with the important questions about *Carmen*—its supposed vulgarity (which she rightly affirms), its supposed "Wagnerism," the Spanish element, the ambiguity of its portrayal of relations between the sexes. Above all, she deals with the last topic not merely in terms of her discussion of the libretto, but as a musical issue. The following paragraph on the death of Carmen may give some idea of the deftness with which McClary unites drama and musical expression:

> In this finale, Bizet gratifies simultaneously two very different notions of closure. On the one hand, José's dramatic and musical trajectories here reach climax and resolution: he has managed to possess Carmen even if it has meant annihilating her. The instability of the final number encourages the listener both to fear his rage and to long for the event which will put an end to this turmoil. The urgency of Bizet's music, in other words, invites us to desire Carmen's death. But, on the other hand, the formal symmetries that had spelled normalcy throughout the opera and the promise of containment by the opening frame likewise achieve satisfaction here. The principal irony of the opera concerns a fatalism that engages with the most basic formal processes: the willful teleology of José's actions results in the "necessary" return of [musical] materials announced [in the overture] before he even appeared. His agency dissolves into the fulfillment of a fate foretold.

It is rare to find so cogent an expression of the way the musical structure alters and even coerces our feelings about the stage action.

McClary's collection of essays, *Feminine Endings*, alternates between splendid insights presented in a macho style and the kind of extravagance that provokes neither refutation nor assent. But her attempt to identify cadential closure in Western music with patriarchal domination in Western society is too facile to be convincing. Since the early Romantics, we have generally accepted that something as primitive as sexual desire and the way its expression is organized socially will be reflected at all levels of culture. Nevertheless, McClary underestimates how tenuous the analogy becomes as we move away from the basic appetites. Masculine and feminine rhymes, for example, are only distantly related to sexual difference, even if the origin is evident. In addition, any binary relationship, like male and female, will find an easy parallel wherever one looks for it: black and white, closed and open form, nature and culture, master and slave, classical and romantic. Some of these parallels may be stimulating, but it is difficult to know where to stop—or, indeed, why.

In a review of this collection, Ruth Solie said that it was full of "Aha" moments, which is true, but it is full of "Ho Ho" moments as well, like McClary's suggestion that "orchestral musicians dress in black so as to minimize the embarrassing presence of their physical beings." McClary knows that soloists dress in black, too, and waiters, and boys at a prep-school commencement dance or coming-out ball, and, generally, most men and many women on formal occasions; but she is concerned at all costs to draw sympathy for exploited classes like women and orchestral players, and to emphasize the importance of the body in making music. W. H. Auden wrote that our

> greatest comfort is music
> Which can be made anywhere, is invisible,
> And does not smell.
> ("In Praise of Limestone")

but that is not the comfort McClary wants. She knows that sweaty musicians smell, and does not mind. If she deliberately cuts herself off from the ideal but sensuous pleasure that Auden celebrates, she tries with admirable spirit to restore our sense of the physical aspect of musical gesture. This accounts for her remarkable treatment of popular music and Madonna in particular.

Examples of her imaginative response to music and her efforts to force the works into a social and political interpretation are found in the collection of essays by different authors, *Music and Society,* edited by Richard Leppert and Susan McClary. With the essay "The Blasphemy of Talking Politics during Bach Year" she sets up, like so many of the "new musicologists," a straw man to knock down, the dogma that music has no meaning, and no political or social significance. (I doubt that anyone, except perhaps the nineteenth-century critic Hanslick, has ever really believed that, although some musicians have been goaded into proclaiming it by the sillier interpretations of music with which we are often assailed.) McClary writes first on the opening movement of the Brandenburg Concerto No. 5, probably the first keyboard concerto in history, which has an astonishingly long cadenza for the harpsichord alone without the other two solo instruments, flute and violin. She interprets this cadenza as political or social allegory: until then, the harpsichord was an accompanying instrument, always present in a Baroque ensemble, but providing only what is called a *continuo* part, a harmonic support to the bass instrument. She writes:

> Anyone who has served as an accompanist knows the almost complete lack of recognition that comes with that position. As an active keyboardist, Bach was very familiar with this role and—if the narrative of this piece can serve as an indication—with its attendant rewards and frustrations. For in this concerto (in which he would have played the harpsichord part himself), he creates a "Revenge of the continuo player": the harpsichord begins in its rightful, traditional, norm-articulating role but then gradually emerges to shove everyone else, large ensemble and conventional soloists alike, out of the way for one of the most outlandish displays in music history. The harpsichord is the wild card in this deck that calls all the other parameters of the piece—and their attendant ideologies—into question.

But if, as McClary herself recognizes, the harpsichordist was most often the conductor of the ensemble—or, as she says, "a Svengali or puppet master"—are we justified in reading the inferiority complex of the present-day accompanist into the society of 1720 at the court of Cöthen? McClary forgets that today's accompanists are paid considerably less than soloists, whereas in Bach's case, as the well-paid director of music, the leader of the ensemble, and the composer, he was not likely to feel deeply frustrated. The outlandish length of the cadenza has probably a purely artistic explanation (anathema, I suppose, to McClary), a way of celebrating the invention of the keyboard concerto.

In her haste to arrive at a political interpretation, McClary misses the way the harpsichord a few pages before the cadenza starts with pure accompaniment figures, and then gradually—in fact, almost imperceptibly at first—assumes the soloist's role while flute and violin take on accompanying figures. She almost arrives at this insight, but all she can say about this moment is that the parts of the flute and violin "no longer make sense." But they do, just not the sense that McClary wants, and the typical ploy of claiming that some essential element has no meaning or no logic has begun to seem tiresome today.

McClary also treats the duet between Soul (soprano) and Savior (bass) from Bach's cantata *Wachet Auf* to a feminist interpretation. She remarks:

> The duet operates on the conceit that the Soul, unable to perceive Christ's presence, or his responses, longs impatiently for him, continually asking when he will arrive . . . The Soul is presumably gender-

free (male souls are also supposed to long in this manner for Christ's coming, after all), yet the musical images Bach uses mark it as specifically female, or as femininity is frequently constructed in his—and our—culture, in any case. Put quite simply, the Soul here is a nagging, passive-aggressive wife, insecurely whining for repeated assurances of love and not hearing them when they are proffered.

It is true that the Soul asks repeatedly, "When do you come?" and the Savior replies over and over, "I come." Repetition of text is normal in Baroque cantatas, and seeing this as the image of a nagging wife is comic. McClary reminds me of the Major-General in *The Pirates of Penzance,* who hears the policemen's chorus, "We go, we go, we go," and objects, "Yes, but you don't go!" She has forgotten the conventions of Baroque setting of texts, just as the Major-General is ignorant of the conventions of Italian opera choruses.

Clearly even when she is in error, McClary is fun to read, and it is also clear where her force comes from. Her essays on Bach are not only free-wheeling; they employ free association, a willingness to take chances with an engaging recklessness. McClary has faith, not always misplaced, in whatever comes into her head. On two occasions this faith created dismay among musicologists who felt threatened by her positions.

We have first her characterization of the moment of recapitulation in the first movement of Beethoven's Ninth Symphony: "The point of recapitulation . . . is one of the most horrifying moments in music, as the carefully prepared cadence is frustrated, damming up energy which finally explodes in the throttling, murderous rage of a rapist incapable of attaining release." The phrase about the murderous rage of the rapist has since been withdrawn, which indicates that McClary realized it posed a problem, but it has the great merit of recognizing that something extraordinary is taking place here, and McClary's metaphor of sexual violence is a not a bad way to describe it. The difficulty is that all metaphors oversimplify, like those entertaining little stories that music critics in the nineteenth century used to invent about works of music for an audience whose musical literacy was not too well developed. I do not, myself, find the cadence frustrated or dammed up in any constricting sense, but only given a slightly deviant movement which briefly postpones total fulfillment.

To continue the sexual imagery, I cannot think that the rapist incapable of attaining release is an adequate analogue, but I hear the passage as if Beethoven had found a way of making an orgasm last for sixteen bars. What causes the passage to be so shocking, indeed, is the power of sustaining over such a long phrase what we expect as a brief explosion. To McClary's credit, it should be said that some kind of metaphorical description is called for, and even necessary, but I should like to suggest that none will be satisfactory or definitive.

Sex and music have long been associated, although Richard Wagner's insistence that music was female and poetry masculine and his conclusion that Beethoven was the greatest female sex organ in the history of culture are rather at odds with McClary's vision of Beethoven as rapist.[7] The problem is that the significance of music is extremely malleable, and allows infinite room for speculation and free association.

Schubert's sexuality has provoked even more controversy than Beethoven's, and still continues to do so. The instigation of the affair was an article by Maynard Solomon about a passage in the diary of one of Schubert's friends: "Schubert half sick (he needs 'young peacocks' like Benv. Cellini)." This suggested homosexual slang to Solomon, who reinforced his proposal with two passages from Cellini's memoirs, one in which his apprentice was disguised as a girl and compared to the women at a dinner as a peacock among crows, and another in which Cellini and his apprentices, feeling poorly, shot and ate young peacocks and recovered their health. Putting together the use of the image of hunting birds by Cellini's contemporaries to mean cruising for boys and the well-known reputation of Cellini for homosexuality, Solomon concluded that it was probable that Schubert was homosexual: we know of no consummated affair with a woman, only that he caught syphilis from prostitutes of whatever sex. This created consternation among Viennese musicologists and their allies, who saw a takeover of Schubert by the Homintern, and have proceeded to invent an Immortal Beloved for Schubert like Beethoven's and even to suggest that the keys of Schubert's works are a secret code that identifies the name of the lady.

McClary, however, seized the opportunity to suggest that Schubert's homosexual nature was revealed in the modulations and the harmony of the "Unfinished" Symphony, and she gave a sensitive analysis of these modulations. This proposal was received with some skepticism, and McClary has moved to a simple affirmation (printed in *Queering the Pitch*) that Schubert was providing an alternative to Beethoven's phallic style. This turned Schubert into an Other, which is a good thing to be in gay and feminist circles, and it has helped to promote a healthy interest in, and research about, Schubert's work. It is not, however, a critical advance on the first edition of Grove's *Dictionary of Music* more than a century ago in which Sir George Grove described Schubert's music as basically feminine in style.

The slyest and most pointed comment on the issue of homosexuality in music

---

7. There is a brilliant discussion of Wagner and sexuality by Jean-Jacques Nattiez in *Wagner Androgyne*, translated by Stewart Spencer (Princeton University Press, 1993).

was made by Paul Attinello, the editor of the gay musicological review which published McClary's article. In the issue that followed, Attinello remarked:

> So, if Ravel was gay and Debussy was not: tell me, then, the difference between their musics. One interpretation: a subtle but extensive fracturing of the tonal system on the one hand, and on the other a reinscribing of classical structures, each beneath a sensual surface that appears rather similar. Yet which is which? They seem to be the wrong way around, according to my expectations of what a "gay" music might be.[8]

It is clear enough that a composer's life and character, including his sexual behavior, ought to have something to do with his music. The problem is largely that homosexuality is a legal concept, not a character trait. Before we can conclude anything about Schubert and sex, we would have to know exactly what he did with which partners. Homosexual preferences can range from simple cuddling to physical mutilation. I presume—or I should like to presume—that a rapist and a foot fetishist would write different kinds of music, but I am not sure how one would go about confirming this.

McClary is reduced to speculating, not on Schubert's sexual nature, but on the sense of alienation experienced by homosexuals which must have inspired them to produce a music which was satisfyingly "other"—that is, satisfying to modern critics. But is this so certain? Would not the alienated composer try to produce something deliberately conventional, as Schumann, afraid in his late years that he was going insane, tried to make his earlier music seem more normal, less mad? Although it is true that Maynard Solomon misinterpreted a few details, I myself think that his evidence makes it likely that Schubert was gay, but I am not sure that this accounts for the contrast of his style with Beethoven's emphatic and more masculine manner. We must remember that Beethoven was a very successful and brilliant concert pianist from his earliest years, and that Schubert was only a modest performer. This gave Beethoven a large experience of the concert stage that must have shaped his style from the beginning; was his allegedly more "masculine" style a response to the growing importance of public concerts in ever larger halls? He wrote five piano concertos for himself to play, and Schubert wrote none. Beethoven heard all of his symphonies and quartets and his opera performed for a large public; Schubert never succeeded in getting a public performance of his most ambitious works, and his experience of his own music was

---

8. See the editorial "Speaking its Name," GLSG Newsletter for the Gay & Lesbian Study Group of the American Musicological Society, vol. 2, no. 2 (October 1992), p. 15.

largely confined to small, semi-private gatherings of friends. It is only modern prejudice that makes us think that one's sexual proclivities have more influence on artistic style than one's career. I might add that McClary averts her eyes from the frequent outbursts of savage violence in Schubert's scores.

The issue of gay studies has served to illuminate the general difficulties of gender studies. There is no specific homosexual sensibility any more than there is a specific Jewish sensibility, two attractive fictions that Susan Sontag conflated and publicized in her well-known essay on camp. There are various styles of life open to male homosexuals that have traditionally allowed them a certain freedom of expression—interior decorating, leather bars, fashion designing, the theater, ballet, and musicology—just as certain professions have traditionally been more receptive than others to Jews—nuclear physics rather than the chemical industry, medicine rather than automotive manufacturing. This has fostered the appearance of distinctive sensibilities that are of no use in dealing with individual cases, and with a composer like Schubert it is the individual case that counts.

Gender studies have come up against the same problem. It is now widely accepted that it is not the biological difference between men and women that can be studied for its effect on culture but the way society has organized the institutional relation of the sexes, and how men and women are affected economically, psychologically, and aesthetically by the sexual hierarchy forced upon them by different societies. Certain values have been labeled feminine, and women are presumed to be intuitive, subjective, maternal, illogical, and less aggressive than men—or, at least, aggressive in more subtle ways. Not all women or all men are happy with the roles they are expected to play. A female composer, for example, has to struggle hard to impose herself against this system. When she is able to do so, as Ruth Seeger did briefly with the extraordinary String Quartet of 1931, she may end up by abandoning composition and spend the next decade gathering folk songs for her husband. Feminist scholars have worked hard to rehabilitate a mediocre talent like Cécile Chaminade, while a major figure like Ruth Seeger remains neglected (in the *New Grove,* she received only two brief and uninformative paragraphs).

III

Both gender and gay studies have happily insinuated themselves into the vacuum left by the disappearance of Marxist and Freudian criticism; we should be thankful that they are trying to salvage what is most stimulating and valuable in those fields. Gender studies substitute women for Marx's oppressed proletariat, and assume that the forms of culture recreate in various ways the forms of our social and moral organization of which we are largely unconscious. Gender studies are manifestly a polemic in favor of the equality of women, and so they should be, just as gay studies are essentially pursued for the sake of greater acceptance and tolerance of homosexuality. Besides the political benefit of gender studies, the greatest success in this field of literary interpretation has come through the examination of the role of women as consumers as well as creators of culture, and the way literary works can reflect, obliquely as well as directly, the role of gender in society.

Musicologists would like to achieve something similar in their own realm, but the relation of literature to language and to the portrayal of the world around us is obviously more direct than that of music. It is not that music is more autonomous, but more ambiguous, slippery: it will not allow itself to be caught and pinned down like a novel or even like a poem. Music has meaning but very little reference. Critics often forget this and would like to make music speak—which it does, but not often in a language they can easily translate. For example, the title of Schumann's piece "Chiarina," from *Carnaval,* refers both to the music and to Clara Schumann, but the music itself does not refer to Clara although the title enriches the music's meaning.

In short, the problem is to get from the music to a critical interpretation: we assume that different societies and different classes will produce exactly the music they want, and that the text of the music will contain clues to its significance for the listeners for whom it was intended. The difficulty is that music, more than any other art, can accommodate different meanings, different ideologies, different uses. A fugue of Bach does not make sense solely within the society for which it was produced; if it brings some of its original meaning to us, it can attract new ones. In fact, one of its most important functions in history has been its free relation to the meanings that are imposed on it. The greatest disappointment for me in the studies of the "new musicologists" is the failure to appreciate the inherent instability of musical meaning. The search for meaning, historical and analogical, is a necessary condition of listening as well as of understanding, but we cannot impose as dogma what is at best provisional.

An argument about "close reading" between Lawrence Kramer and Gary Tomlinson in *Current Musicology* (no. 53, pp. 18–40) reveals how the intractability of music to being transfixed by meaning has made a dilemma for critics. Tomlinson would like to dethrone close reading, the unswerving examination of the formal details of a work, from its central role in musicology: not only does this kind of analysis remove music from history, Tomlinson feels, but it also involves the musicologist too closely in the values of the music he is studying. Neither Kramer nor Tomlinson observes that the intense concentration on the text of a work of music is a joy, sensuous as well as intellectual, one of the main reasons for becoming a musicologist. Tomlinson deplores the way even ethnomusicologists transfer "onto the musics they study precisely the western pre-sumptions—of internalism, formalism, aestheticism, transcendentalism—that we need to question." This transference does sound very wicked, but of course the ethnomusicologist properly starts by trying to enjoy the music he is study-ing, relating it to the music he already knows, and he gradually widens his expe-rience and loses his deplorable prejudices as he becomes more deeply involved with his field.

It is, however, precisely this deep involvement that arouses Tomlinson's suspi-cions. Kramer, whose heart is in the right place, argues for the importance of close reading in order "to trace out the interrelations of musical pleasure, musi-cal form and ideology. Not to pursue that possibility," he continues, "is tanta-mount to denying . . . the two cardinal, historically grounded truths that music (or art) is meaningful and that music (or art) gives pleasure." The difficulty for the historian, however, is to connect historical meaning and pleasure: they do not work separately. Tomlinson, on the other hand, urges us to "dredge up our usual impassioned musical involvements from the hidden realm of untouch-able premise they tend to inhabit, and . . . make them a dynamic force—to be reckoned with, challenged, rejected, indulged in, whatever—within our study." "Whatever" is the right word here. Evidently it does not matter to Tomlinson what happens to our passion for music, even rejection, as long as the involve-ment ceases to determine our interests and affect our judgments. He ends by asking, in short, for a value-free history, although he knows that this ideal of ob-jectivity is impossible. (He cannot accept the term "objective," because today that is a word equivalent to "modernist," "positivist," "aestheticist," and "phallo-centric," all curiously synonymous.) As a practical matter, I have found that the attempt completely to divest oneself of all one's modern prejudices ends up by making us blind to how much of later history was already active in the past. When Tomlinson says that "we might even find that Beethoven and Mozart are not so like ourselves," he seems to be hoping that these figures from the past will turn to be absolutely Other, untranslatable for modern taste, incapable of receiv-ing our appreciation. This is the view of history that Walter Benjamin called deeply melancholy.

The effort of the "new musicologists" to escape from the formalist view of music by what they call "contextualization"—resituating the music in history in order to reconstruct the various musical and extra-musical meanings of which it was the bearer—can be vitiated at the outset by a failure to realize that through-out history music has resisted, and has been intended to resist, such constraint. It is, in fact, a historical distortion to anchor music too firmly in history.

Paradoxically, "contextualization" can often turn out to be unhistorical. The "particular kind of aesthetic engagement" that Tomlinson locates in the eighteenth century is already found in the Renaissance: vocal settings of the ordinary of the mass were transcribed and played on the lute in the sixteenth century, and the music was enjoyed in and for itself without regard to its original liturgical purpose. Tomlinson's identification of the formalist approach with modernism will not wash; I should imagine it started with the Greeks or Egyptians in some form or other. Detaching music from its original meaning or function continues to be one of the ways that music is traditionally intended to be used. The musicologist Alfred Einstein, disappointed that he could hear no opera in Italy on Sunday, found that arias by Donizetti and Verdi were sung with Latin words during the church services.

Tomlinson's goal is a grand one: to widen our understanding and extend it to other musics besides our own, to comprehend how music has been present in history. It is only the restrictiveness of his practice and of his theory that is regrettable. What is curious, above all, is his psychology. Without a passionate involvement in a particular form of music, an involvement largely unquestioned and unchallenged, the field of musicology will shortly become uninhabited.

Both Tomlinson and Kramer raise essential questions about how one can write properly and improperly about music. What they seem never to have asked themselves, however, is who wants to read about it. The most responsive audience for their brand of writing is found among literary critics, for whom musical detail or its accuracy does not matter, and among younger musicologists hungry to keep abreast of the latest news in their profession. It seems to be almost impossible now to write a book that both engages the specific form of the music accurately and intensely and, at the same time, assesses its role in cultural history, like Hermann Abert's great book on Mozart, or Joseph Kerman's books on opera and on the Beethoven quartets. Composers, performers, and listeners are being shut out by the latest trends in musicology, although the most specious popular treatments still fill the gaps as they have always done. I suppose that it is cheering, however, to reflect that just as bad theories of music have stimulated some wonderful compositions, so defective theories of history may still inspire some criticism good enough to survive.

PART FIVE

The Crisis of the Modern

CHAPTER SIXTEEN

Schoenberg: The Possibilities of Disquiet

O N March 12, 1912, the day he began to compose *Pierrot Lunaire*, Schoenberg noted in his diary, the *Berliner Tagebuch:*

Had this morning suddenly a great desire to compose. After a very
long time! I had already envisaged the possibility that I might never
compose again. There seem to be many reasons to give for this. The
obstinacy with which my students tread on my heels, as they strive to
outbid what I offer, puts me in danger of becoming their imitator, and
prevents me from consolidating what I have built on the ground
where I already stand. They raise everything at once to the tenth
power. And it works! It is really good. But I do not know if it is necessary. This is why I now am forced to decide yet more carefully than before whether I must write. Since:—I do not attach so much importance to my originality; but it often gives me joy, and in any case I
prefer it to unoriginality. Then came the occupation with theoretical
questions [his recent writing of the *Harmonielehre*]. This decidedly
dries one up. And perhaps that is why I suddenly after two years no
longer feel so young. I have become remarkably tranquil. That is even
noticeable in my conducting. What I lack is an aggressive spirit. The
quick going-outside-oneself, and the ability to attack, to grab. Perhaps
it will be better that I do nevertheless compose again. Or, indeed, it is
better. I remember that I wrote a poem about ten or twelve years ago,
in which I wanted to become old and without ambition, tranquil.
Now that I suddenly see the earlier possibilities of disquiet again, I almost long for them. Or are they already there once more?

Originally written in 1975 as a review of Josef Rufer, ed., *Arnold Schoenberg: Berliner Tagebuch,* and
Leonard Stein, ed., *Style and Idea.*

In this page, perhaps the most revealing that Schoenberg ever wrote about himself, the major psychological forces that shaped his work appear pell-mell, but in a disorder that suggests their interdependence: we find the reluctance and perhaps the fear with which he embarked on one of the most important and influential revolutions in the history of music; the pride in his students' work, and the resentment—even the touch of paranoia—sparked by the way they pushed forward with his ideas, driving him ahead faster than he wished to go (or was this only an excuse, a cover for the forces that were driving him from within?); the awkward, grudging, suspicious sense of his originality, revealed even in the rhythm of those graceless sentences acknowledging its weight; the opposition between theory and practice, between the rational understanding and creation; and finally the late Romantic, almost consciously "decadent" identifiction of artistic creation with anguish, of contentment with the death of inspiration.

The opposition of the critical understanding and artistic creation is fundamental to Schoenberg's thought. It is an inherited Romantic topic, a sacred commonplace to which one may return again and again for meditation and for exegesis. It often serves to show critics the door, but properly understood it embodies a mystery: it is only really useful when it is believed because it is absurd. This sense of the topic supports Schoenberg's defense of his teaching. The greatest difficulty for students, he wrote in a letter to Douglas Moore (printed as an appendix to his *Fundamentals of Musical Composition* [London, 1967]), "is to find out how they could compose without being inspired. The answer is: it is impossible. But as they have to do it, nevertheless, advice has to be given."

Schoenberg wrote almost all his music in a fury of inspiration. The opera *Erwartung,* for example, was finished in seventeen days. He had enormous difficulty picking up the thread of an inspiration once abandoned, as if it were beyond rational calculation. Even the development of twelve-tone technique came more as the result of a series of instinctive moves than as a conscious plan. But he was also a magnificent critic, and we must be grateful for the new edition of *Style and Idea,* his collected prose writings.

It is neither precisely a new edition nor the collected prose. It contains all the articles of the original 1950 edition of *Style and Idea,* with one omission; but to these fourteen articles are added ninety more, many of them never edited before (some of them, indeed, unfinished essays or even informal jottings). The selection, however, is far from complete: in particular, all of Schoenberg's analyses of his own compositions have been set aside for a later publication.

Most serious is the omission of a 199-page manuscript, "The Musical Idea and Its Presentation," that Josef Rufer has called Schoenberg's most fundamental theoretical work; it contains his ideas, developed and reformulated over many years, on theme, motif, figure and phrase, laws of comprehensibility, laws of coherence, and so forth. Even if much of this important manuscript is in the form of notes, many of the essays now published are only incomplete and fragmentary. It is hard to discover on what the present selection is based, and a considerable part of the new material will do Schoenberg's reputation no service. The sarcastic letters to critics, written in a kind of disastrous pastiche of the style of Karl Kraus, do him little credit; nor do the grouchy, heavily ironic sallies at other composers—but then Stravinsky, too, published silly remarks about his contemporaries and wrote unnecessary, exasperated letters to critics.

It is a pity, however, to have published Schoenberg's most brilliant and important essays with this mass of second-rate material. Much of it, including the essays on politics and human rights, has only an ephemeral and superficial autobiographical interest that even in this respect cannot be compared with the recently published diary of 1912, or the wonderful lecture, printed in the first section of *Style and Idea*, entitled "How One Becomes Lonely"—at once an assessment of his life and his music.

There is, of course, hardly a page where Schoenberg does not produce an observation characterized by his extraordinary penetration, his inspired shrewdness, but we must pay for these details by suffering his ill-tempered suspicions and sour complaints—almost all justified, no doubt, which does not make them more agreeable to listen to (we prefer our victims to maintain a silent dignity). Schoenberg had to pay as well, as he himself understood in a moment of blinding lucidity after writing a particularly obtuse paragraph about Stravinsky's *Oedipus:*

> My remarks about Stravinsky now strike me not only as less witty than they did a few hours ago, but as something almost equally bad: rather philistine. Naturally I can do nothing about it, even though it is evidence against me and for the work. I know, after all, that the works which in every way arouse one's dislike are precisely those the next generation will in every way like. And the better the jokes one makes about them, the more seriously one will later have to take them.

This is no *mea culpa*—Schoenberg takes nothing back—but critical intelligence so powerful that it replaces introspection as a form of self-knowledge.

The finest essay is "Brahms the Progressive," with its unsurpassed discussions of Mozart's and Beethoven's phrasing and motivic technique, along with its homage to Brahms. "Folkloristic Symphonies" is less rich but no less impressive, as it reaches the heart of Schoenberg's preoccupation with musical theory: the nature of the motif or the theme that can be used to create a work on the largest scale.

The most provocative of the writings, however, is the early essay "The Relationship to the Text" published in the *Blaue Reiter* in 1912, in which Schoenberg proclaims the impotence of the critical intellect. He starts from Schopenhauer, whose derivative and oversimplified version of the early Romantic theory of art provided the basis for so many of the later nineteenth century's platitudes in aesthetics:

> Even Schopenhauer, who at first says something really exhaustive about the essence of music in his wonderful thought, "The composer reveals the inmost essence of the world and utters the most profound wisdom in a language which his reason does not understand, just as a magnetic somnambulist gives disclosures about things which she has no idea of when awake"—even he loses himself later when he tries to translate details of this language which *the reason does not understand* into our terms. It must, however, be clear to him that in this translation into the terms of human language (which is abstraction, reduction to the recognizable), the essential, the language of the world, which ought perhaps to remain incomprehensible and only perceptible, is lost.

The surface paradox of "perceptible and incomprehensible" reappears elsewhere in Schoenberg's thought: it was an escape hatch that allowed him to pursue his separate critical and creative ways. But it did not save him from the inconsistency that we find in his own writings, in which a brilliant appreciation of other men's music (when his prejudices remain uninvolved) is accompanied by a misunderstanding of many aspects of his own music, and even by a curious underestimation of his most radical achievements.

The confidence with which he confronted the music of Brahms and Mozart oozed away when he faced his own works, above all those of the years from 1908 to 1914. These works had a logic of their own, he sometimes felt, but he could not yet explain it. Often he placed this logic outside the music itself. In 1923 (in "Composition with Twelve Tones") he wrote that he had discovered in 1908 how to construct large works only by following a text, as the abandonment of tonality had put the traditional structures out of reach. A few years later (in "Opinion or Insight"), he was even more emphatic about the non-musical nature of his large musical patterns:

> Renunciation of traditional means of articulation made the construction of larger forms temporarily impossible, since such forms cannot exist without clear articulation. For the same reason, my only extended works from that time [i.e., 1908–1914] are works with a text, where the words represent the cohesive element.

Yet this represents a flat violation of his critical doctrine, as he had already expressed it in "Composition for Twelve Tones":

> Prior to Richard Wagner, operas consisted almost exclusively of independent pieces, whose musical relation did not seem to be a musical one. Personally, I refuse to believe that in the great masterworks pieces are connected only by the superficial coherence of the dramatic proceedings. Even if these pieces were merely "fillers" taken from earlier works of the same composer, something must have satisfied the master's sense of form and logic. We may not be able to discover it, but certainly it exists. In music there is no form without logic, there is no logic without unity.

It would be odd to maintain that "the words represent the cohesive element" in *Erwartung;* for this most convincing and most masterful of Schoenberg's large-scale works, very few critics could give an account of exactly what happens on the stage or of what the libretto means—nor, indeed, is it necessary. *Erwartung* may be grasped comfortably, conveniently, and persuasively as a work of pure, abstract music. It is certain that Schoenberg would not have it otherwise. The music has clearly a logic of its own which is at the very least *almost* independent of the text and action, and perhaps more so than the operas of Mozart to which Schoenberg is clearly referring in the above quotation. Once the inspiration that created *Erwartung* had fulfilled itself, however, the composer could no longer retrace the steps of its composition.

The problem was that by the 1920s Schoenberg had lost some of the assurance, the artistic faith of a decade earlier. About the great period just before the First World War, he remarked nostalgically in 1949 when writing "My Evolution":

> Intoxicated by the enthusiasm of having freed music from the shackles of tonality, I had thought to find further liberty of expression. In fact, I myself and my pupils Anton Von Webern and Alban Berg, and even Alois Hába believed that now music could renounce motivic features and remain coherent and comprehensible nevertheless.

The 1920s were a more sober era. Looking back at his earlier works, Schoenberg refused to believe in the renunciation of motivic and thematic form, and tried to explain them by motivic analysis—with a success that was naturally only partial. *Erwartung* and the Four Songs for Orchestra do not lack motivic elements, but these elements are no longer (and not yet) at the center of the musical construction. With the twelve-note system, Schoenberg reinstated motivic form—or thought he had. It was, of course, just this aspect of twelve-note composition that many later composers were to dissolve.

This question of motif haunted Schoenberg for the rest of his life. More than anyone else, he understood that the motif, as conceived in Western music, was basically a tonal form. "In every composition preceding the method of composing with twelve tones," he write in 1941, "all the thematic and harmonic material is primarily derived from three sources: the tonality, the *basic motive*, which in turn is a derivative of the tonality, and the rhythm, which is included in the basic motive" (*Style and Idea*, pages 225–226). The method of "composing with twelve tones" was invented above all to replace tonality as a source for motifs, which can now be derived from the row. But this places the motifs of works like the Four Songs for Orchestra in a curious limbo: no longer tonal and not yet twelve-tone, from what are these motifs derived, what supports them? It is no wonder that Schoenberg, no longer willing to envisage a basic, non-motivic structure, professed himself baffled by the logic of these works even as he affirmed it. He declared that the future would prove that in their style there was a "centralizing power" comparable to tonality, but he himself could not say what it was.

For the most part, he speaks of the motifs of these great atonal, pre-twelve-tone songs not in terms of pitch but of contour—an aspect that analysts have largely neglected. But then the twelve-note system was to reaffirm tyranny of pitch, and to push the great experiments with tone-color and texture of the atonal period into the background. The tone-row is conceived by Schoenberg entirely in terms of pitch and as a quarry for motifs. This makes the relation of the row to the thematic material of a work fundamentally different from the relation of tonality to motif emphasized by Schoenberg: the row with its transformations is the sum of the motifs, and it has no identity independent of them. The work, too, is the sum of these transformations—at least theoretically; practically Schoenberg was to retain a freedom of style and procedure until the end, although the expansive and miraculous freedom of the years 1908 to 1914 was only to be recaptured in a few rare works, above all in the late String Trio.

The malaise, the contradictions concerning thematic form lie very deep in Schoenberg's criticism. Two quotations show how inconsistent his stance may appear; in one, he presents his ideas on motivic form, in the other—much earlier, but revised much later—he brilliantly defends the music of his beloved Mahler:

> Whatever happens in a piece of music is nothing but the endless reshaping of a basic shape. Or, in other words, there is nothing in a piece of music but what comes from the theme, springs from it and can be traced back to it; to put it more severely, nothing but the theme itself.

Or, all the shapes appearing in a piece of music are *foreseen* in the "theme." ("Linear Counterpoint," 1931)

Incredibly irresponsible is another accusation made against Mahler: that his themes are unoriginal. In the first place, art does not depend upon the single component part alone; therefore, music does not depend upon the theme. For the work of art, like every living thing, is conceived as a whole—just like a child, whose arm or leg is not conceived separately. The inspiration is not the theme, but the whole work. And it is not the one who writes a good theme who is inventive, but the one to whom a whole symphony occurs at once. ("Gustave Mahler," 1912, revised 1948)

The contradictions here are not superficial (although we may envisage a reconciliation): they express the opposition between criticism and inspiration. The affirmation of thematic unity is made by the critic, while it is the composer that claims priority for the total work seen *in advance* as a whole. The same tensions may be found in E. T. A. Hoffmann's analyses of Beethoven. The two claims are united only in Schoenberg's intuition of the "incomprehensible and only perceptible," which is the fundamental condition of music for Schoenberg.

He was not always pleased when his performers worked out the row, and wrote a disagreeable letter to Rudolf Kolisch, who had figured it out for the Third Quartet:

You must have gone to a great deal of trouble, and I don't think I'd have had the patience to do it. But do you think one's any better off for knowing it? (*Letters*, edited by Erwin Stein [London, 1964], page 164)

Nevertheless, he reported with considerable satisfaction in 1946 that when one of the singers of his opera *Von Heute auf Morgen* became "familiar with the basic set, everything seemed easier for him." For Schoenberg, this was a vindication.

He evidently was determined to have it both ways. That was his greatness both as composer and critic. Lesser men are flaccidly and hazily inconsistent, Schoenberg violently and passionately so. This violence led him ultimately to a way of reconciling even the contradictions in his conception of motif: in a crushing indictment of the theories of poor Joseph Hauer, who had worked out a silly theory of twelve-tone compositions, Schoenberg referred—almost in passing—to the "artistic way—the way, for example, that motivic working-out needs to be concealed and yet effective, basic yet also felt on the surface." And he might have added, "incomprehensible and only perceptible."

It is only just to add (and it would have pleased him) that his instinct and his sense of adventure served him even better than his critical intelligence. The day after he began *Pierrot Lunaire,* he noted in his diary: "I am moving absolutely to a new expression. The sounds become here a frankly animal and immediate expression of sensuous and spiritual movement. Almost as if everything were directly translated. I am curious to see how it will go on."

CHAPTER SEVENTEEN

The Performance of Contemporary Music: Carter's Double Concerto

C AN a new work of music be played brilliantly by musicians who think that it is impossible to get through it technically with confidence, and also be wildly cheered to the galleries by a public most of whom would claim that it is too complex to understand? So it would seem from the first performance of Elliott Carter's Third Quartet by the Juilliard String Quartet in New York on January 23, 1973. It appears certain that, for all its alleged difficulty, this fascinating work will become a permanent addition to the chamber repertory. Carter's first and second quartets, generally acknowledged as the greatest works in their medium since Bartók, have already achieved this status.

Orchestral works have a harder time making their way. However, at the end of April last year, Carter's *Variations for Orchestra* was played four times in one week in New York: three times by the New York Philharmonic and once by the Chicago Symphony. Although this work is a regular part of the Chicago Symphony's repertory (they have played it all over Europe), it was the first performance by the New York Philharmonic.

Variations for Orchestra was written in 1955, and it was Carter's only major symphonic work before the *Concerto for Orchestra* of 1969. That Carter should have had to wait seventeen years for its performance by America's reputedly most distinguished orchestra is typical of the difficult relation between American composer and orchestra today. During these seventeen years—and early enough in them—Carter had been recognized internationally, and considered by many as the finest and most interesting American composer now writing; for most of these seventeen years, in spite of this widespread recognition, the New York Philharmonic had chosen to act as if he did not exist.

The myth of the unrecognized genius is a necessary part of the public aspect of art today. It is important for a radically new work to be understood only little by little and too late. That is the only tangible proof we have of its revolutionary character. There has never, of course, been a truly neglected genius in the history of music—at least not since the time when we have any real data on the lives of composers. Even Schubert, who died so young that appreciation of his stature was only beginning to grow, was already well enough known beyond the small world of Viennese music for the young Schumann, when he heard of his death, to have wept uncontrollably all night.

Nor is Carter himself in any way a neglected figure. With the appearance of his first string quartet in 1949, he almost at once achieved the kind of international fame that would satisfy any ambition. The New York Philharmonic's neglect of his work is therefore an empty ritual, a symbol of the gap that has opened up in our time between performance and composition.

In 1969, the Philharmonic took notice of Carter, but not to play the *Variations*. It commissioned a new work, to be written especially for the celebration of its centenary. The *Concerto for Orchestra*, as its title implies, is a work requiring exceptional virtuosity from the players and was immediately accepted as one of Carter's most imaginative achievements. It would, of course, have been much easier to play for an orchestra that was already familiar with Carter's style through the *Variations*. (It would also have been easier to grasp by a public that was not listening to a work by Carter for the first time—a work, too, of far greater difficulty than the *Variations*.)

All these barriers to appreciation would no doubt create a reputation for difficulty with any composer. But it is important to note that Carter's distinction has been won neither in spite of this reputation nor because of it. To a great extent—and this is one of the paradoxes of American musical life—it is assumed that because Carter has developed an original style by purely musical procedures and with no recourse to the doctrinaire shenanigans of many of his contemporaries, his music must *therefore* be hard to grasp. To the normal difficulties of playing any new music of any originality is added our expectation that avant-garde art must puzzle, shock, and, above all, resist immediate understanding. Both performer and listener come to a new work by Carter with a conviction of initially insurmountable problems. Our sense of history and the organization of our musical life combine to help us realize these comical fears.

The problem of difficulty in contemporary music is most often wrongly posed. It is generally believed that music is difficult to comprehend either when there is too much going on for the ear to distinguish or when the composer's form—harmonic, melodic, or architectural—is in some mysterious way beyond the grasp of the mind of the listener. Yet both these conditions may be fulfilled and the music still seem lucid and even popular in style.

In the music of Richard Strauss—to take only the most notorious example—not only do a great many of the notes remain totally indistinguishable from an enormous mass of busywork, but the composer was clearly far from caring if they were. "Gentlemen, you are playing all the notes," he is reported to have gasped, appalled, at a rehearsal of *Don Juan* with the Boston Symphony.[1] As for the understanding of form, I remember a group of college students, all music majors, who did not realize that in a sixty-bar piece of Bach I had just played for them, the last twenty bars were the first twenty repeated without alteration. The appreciation of form of the average audience cannot, I think, be rated very high, and yet it has never prevented their enjoyment. Yet those who take in their stride the most abstruse complexities of Beethoven, the subtlest nuances of Mozart, and the most complex effects of Wagner or Mahler, will stalk angrily out of the hall when presented with, say, the enchanting simplicities of Alban Berg's "postcard" lieder.

It is paradoxically not what is actually to be heard that makes music difficult, but what cannot be heard because it is not there. It is the lack of something which the listener expects to hear but which is refused him that makes his blood boil, that brings the aged Philharmonic subscriber to the verge of apoplexy.[2] Every original work represents an omission, even a deliberate erasure of what was previously indispensable to art, as well as a new ordering and new elements. The real irritant for the listener is that what he has so far considered as essential to a work of music he now cannot perceive. The composer has left it out. The appreciation of a new style is as much an effort of renunciation as of acceptance.[3]

To see what Carter refuses to allow the listener is a preliminary necessity to a comprehension of his art; in the end it will be the same as seeing what he has brought to music. What an original composer "leaves out," however, is rarely what the public, or the average musician for that matter, thinks. We have only to remember the reproaches that there was no melody in Wagner, no form in Beethoven, no coherence to Schumann, or that the music of Mozart could appeal only to the head and not to the heart.

To show something of the gradual process of understanding a new composer's thought, I can mention my own experience with Carter's most brilliantly attractive and apparently most complex work, the *Double Concerto* for the piano, harpsichord, and two small chamber orchestras. This is a work which has had, happily, a considerable history of performance. At its premiere (in which I

---

1. Perhaps even more revealing was his ironic reproach to Toscanini: "In my music there are good and bad notes; when I conduct it, I can hear only the good ones, but when you conduct it, I can hear *all* the notes."

2. We should not underestimate the physical effects of incomprehension. I recall that when, at the age of seventeen, I first heard the Bartók String Quartet No. 5, it made me physically sick.

3. And not only in music. I see from Leo Steinberg's splendid collection of essays *Other Criteria* (Oxford University Press, 1972) that back in 1962 he made a similar point about modern painting.

played) it was felt that future performances would be rare. The requirement of four virtuoso percussion players, each playing more than ten instruments, was alone sufficiently dismaying. Yet it has been recorded twice, and given more than thirty performances, by many different groups. I have played in more than a third of the performances and in both recordings, so that for once I have some personal knowledge of the unfolding history of our understanding of a work of music. The original difficulties of performance—and of hearing—transformed themselves, becoming at once easier to deal with and more problematical, both more traditional and tied to a new vision of the art of music.

II

In the summer of 1961, I received the last pages of the piano part of the *Double Concerto* in Paris a few days before flying to New York for the first rehearsal. It is not only eighteenth-century musicians, waiting for Mozart to blot the wet ink on the score, who have had to learn a new work at the last minute. (Recently for Boulez's *Eclat-Multiples* the copyists were working until the day before the first performance.)

This final section or coda of the *Double Concerto* contained the most complicated rhythmic passage I had ever been asked to play, a few measures of moderately fast septuplets against triplets—that is, while the right hand plays seven even notes to each beat, the left hand plays three. The real complication comes from the division of the septuplets into groups of four by a melody (marked *singing and expressive*) whose line consisted of every fourth note. The most complicated cross-rhythm I had seen before this was the famous eight against nine in Brahms's *Variations on a Theme by Paganini.* The Carter seven against three was more difficult because of the internal subdivision of the sevens and, paradoxically, because of the slightly slower beat so that the irregularities were easier to hear. (As we shall see, this passage will turn out to be not a true cross-rhythm at all, but something quite different.)

I had not yet succeeded in persuading my left hand to ignore what my right hand was doing when I had to leave for New York and one of New York's late-summer heat waves. Rehearsals took place during a ten-day period in which the weather frustrated a sane and cool approach to a difficult new work. The luxury of ten days' rehearsal was due to the generosity of Paul Fromm, who commissioned the work and allowed the composer his choice of performers. The small chamber orchestra was made up of the best of New York's freelance players with a considerable awareness of contemporary style. The conductor was the young Swiss, Gustav Meier; the harpsichordist, the older and more experienced

Ralph Kirkpatrick. Kirkpatrick's experience, however, was almost entirely in eighteenth-century music; his style of playing was heavily dependent on the kind of freedom (or *rubato*) most appropriate for Baroque music. This did not prevent him from giving an impressive account of the work, the solo cadenza in particular; one of the graces of his performance was indeed a tension between an older style of playing and a newer style of writing.[4]

But Kirkpatrick had recently undergone an eye operation which exacerbated the most ticklish problem of the *Double Concerto:* the seating arrangement. Each of the two solo instruments is placed in front of its own small orchestra of six players: two strings, two winds, and two brass. The separation between the two orchestras (and, therefore, the two soloists) would be both visually and audibly evident. Spread out over a half-circle behind the two orchestras are four percussion players, each with a formidable array of about a dozen instruments to cope with. The harpsichordist, in front of his orchestra, and two percussion players are on the left of the stage as the audience sees them; the pianist and his ensemble are to the right. The problem is to place the conductor so that he can see and be seen by both soloists and both orchestras. There are various solutions possible, but the wide separation of the two chamber orchestras and the danger that the raised lids of the two solo keyboards might hide the conductor from part of the orchestra created unexpected difficulties.

This new technical obstacle arose from a new and even revolutionary conception of the use of space in performance. Contrast of two or more groups, echo effects, and other static devices are common enough, and have been since the sixteenth century when the Venetians decided to exploit the immensity of the interior of St. Mark's. In Carter's *Double Concerto,* however, the choirs are not merely set off against each other, but the music describes arabesques in space as rhythms are passed from one musician to another. The simplest example of this is a roll on the cymbals that goes from right to left as each one of the percussionists takes it up, overlapping with the previous one.

The most elaborate use of the spatial arabesque is in the slow movement, where the winds and brass intone a soft chorale-like texture in strict time and—imposed like a grid over this—a continuously and uniformly accelerating (and, later, decelerating) rhythm is played with great delicacy by piano, harpsichord, and percussion *staccato,* and strings *pizzicato,* each instrument playing only one or two notes as the steadily changing rhythm passes around the orchestra. It is a beautiful conception, but difficult to notate: everybody's part must be written to

4. In most of the recent performances, Paul Jacobs has been the elegant and brilliant harpsichordist.

refer to the conductor's beat; the conductor must direct the continuously accelerating instruments; and when an absolutely simple and even rhythm is written to conform to a continuously changing beat, it comes out looking very queer indeed.

Some of the members of the orchestra in many of the performances had such difficulty trying to place their notes relative to a uniformly changing beat that they never realized that their own parts are actually played in strict time. Their difficulties, indeed, were aggravated by the fact that when the acceleration has proceeded to a certain point, the conductor's beat has become so fast that for purely physical reasons he must shift to beating only the longer note values— without, however, interrupting the acceleration. At these moments the beat becomes three times as slow, and the notation three times as fast, and it is difficult for most musicians to make the shift imperceptible to the audience.

At the first rehearsal, the passage in the coda that had so frightened me in Paris (three against seven, with the sevens accented in groups of four) became far more terrifying when I at last saw the full score. The piano and its small orchestra have their parts notated in 3 beats to the measure, the rhythm of septuplets in the right hand therefore coming out to 21 notes against the 9 (3 triplets) per measure in the left; but the harpsichord and its orchestra have their music written in 2 beats per measure, the harpsichord playing 5 notes per beat in the right hand against 4 in the left, or 10 against 8 per measure—with the quintuplets accented every third note, the quadruplets every fifth, *so that the accents of all four lines in piano and harpsichord never coincide.*[5] The already complex cross-rhythms of 21 against 10 against 9 against 8 were made infinitely more difficult by the subdivisions of phrase and accent.

It was some time afterward that I began to realize slowly and painfully (how slowly I am ashamed to confess) that these were not cross-rhythms at all, at least not as they had always been understood so far in music. Brahms's eight against nine in the *Variations on a Theme by Paganini* is a true cross-rhythm because the beginning of each group of eight and nine—their moment of coincidence—is

---

5. The complexity here is exceptional, as the coda sums up the work. The following table may make the system of notation clearer:

Piano right hand: $3 \times 7 = 21$ (accented groups of four)
Harpsichord right hand: $2 \times 5 = 10$ (accented groups of three)
Piano left hand: $3 \times 3 = 9$ (accented groups of seven)
Harpsichord left hand: $2 \times 4 = 8$ (accented groups of five)

The tempo is moderate, the dynamics very soft, all rhythms exactly even, and the texture transparent. (The accented notes are made by allowing them to continue to sound during the unaccented ones.)

clearly marked. There is, in short, a central beat in Brahms which occurs every eight (or, in the left hand, every nine) notes, and which provides a frame. We hear a larger, slower rhythm within which the cross-rhythms are to be understood.

What Carter has done is to remove the central beat—except for purposes of pure notation. No central beat can be heard: the rhythms therefore do not cross, but proceed independently. They are, in fact, cross-tempi or cross-speeds, if you like. The occasional coincidence of accent in two parts no longer refers to the existence of a slower and all-governing beat, but to periodic movements which have momentarily come together and are about to spread apart once again. There is a central rhythmic frame of reference in the *Double Concerto,* but it is no longer a static and immovable principal beat; the frame is the system by which one tempo is transformed into another in the course of the piece. The central rhythmic conception cannot be heard as completely revealed at any one moment of the work, but is a function of the work as a whole.

In other words, those complicated-looking septuplets divided into groups of four in the right hand of the piano part were not septuplets at all, and not in the least complicated; they were simple groups of four. They coincide with the left-hand rhythm every seven notes, but the moments of coincidence are not supreme, have no privilege. But they are what the conductor must beat to keep the ensemble together.

Music is "difficult," as I said above, when we are listening for something which is not there. It is not the multiplicity of rhythm in this passage that creates the initial impression of obscurity. The four different superimposed tempi are clearly audible: we can all hear, in a beautifully transparent texture with ravishing tone color, four lines moving at four different rates of speed. Four different lines are, surprising as that may seem, very easy to perceive when clearly different in rhythm, and have always been easy in music from Bach to the present; they merely demand a carefully nuanced and sensitive performance.

But when we ask—as we do after our experience of traditional music—"What is the *basic* rhythm?" we receive no answer from Carter where we have always had one from Bach. Debussy's writing, for example, is always exquisitely balanced, rich, and harmonious, but when his public asked, "What is the key?" "What is the central chord?" and received no answer, the music seemed an intolerable succession of dissonances. Critics have sometimes complained of Carter that many of his notes cannot be heard, whereas in fact everything in his work is as easy to hear, as transparent as the scores of Mahler, Berg, Ives, or Tchaikovsky. Paradoxically, the *Double Concerto* appears most difficult to musicians who are trying to follow the score. The bar lines traditionally mark a regular strong beat:

in Carter they are often a purely visual aid to the ensemble with only occasionally a genuine significance for the ear.[6]

The reliance of the public upon the conductor's movements for the sense of what they are hearing leads to an analogous misunderstanding. For many people the gestures of the conductor are a guide: they interpret the piece, clarify its rhythm, indicate the climaxes, tell them what to feel. In the *Double Concerto* the conductor's beat does not indicate a central rhythm, but only one of two or more equally important lines, and the public is often puzzled to hear nothing fundamental that corresponds to the most vigorous gestures. They conclude that something has gone wrong with the ensemble—and matters are not helped by the fact that occasionally something has.

Musicians take almost as long and sometimes longer than the public to accept and understand something new in music. They are as dependent upon the gestures of the conductor for a feeling of security. But the conductor's beat largely must correspond to the notation. The bar line is the traditional place for the conductor's down beat, and it generally means the strong beat, the mark of the dominating central pulse which often disappears from Carter's music.

At one point, indeed, in the *Double Concerto,* traditional notation is stretched beyond its limits and even abandoned, if only briefly. The climax of the slow movement is a brilliant and enchanting one: the piano and the harpsichord have been softly accompanying long melodies in the wind instruments; then, as the harpsichord and both orchestras begin to slow down in an immensely long ritard, the piano begins gradually to accelerate more and more until its notes end in a soft, resonant blur. It is a beautifully poetic effect, and an extraordinarily simple and direct one. A gradual acceleration against a gradual deceleration, however, would require for its exact notation the solution of a differential equation of the second degree. The points of coincidence between piano and orchestra are therefore only approximately notated in the score. In playing this passage, I have always found it best not to look at the conductor at all and just pray that it will come out right. It generally does, as the extreme speed of the repeated notes at the end demanded by Carter represents the technical limits of the instrument as well as of the performer.

The mood of the first performance was one close to panic. In particular the last section of the piece, with one orchestra's part notated in $\frac{6}{8}$, the other in $\frac{3}{4}$, caused special anxiety. "I feel more like a traffic cop than a conductor," said Gustav Meier, trying to balance the sonority of one orchestra against another.

---

6. It should be remembered that the score is a late Renaissance invention. The complicated polyphonic music of the fourteenth and fifteenth centuries was sung and played without a score and without bar lines.

Would we get through the piece without breaking down? We made it to the end. I had no clear idea how the performance went, but it turned out to be an enormous success with the public and, the next day, the critics.

III

The poetic content of the *Double Concerto* and its dramatic conception imposed themselves at once. The fragments of the introduction that seem to grow together in a continuous organic movement, the end of the slow central section in which the extreme slowing down of the orchestra suddenly becomes identical in its total suspension of movement with the extreme speeding up of the piano carried so far that no increase of motion is audible (like two opposed infinites that meet), the scherzo dramatically broken twice by the violent cadenzas of the piano, and the fierce coda that superimposes all the rhythms of the work in one great sonority and then falls to pieces "and in a flash expires" (like the end of Pope's *Dunciad*, as Carter himself has remarked)—all this was immediately obvious in spite of so much about the music that was not yet clear to the musicians or to the public.

Stravinsky, indeed, spoke of the *Double Concerto* as the first American masterpiece. What was most evidently masterly, most easily accessible to the general public, was the rich play of sound, not only in contrast and blending of sonority, but in a dynamic conception of one kind of sonority moving into another—piano *staccato*, violin *pizzicato*, and bongo drums clearly taking over the successive notes of a single rhythmic phrase, for example. Virtuosity, too, is still a direct and legitimate way to the public heart, and the virtuoso passages in the *Double Concerto* for the harpsichordist, the pianist, and four percussion players are spectacular. So difficult, in fact, are the percussion parts that these players generally tend to swamp the others—less from an inability to damp their instruments than from an attempt to give themselves confidence by more vigorous and hearty thumps.

No matter what the performance is like, the work is almost player-proof, always a success. The only exception occurred the following year in London when it was directed by the greatest conductor to have done the piece to this day, Hans Rosbaud. The work had already been played in London a few months previously under Jacques-Louis Monod, one of the finest and most intelligent young conductors. His performance was exciting, with great vitality, but half the rehearsals were devoted to changing the seating arrangements of the orchestra and soloists. In one of these periodic redistributions, I bumped my head on a pendant microphone and had three stitches sewn in my scalp (the BBC refusing to let me leave for the hospital until I had filled out a long official form describing the accident).

Rosbaud, a courteous, gentle man, beloved by orchestral musicians, had devoted a great part of his life to contemporary music. When he directed the *Double Concerto* at a festival of the International Society for Contemporary Music in London, he was a dying man, the cancer that was to kill him six months later already far advanced. The program, as at most such international occasions when each country must be represented, was far too long. On this one evening there were major works from England, France, Italy, and Poland, as well as the *Double Concerto*.

Rosbaud was fascinated with the *Double Concerto* but had not realized its difficulties when studying it (if, indeed, he had been able to study it at all). He confided to me that it was the only work on the program he liked, along with a beautiful song cycle by Tadeusz Baird. Accordingly, he rehearsed the *Double Concerto* and little else, as the Baird songs were much easier. Rehearsals took place in an atmosphere heavy with resentment, smoldering with tension, as other composers and soloists waited around for their scheduled turn, only to be told that Rosbaud wished to continue rehearsing Carter's work.

It was a measure of the greatness of Rosbaud's character as well as a poor omen for the performance that, as we were about to step onto the stage, he turned to me and said, "Tell me, where were those places I was beating wrong this morning?" The performance did not break down, but it was a dead one, drained of all vitality; in part this was due to one of the lead players then in the BBC symphony, who hated contemporary music and was doing his discreet best to sabotage the festival. Carter, who was there, was ashen afterwards. It is a terrible thing for a composer to hear one of his works played with most of the right notes and no musical life.

At all other times, the *Double Concerto* seems to have created excitement against whatever odds. There have been beautifully controlled, relaxed, convincing performances by Gunther Schuller. There have, of course, been many performances that I have neither played in nor heard. A measure of the progress of our understanding of the work was a recent performance in New York under Dennis Russel Davies at Tully Hall. When the work was first played in 1961, there were ten full days of rehearsal. In 1972, for a completely relaxed execution, less than half that was necessary. The New York musicians were beginning to learn how to deal with the piece.

It was in these recent performances that certain aspects of the music began to be clear. As we all gradually shed our fears of getting lost, of the performance breaking down, as we stopped accenting the down beat in a desperate effort to keep together, and started phrasing the music as it asked to be phrased, making the delicate nuances that Carter had written, we began to hear things we had never suspected in the work. The enchanting play of intervals, each with its own periodic rhythm, moving in and out of phase with each other, suddenly became clear.

We realized that the absence of one dominant pulse did not mean a loss of control, but that it made possible a new and powerfully expressive set of relations between the apparently independent voices. In fact, Carter's rhythmic innovations—which are now famous—can be seen as affecting all the other elements of music, and even as radically altering our conception of the nature of music itself. Carter's recent works—the Third Quartet in particular—can no longer be heard as purely linear, narrative progressions in time, but as the intersection of opposed forces in a kaleidoscopic pattern.

Paradoxically, the most satisfying performance of the *Double Concerto* I have played in took place a few years ago with students at the New England Conservatory in Boston, directed with love and understanding by Frederick Prausnitz. Students have a great advantage over full professionals for a work of this kind: they don't have to be paid for rehearsals, and they are usually eager to take the music home and really work on it. The *Double Concerto,* too, needs only one violin, one cello, one oboe, etc., and any important conservatory can generally provide one first-rate player on every instrument. The New England Conservatory has a uniquely deep stage, and the problems of the seating arrangement solved themselves at once with an incomparable gain for the spatial conception of the work.

The history of the *Double Concerto* is one of a gradual but irregular progress of understanding, perception, and sympathy. When the work first appeared, there were hardly any performers who did not, at least secretly, regret the absence of the central pulse that made ensemble playing so much easier, just as those who saw the first cubist pictures must necessarily have felt—along with a liberated excitement—a curious anxiety at the loss of the central point of view destroyed by cubist fragmentation. A multiplicity of vision has become central to the artistic imagination of the twentieth century. Carter's is the richest and most coherent realization of this multiplicity in the music of our time. The simplicity and directness of his achievement, however, its permanence and its solidity, are only beginning to be felt.

CHAPTER EIGHTEEN

The Irrelevance of Serious Music

There are three ways of measuring the success of a musical style: the gradual win-
ning over of a large public willing to pay to hear it; the continued presence of an im-
portant group of musicians who passionately want to perform it; its influence on
succeeding generations of composers who are inspired by it. If modernism has par-
tially failed by the first of these criteria, the failure is due as much to economic as to
artistic reasons. It has triumphed by the second. It remains to be seen if the music of
the next century will continue to find inspiration in the great modernist achieve-
ments of this century. Experience teaches us that it is unlikely that much of the easy
music of our time promoted by the enemies of modernism will survive into the
future.

This essay is a combination of two articles written a few weeks apart. It provoked
some correspondence, and even answers in journals and newspapers. (Subsequent
to the publication of the second article, Peter Gelb canceled a compact disc about the
piano that I was supervising for Sony, in collaboration with National Public Radio.)
Most of the replies merely reiterated that the writers did not like difficult modern
music, that tonal music is easier than atonal for most laymen to understand at first
hearing, which is not exactly news, and that modernism has not been able to gain a
large audience, which proved that there was something wrong with it. Music which
does not appeal to a large mass audience does indeed have something wrong with it:
it does not have popular appeal—but that is about all that one can conclude except
to repeat the charges in different forms. Perhaps I should note here that the verdict is
not yet in on even this failure: of the three great Viennese dodecaphonic composers,
Berg has been able to win an international following (still contested, of course, by
part of the audience), but his success on this scale came almost forty years after his
death. Boulez, Carter, Berio, and Stockhausen—among the grand figures of the
1950s and 1960s—are still with us. No discussion of the difficulty of contemporary

style has any value if we do not see it as a part of a general problem of organizing our musical life to make serious music reasonably available for the important minority interested in it.

T HE death of classical music is widely proclaimed today in books and journals, although the villains responsible are variously identified. For some critics, the assassins are the star conductors and the operatic tenors who demand exorbitant fees; for others, the orchestral managers and the agents who attempt to impose ruthless commercial standards on high artistic ideals; still others blame the composers of difficult modernist atonal music or the performers who insist on playing Mozart and even Chopin on antiquated period instruments.

Nevertheless, the death of classical music is perhaps its oldest continuing tradition. In any case, it has been going on for a long time. Most music lovers know that terrified critics foresaw that Stravinsky's innovations around the time of *Le Sacre du printemps* in 1912 would destroy Western music, and that similar predictions had been made for many decades about Wagner. Sometimes all the arts were thought to be in danger of being perverted into an irreversible decline: at the end of the nineteenth century, Max Nordau published an influential book which claimed that all modern art, that of Zola and Cézanne as well as Wagner, was produced by moral degenerates. Earlier, the feeling that Verdi was ruining the great old *bel canto* tradition with the violence of his dramatic style was widespread among Italian academics. Chopin lamented that the fundamental importance of counterpoint was being lost with the new fashion for teaching harmony before anything else. For many music lovers in the first decades of the nineteenth century, the growing influence of Beethoven was certain to have fatal results. In the early eighteenth century, Roger North claimed that the old tradition of private music-making in the English country houses was being wiped out by the importation of Italian virtuosos. In the first decades of the seventeenth century, old-fashioned musicians felt that Monteverdi's novel and overly expressive manner was killing the basic madrigal tradition. The disappearance of an old way of performing or composing, the displacement of one music by another, is an eternal part of history.

Recent complaints, however, have a slightly different slant: they are all specifically listener-oriented. What is disappearing today, for one reason or another, is the audience. The standard, banal repertory, it seems, is driving listeners off—or, alternatively and paradoxically, too many new and unfamiliar works on concert programs are alienating them. High fees for the most famous artists or demands for higher wages by greedy orchestral musicians are forcing ticket prices up beyond the means of the average concert-goer. Concert organizers do not understand the market well enough to attract a public that would make classical music commercially viable.

There is some truth to these attacks, of course, but they all overlook the essentially artificial nature of a system that makes music depend principally on the listener. The life of music is based not so much on those who want to listen, but on those who want to play and sing. Public concerts are a relatively recent phenomenon in the history of mankind, dating largely from the latter half of the eighteenth century. They were a way of enabling musicians to make a living doing what they like to do after much of the patronage of church and court had been withdrawn. Musicians need and want an audience from time to time, but the public concert is only a small part of the making of music, not the whole of it: playing for a few friends, playing with other musicians, and even playing for oneself still provide the foundation of musical life. Making the public concert the economic basis of music has somewhat obscured the reason that music exists.

Most of the contemporary problems of the public concert, however, are nobody's fault. Expenses that have nothing to do with music play the most important role. It used to be possible for pianists to earn enough money by traveling from one small town to another as well as to large cities. That is now impossible. Without subsidy, no concert series today can afford to pay fees high enough to cover the incidental costs of travel and leave enough left over for the pianist to live—and when the concert is not just a single pianist, but a violinist with an accompanist, or a string quartet, or a chamber orchestra, the problem is raised to a higher power. Whether the subsidy is from rich patrons giving tax-deductible donations or directly from the government, in the end the money comes out of taxpayers' pockets.

The man who used to organize all of the classical music in Chicago except for the opera and the Chicago Symphony, Harry Zelser (and he even managed the opera for a while), claimed to run the only unsubsidized series of piano recitals in the United States. He once told me that Josef Hofmann, perhaps the greatest pianist I ever heard, never made a success in Chicago. "We plastered Chicago with posters one year," he said, "and we only took in fifty dollars more at the box office. After that he played in Studebaker Hall." This hall, now a movie theater, seats about five hundred; by the time I was playing in Chicago, Harry could not have afforded to book a concert that sold only five hundred tickets. In a hall with two thousand seats, his piano recital series (generally about fourteen concerts a year, as I remember) regularly attracted about fifteen hundred subscribers. Along with the most famous pianists, Harry always introduced young newcomers, and everyone, even the most distinguished performers, cut their fees for

Harry in order to play in Chicago. (To my surprise, one year he raised my fee slightly, and explained, "Well, last year we sold some extra single seats for you at the box office, so you're paying your way.") When he died, Harry willed his agency to the Chicago Symphony, a non-profit organization dependent on tax-free subsidy, and all pianists raised their fees immediately.

Recitals in the United States now depend almost entirely on the sponsorship of non-profit groups—universities, symphony orchestras, or cultural foundations. The aim, nevertheless, is to fill the hall—and, if possible, the largest hall in town. Even if every seat in a hall of two thousand is sold, however, it is not always possible to make much of a profit. It costs about a thousand dollars to move a piano in New York from Steinway Hall a few yards across the street to Carnegie Hall. And when the rental of the hall is still reasonable, the price of newspaper advertising in a large city like New York is likely to eat up half the receipts of the concert. Giving recitals was already a precarious way of making a living in the early nineteenth century: there was always the danger of arriving in a small town just after someone else had played, and the taste for music was momentarily sated. Today it can no longer guarantee a livelihood; to some extent the most famous musicians are dependent on societies subsidized in one way or another.

With opera and symphonic concerts, the situation is notorious. Even if the Metropolitan Opera in New York or La Scala in Milan sold every seat in the house for every performance of the season, the deficit would still be in the millions of dollars, and it should be added that the ticket prices are already beyond the means of most people interested in going to the opera. This is not, however, a recent development. Almost from the beginning, serious opera has been a losing economic affair, paid for directly or indirectly by the government. The memoirs of Doctor Véron, the man who took over the affairs of the Paris opera for a few years when it was privatized in 1830 by the new régime of Louis-Philippe, are delightfully instructive. He intended to make money running the opera, and he did make a fortune. He decreased the size and increased the number of the high-priced boxes, so that he could sell more subscriptions to middle-class families. He cut costs. It was no use trying to reduce the fees of the outlandishly high-priced international singers: they could not be touched. It was no use, either, to try to reduce expenses on scenery and staging—that was what people came to see. He was, however, able to lower the salaries of the only people who were relatively helpless (and he admits this somewhat shamefacedly): the members of the orchestra. In the end, he adds, when he was asked how he was able to make a fortune by managing the opera, he replied, "Because I got out before the government lowered the subsidy." The privatization of the Paris opera was, typically, still paid for by the taxpayers.

II

Employing marketing techniques for the selling of classical music is clearly not an option without its dangers. Even if one could interest twenty thousand people for a single concert, this kind of music cannot be played in a large stadium with amplification and still survive. Performances of that kind occasionally occur; operas are produced in the baths of Caracalla in Rome, but it is only a curiosity for tourists. I once played the Liszt Concerto No. 1 outdoors at Hartford, Connecticut, for what I was told was an audience of fifteen thousand, but I cannot imagine that this was an experience that would satisfy the average music lover or even convert the uninitiated.

It is understandable that the promoters of classical music deplore the small size of the audience, but something very much more serious goes almost unrecognized. All these generally vain attempts to fill large halls with bodies for classical concerts hide the fact that most of the halls are already too large for the greater part of the standard repertory. For example, no Mozart opera is fully audible in the opera houses of the major cities. To take one famous dramatic moment: the three orchestras on the stage at the end of the first act of *Don Giovanni* cannot be heard properly beyond the fifth row of the opera houses in Milan, New York, London, Vienna, or in any theater that seats more than eight hundred or a thousand. Each orchestra plays a different dance tune in a different rhythm, and the second and third orchestras tune up harmoniously while the previous one has already begun to play: it is one of the most stupefying displays of contrapuntal virtuosity since the English Renaissance, and very few lovers of Mozart have ever heard it in anything like all its detail. (It is sometimes claimed that one can hear the three orchestras on records, but of course on a recording one cannot distinguish each orchestra from the others in space and appreciate the cross-rhythms of the counterpoint—the effect demands polyphony made visual in order to become audible.) *Don Giovanni* was composed for a house of about 750 in Prague; a performance in a hall of that size is a revelation. Details never noticed except on the page can suddenly be heard.

Even in a house of such a small size, care has to be taken to ensure audibility; Mozart was notorious for making it difficult to hear the singers with his elaborate orchestration and rich polyphonic inner voices. In the great sextet in *The Marriage of Figaro,* when Susanna is distressed to discover Figaro kissing a lady who turns out to be his mother, one of the most beautiful passages in Susanna's part cannot be heard unless she is placed a few feet in front of the other five singers. I do not think that I have ever clearly heard the descent of this wonderfully expressive line in performance:

Sus.

With Mozart's first operatic masterpiece, *Idomeneo,* written when he was twenty-one, the problems are even greater—and rarely appreciated because they are largely insoluble in almost every modern opera house. *Idomeneo* was composed for the tiny Residenz-Theater in Munich, an architectural delight designed by Cuvilliés which seats only 350. The tenor part, intended for a famous singer already long past his prime who had lost a lot of his power but had retained his coloratura technique, is very elaborate: it makes sense only if sung lightly in a small space. Famous tenors bellowing the role in the large arenas now considered economically necessary provide an absurd spectacle. It should be clear that the greater the number of people that can be enticed into a performance of one of these Mozart operas, the greater the musical disaster.

Solving the economic problems of classical music, therefore, will not help if enjoyment and comprehension are diminished by the financial improvement. We might even predict, with only some small rhetorical exaggeration, that any viable economic solution will end by destroying much of the pleasure in the music. At least with the music from 1700 to 1850, from Bach to Chopin, the consistent efforts over the last century to reach a much larger audience have only succeeded in giving a false image of a major part of the repertory. Only two of the thirty-two sonatas of Beethoven were played in public concerts in Vienna before his death. The piano sonatas of Schubert were never played during his lifetime for an audience of more than twenty or thirty people. It is true that the cantatas composed for huge forces during the French Revolution by Grétry and Méhul were intended for mass audiences—this was the tradition inherited by Berlioz for his own music and for his extraordinary production of Beethoven's Fifth Symphony with five hundred musicians. Nevertheless, the symphonies of Haydn and Mozart and even Beethoven were performed in relatively small concert rooms, even if Mozart once enjoyed a performance of one of his symphonies (K. 338 in C major) with forty violins, eight oboes, and ten double-basses. Only symphonies, concertos, and overtures at that time were fully public, and everything else—sonatas, trios, and quartets—was performed in settings which would seem very intimate to us today.

A growing awareness of how inadequate or irrelevant so much of our interpretation of the works of this period has become is the principal stimulus for the attempt to revive the original instruments on which they were played. The brilliance and power of modern instruments developed gradually in response to the ever-larger concert halls that were being constructed as well as to the louder music that was being composed for them. Not only pianos and wind and brass instruments have been radically modernized: every Stradivarius has had its neck lengthened in order to give greater tension and carrying power to the strings. Furthermore, we inevitably play very differently in reaction to the larger spaces that must be filled with sound. Pianists use the pedal almost continuously in Beethoven, so that its function for him as a special effect is lost. Most string players now employ a continuously fast and unvarying vibrato in order to give greater presence to their sound, and delicate variations of vibrato no longer contribute to the interpretation. Performing private works in public in a large hall alters the style of playing in many ways, some subtle and some gross, all largely unconscious as every one of us has become conditioned to think of all music in terms of public performance.

The popular movement to revive so-called "authentic" instruments and stylistic habits is, in sum, a natural reaction when we become aware of the inevitable distortions of modern instruments created for larger concert halls. It is, unfortunately, subject to the same commercial pressures, the same problems, as less "authentic" performance. In order to sell the authenticity, to make it commercially attractive, it has been only too tempting to claim with each new interpretation that the unique true method of performance has at last been resuscitated, although in the eighteenth century there was as much, if not more, possibility of individual stylistic variation than there is today. Above all, playing the ancient instruments with their weaker, subtle, and more fragile tone in a large space with modern acoustics only exacerbates the problem of revealing the music to the public. Reviving the sonority of an eighteenth-century piano is defeated when it is played in a hall that seats more than two or three hundred people even when it is completely audible, which is not always the case: it may be the same instrument, but it is not at all the same sound. Recordings are a more successful means of transmission, but more than anything else, the emphasis on the recorded performance has only reinforced the modern delusion that music is intended more for listening than playing. Nevertheless, the "authenticity" movement has been salutary and beneficial. Few pianists today would want to perform a Beethoven sonata without at least taking into account the sonority it might have had during the composer's time.

The music that works most easily for the way our musical life is organized at present is the music written since 1850 for public performance in large halls: it gives rise to the least amount of misrepresentation in performance today. It is also this kind of music, splendid as so much of it is, that has caused us to misunderstand the music of earlier periods. We take a work of music specifically written for a public concert as the norm, and we do not realize to what an extent it is actually an anomaly in the history of music. Most works, when not improvised or simply handed down without ever being transcribed, were composed for a specific social function: court music or ecclesiastical music (both to be played on traditional occasions); or chamber music and house music (to be played for friends and invited guests); or educational music (to be played by professional students and musicians in private). Almost all the best-known works of Johann Sebastian Bach, for example—the *Well-Tempered Keyboard,* the Goldberg Variations, the Partitas, the Italian Concerto, the *Art of Fugue*—are educational, models of composition to be studied and played at home: the kind of public concert at which they could be played did not exist during Bach's lifetime, and he could never have envisaged a concert performance of any of them. In fact, public performance of most of these works is largely an invention of the twentieth century.

III

The public concert is like a museum: they are both institutions developed at roughly the same time and for the same reason. They both provide works of art with what seems to be a perfectly neutral framework, and they both claim to detach the works from their social and ideological setting. The purpose is to advance purely aesthetic values. The claim of a perfectly neutral frame cannot be sustained, of course; museums and symphony concerts embody pretentious social values, but that is beside the point. You may buy a subscription to the symphony because it marks you as a person of culture and good breeding, but you are supposed to go because you sincerely enjoy it, and many people do enjoy it— and many others succeed at last in honestly persuading themselves that they enjoy it, which in the end is the same thing. This snobbish social aspect has given rise to the sociological fantasy that serious music is tied to a structure of class distinctions, but that will not hold water. It is unfortunately true that the rich can better afford to go to concerts than the poor, but there is no reason to think that the possession of wealth gives one a deeper interest in, or understanding of, classical music. Appreciation of music, like a love of sport, is not tied to class.

The isolation of a work of art in a museum inevitably removes some of its significance along with the removal of context: it allows the purely aesthetic values to come forward only by pushing every other kind of meaning into the background. A public concert does the same with pieces of music. The abstract formality is emphasized by evening dress, and by the element of ritual that surrounds a concert. The Goldberg Variations are no longer a model of how to write many different kinds of canons on a descending bass as well as an encyclopedic survey of different styles and different forms: it has been stripped down to its direct emotional and musical power, and this is a gain as well as a loss, an advantage rather like that of removing a picture by Caravaggio from a church into a museum where it can be seen in a better light. There is an important loss of meaning, nevertheless, and we look at the picture in a different way, disregarding much of its content in favor of painterly values. Music, however, is not an art to be passively appreciated like painting; it must be actively recreated at each playing, and we not only listen to a private work differently in a concert hall, but we play it in a different way as well.

Composing music directly for public performance results in a work of a special abstract character, rather like painting a picture solely to be hung on the walls of a museum. That is why so much of even the finest public music of the late nineteenth century resembled the contemporary academic history painting in both its grandiose pretensions and its rhetoric. It is also why chamber music and solo piano sonatas have taken on a grandiose character often so much at odds with the genre: the performance of a nocturne now seems to be almost as dependent on the presence of a mass audience as that of a symphony or a requiem mass. (This is also true of "authentic" interpretations, which tend to be even more dogmatic and pompous than the standard thoughtless and banal performances of the average conservatory graduate.) From its inception, the public concert was a conservative institution. The most important concert society in mid-eighteenth-century London was the Society of Ancient Music, which forbade the performance of any work less than thirty years old. In this light, it is easy to explain the contradictory complaints about the repertoire: it is all old hat and/or the new works are unintelligible. The audience traditionally wants something new and detests innovation. The paradox can be extended even to the composers themselves. Anton von Webern hoped for the day when the postman would whistle a twelve-tone tune while delivering his mail. He did nothing, however, to make his work more accessible, and there is no reason to think that there was anything he could have done.

As concert halls became bigger and audiences became larger, music became gradually more and more difficult to understand at first hearing. That paradox is essential to the history of modern culture. Mozart was already difficult for his contemporaries, who were distressed by unintelligible modulations and overcomplicated textures. Beethoven was much harder than Mozart, and polemic about the insanity of some of his late conceptions continued literally until the end of the nineteenth century. Wagner made Beethoven's music sound simple by contrast for most amateurs. A devoted Wagnerian like Ernest Newman found parts of Strauss's *Electra* unintelligible nonsense at its English premiere. Debussy was much less acceptable than Strauss.

Although Mozart's music was disliked in early nineteenth-century Paris by both public and critics, it was played anyway, simply because enough musicians liked it, and finally everyone else came around. Beethoven was performed by those who loved his music until he became popular. Eventually in our century even his Great Fugue for string quartet is sometimes listened to with awe and pleasure. Wagner, too, became popular: his admirers obstinately insisted on performing his music-dramas against the prevailing distaste.

The music that survives is the music that musicians want to play. They perform it until it finds an audience. Sometimes it is only a small audience, as is the case so far for Arnold Schoenberg, and I am not sure if he will ever capture a large one, but he will be performed as long as there are musicians who insist on playing him. The most significant composers are those who gain the fanatical loyalty of some performers. There are good composers who never inspire that kind of devotion: they are the ones whose music is briefly revived from time to time and then dropped again.

Nothing is more comic than the resentment of contemporary art, the self-righteous indignation aroused by its difficulty. I remember once being invited to lecture in Cincinnati on the music of Pierre Boulez and Elliott Carter. In the question period afterward, a woman posed what she evidently conceived not as a question but as an aggressive and defiant challenge: "Mr. Rosen, don't you think the composer has a responsibility to write music that the public can understand?" On such occasions I normally reply politely to all questions, no matter how foolish, but this time I answered that the question was not interesting but that the obvious resentment that inspired it was very significant indeed. To understand the frame of mind in which such challenges are made, we must remember that the disastrous first performance of *Le Sacre du printemps* (at which the members of the fashionable Jockey Club organized a riot of booing and hissing) was inaudible after the first few seconds. It is true that the high bassoon note that opens the ballet was a shock at the time, but it is clear that nobody was prepared to listen. Condemnation was decided in advance. (It seems not to be widely known that the second performance was a triumph: the work was listened to this time.) History continues to repeat itself: When Beethoven's Quartet in C-sharp Minor, op. 131, was first played in Paris in the 1830s, the leader of the conservative critical faction, François-Joseph Fétis, claimed that the music-lovers who said they admired the quartet were insincere: they must have been lying. As we shall see, this ignoble argument continues to surface in our time with the enemies of modernism.

IV

In the debates on the so-called crisis of classical music, the same rancor and a similar determination not to listen were displayed by Roger Scruton in an article in the *New Criterion* (November 1996), in which he blamed the imminent death of serious music on the refusal of composers to write tonal music. (He doesn't much like any of the new tonal music, however.) He added a comic political note to the discussion by equating tonality with unregulated capitalism. "The suspicion of tonality," he wrote, "like Marx's suspicion of private property, should be seen for what it is: an act of rebellion against the only way of making sense of things." Even less convincing was Scruton's claim that Western triadic tonality is the only way music can make sense.[1] He draws back somewhat from this extravagance, and admits that experts can make sense of contemporary non-tonal music. But, according to Scruton, even the expert cannot understand it from *experience,* but only because he has decoded it.

There is a Jewish joke about which language is the best: the Englishman claims English for its richness; the German insists that German is the most poetic; the Frenchman elects French because of its clarity and logic; but the Jew insists that Yiddish is the best because you can understand every word. Scruton impugns the honesty and the credibility of all the non-experts who have listened with sympathy, understanding, and pleasure to the music of Berg and Webern. Yet the belief that nobody really enjoys the music of Schoenberg or Boulez is curiously persistent. The great pianist Edouard Steuermann was once approached after a concert by a man who told him that he had written an essay to demonstrate that one cannot play twelve-tone music from memory. "But I do play twelve-tone music from memory," returned Steuermann. The man, nonplussed, was silent for a moment, but he finally found a solution: "You're lying," he said. I myself once received a favorable review for a short book on Schoenberg, but the reviewer was puzzled by my discussion of the emotion in Schoenberg's work. He could not believe there was any. To those who admire Schoenberg's music, the emotion can often seem all too intense to the point of hysteria. In the same way, Bach's music was admired for its contrapuntal art in the latter part of the eighteenth century, but he would have been as great as Handel, it was said, if only he could have shown some understanding of sentiment. For many music-lovers today, Bach's handling of sentiment has greater intimacy and power than Handel's.

There has never been a dearth of acceptable tonal music. Those who do not want to listen to Berg and Schoenberg could always choose Hindemith, Britten, or Shostakovich. Scruton's lack of good faith was revealed by his remarks about

---

1. Scruton wants to have nothing to do with non-tonal Oriental systems. "For three hundred years," he writes, "Japan remained cut off from Western art music [Does he mean to suggest that before that the Japanese were enjoying the fourteenth- and fifteenth-century compositions of Guillaume de Machaut and John Dunstable?], locked in its grisly imitations of the Chinese court orchestras, dutifully producing sounds as cacophonous to local ears as the croaking of jackdaws." This is not politically correct.

Milton Babbitt: "It is possible for a mathematician versed in set theory to get a kick out of Milton Babbitt's ingenious permutation of hexachords" (p. 8). The mathematics in the music of Babbitt is far too simple to interest anyone versed in set theory: this only betrays Scruton's ignorance of mathematics. Advising a composer to write in a style that he does not believe in is insolent. Scruton's criticism is informed by resentment, an inability to believe that anything he cannot take the trouble to understand might be any good.

You do not have to love a work of art or a style in order to criticize it, but you need to understand its attraction for someone who does. Those who, like Scruton, hate contemporary music believe that their dislike has equal weight with the love that others have for it. But their criticism has no significance and no importance if it is not accompanied by understanding—and that implies the comprehension of at least the possibility of love. That is what the enemies of modernism cannot concede, and that is why their criticism comes down to nothing more than an admission that they don't like modern music (which we knew) and can't appreciate it (and we are sorry for them).

The lack of sympathetic comprehension is often the occasion for the claim that only professionals can understand difficult contemporary music, which is demonstrably false, or the more ignoble assertion that those who say they love the music of Schoenberg, Boulez, or Carter are only shamming. This last position is simple cowardice, a refusal to face the consequences of one's own failure to understand, a failure all the more profound as it reflects most often a willful withholding of sympathy. It would seem that the enemies of modern art are frightened by a love they do not want to comprehend.

V

Who's afraid of the avant-garde? Julian Lloyd Webber, for one. A well-known British cellist, he is the brother of the much better known Andrew Lloyd Webber, composer of the successful pop musicals *Jesus Christ Superstar* and *Cats*. He gave a speech in February 1998 at the World Economic Forum in Davos, Switzerland, attacking what he called "the new führers of the classical music establishment." It received surprisingly generous media coverage, including a reprint of the speech in *The Daily Telegraph* in London (February 1998), a sensible answer in *The New York Times* (Sunday, March 22) from Paul Griffiths, and a long interview in *The Independent* (in London, February 2) with the headline "STOP THE DICTATORS OF MODERN MUSIC."

I should have thought that the modernist style in music was no longer a threat, but if it is still frightening, then this attack is an encouraging sign that modernism is alive and in good health. The earliest figures, of course, are now long dead and have entered the Pantheon: Schoenberg, Stravinsky, Berg, Webern, Bartók are an unquestioned part of our musical heritage. The most radical revolutionary masters of the generations that followed—Olivier Messiaen, Pierre Boulez, Elliott Carter, Luciano Berio, György Ligeti, Karlheinz Stockhausen, Sir Harrison Birtwistle, Sir Peter Maxwell Davies, Milton Babbitt—are all aging and respectable members of society. Pierre Boulez, indeed, is almost a public institution. It is, I suspect, this respectability that terrifies Lloyd Webber. Forty years ago, it used to be feared that these young Turks were out to destroy classical music: they have all turned out to be admirers of Bach, Mozart, Beethoven, Chopin, Schumann and Verdi, Wagner and Debussy (if not always of Rachmaninoff and Puccini). What the enemies of modernism cannot accept is the way the avant-garde have taken possession of the mainstream of the great Western tradition.

Nevertheless, with all the devotion and passionate enthusiasm that these composers can inspire, it is true they have not won the hearts of a mass audience. Not even the early generation is fully accepted by the general public, with the exception of Stravinsky—and in his case only the early Russian ballets are truly popular, while the neoclassic and later atonal works remain appreciated mostly by connoisseurs. Lloyd Webber's contention is that the decline in public interest in classical music in general is mainly due to the modernist composers, who pigheadedly refused to compose the kind of music the public would like, and to their allies in the musical establishment, which has mercilessly forced their works on a helpless public.

The absurdity of this thesis was recognized immediately, and Paul Griffiths' article (*The New York Times*, March 22, 1998) is headed "Don't Blame Modernists for the Empty Seats." He writes:

> Moreover, the idea that these composers, or any others, had the power to turn people off Beethoven is laughable. On the contrary, classical composition has remained deeply attached to its roots: veneration of the past, not dismissal, has been its hallmark. And any listener who has had a bad experience with new music would surely be more, not less, likely to rush back to the "Eroica" Symphony and the "Waldstein" Sonata.

This is the eminently judicious and reasonable response. What is worth taking seriously, however, is not Lloyd Webber's claims, but the bizarre language in which they are couched, and the reason for the strange inflation of his obviously ludicrous speech by the media.

A few sentences from Lloyd Webber should give us a taste of his language and logic:

Composers who had pursued a logical development of the music of the great masters [these, of course, for Lloyd Webber, are decidedly not the modernists] were increasingly disparaged and derided by the new führers of the classical music establishment, for whom tonality and harmony had become dirty words. I am not necessarily criticizing that style [why ever not?], but it cannot be good for music to strait-jacket its composers. In the years after the war, Western classical music created a pernicious politburo which proved as effective as its counterpart in the East. In America, composers like Aaron Copland and Samuel Barber found themselves dismissed as dated. In Germany, Bertold Goldschmidt couldn't even get a hearing.

The vocabulary—"führers," "politburo"—is considerably more interesting than the absurd propositions: Goldschmidt had difficulty in getting a hearing in his native Germany after the war principally because he emigrated to England in 1935 and became a British national; both Copland and Barber, however, were performed from 1945 to 1975 with much greater frequency in the United States than any of the more "radical" composers like Elliott Carter or Roger Sessions. Lloyd Webber makes it seem as if it had been easy to hear the works of modernist composers during this period, as if the public could not have escaped their dread dissonances. Of course, just the opposite is true. In addition, Lloyd Webber's style betrays his intellectual confusion: I have never met any admirer of avant-garde music for whom "harmony" was a dirty word, but the combined smear of *führer* and *politburo* makes a nice balance between Nazi and Communist.

Lloyd Webber's rancor is international, but its form has a peculiarly British aspect. His speech recalls the protests launched against Sir William Glock when he took over the direction of music at the BBC in the 1950s, and opened it out to the most interesting recent musical developments. At the time, the BBC Symphony was in a terrible state, with an incompetent musical director (I played a Mozart concerto with him at the Cheltenham Festival, so I had some experience) and a concertmaster who systematically sabotaged performances of difficult contemporary music. The famous Prom concerts in the summer at the Albert Hall had fallen from the high standard set at the beginning of the century by Sir Hamilton Harty, and had become a largely undistinguished set of programs of popular warhorses. Glock (not yet Sir William), a fine musician and an excellent pianist who had studied with Schnabel, was the editor of *Score*, at that time the most important magazine in the world dealing with contemporary music. He transformed the Prom concerts into one of the most distinguished festivals of music in Europe. "We have a public of 3000 every night, and nobody knows why they come," he said to me. "We're going to change the programs and see what happens." In addition to the usual Tchaikovsky, Beethoven, and Gilbert and Sullivan, there were now performances of Mozart's wonderful unfinished opera *Zaïde*, the Berlioz Requiem, and Stockhausen's *Gruppen*, with many other unfamiliar old and modern works. (The Stockhausen work attracted only 2500 listeners, but Glock seemed pleased enough with that.) The BBC orchestra was revitalized with the appointment of Antal Dorati and then Pierre Boulez as chief conductors, and a series of broadcast chamber music concerts was created (the Thursday Invitation Concerts) which combined classical works and avant-garde contemporary pieces with music from the medieval and Renaissance periods.

The BBC has enormous power in British culture, and musical London was transformed by Glock in a year or so from an uninteresting backwater into one of the great centers of music, receptive to works of all kinds. Glock's policies raised an outcry, however, and he was attacked in Parliament in terms exactly like those used by Lloyd Webber. "Gauleiter Glock" he was dubbed, as if he were terrorizing honest music-lovers, forcing them to listen to a debased foreign art against all British tradition. What was resented, in fact, was not the programming of contemporary music (one can always turn off the radio, after all) but the new prestige and acceptance accorded to it. Some of the staff at the BBC were, however, indignant: they complained that the media acted as if Glock had introduced contemporary music for the first time to the BBC, and ignored all the performances they had previously organized over the years. The new respect paid to new music was the point, however. I am not sure if much more contemporary music was really played after Glock's arrival at the BBC than before, but he had found a way of calling attention to it, investing it with a new prestige. He sent the BBC orchestra on a tour of America in which they played six programs of difficult twentieth-century music in three weeks in Carnegie Hall under Dorati and Boulez, something no American orchestra at the time would have been able to equal. That was the true beginning of Boulez's dazzling international career as a conductor; a few years later he was to become the director of the New York Philharmonic.

Gauleiter, führer, politburo—these revealing expressions are clinical symptoms of irrational resentment.[2] The irrationality springs not simply from a distaste for

---

2. Lloyd Webber may have a more personal reason for hating the modern style. His father gave up writing music just as the English musical scene was opened up by Sir William Glock to all the latest international movements. He writes: "A composer like my father stood no chance . . . Although his early works pushed at the boundaries of tonality, his roots were firmly based in the romanticism of Richard Strauss and Rachmaninov—composers whose music was adored by audiences but increasingly dismissed by the 'politburo.' My father found it an impossible climate to write in and ceased composing almost completely in the early Fifties—his spirit disillusioned and broken at the age of thirty-eight."

a style we cannot understand or appreciate, but from an unacknowledged or un-conscious distress at being shut out from the comprehension of something that we dimly feel we ought to be able to admire. That is the reason so much of the criticism of the past can seem wildly irrelevant. In his time, Beethoven's works were called, literally, sexual monstrosities by his enemies. The works of Wagner and Schoenberg as well were equally improbably classed as sexual perversions. Whistler's paintings were described as an insulting fraud by Ruskin.

Typical of this irrational reaction is the belief that a work we do not under-stand must be devoid of all meaning. This leads to a paranoia like Lloyd Web-ber's, the claim that there is some kind of conspiracy to impose a fraud on the public. Ned Rorem, for instance, has written that nobody really likes the music of Elliott Carter: his many admirers only pretend to like it. They must therefore be lying. This truly loony statement is a characteristic expression of resentment, of hatred for an art that one does not understand—or, rather, for an art that one is unwilling to understand.

Taste is, after all, a matter of will, of moral and social decisions. To take a fa-mous example from the modernist tradition in literature, we are assured that Joyce's *Ulysses* is a difficult masterpiece, and we try it, determined to prove our cultural superiority by our appreciation. After the initial repugnance for much of the book experienced by most readers, many of us have succeeded in the end in deriving great pleasure from all of it. Similarly, in the history of music from Bach to the present, by repeated listening we have learned to love the music that has at first puzzled and even repelled us. There is, however, always the megalo-maniac critic or amateur who is convinced—and glories in that conviction—that he is the innocent little boy who sees that the emperor has no clothes.

It is perhaps not healthy or reasonable to develop a taste for absolutely every-thing. "I hate anything Egyptian," Goethe once said at a dinner party, "and I'm glad: one must always have something to dislike." Our limitations, however, are not a sign of moral or aesthetic superiority, as Lloyd Webber implies with his talk of dictators and his foolish claim that the avant-garde composer thinks "harmony" is a dirty word. I myself, for example, do not care for the music of Messaien, and am put off by its air of unctuous piety: when I am mean-spirited, I even describe his opera as Saint Francis Walking on the Birds. But when I reflect that some of the finest musicians today like Peter Serkin adore Messiaen, I realize that I, too, would learn to love his music if I decided to put my mind to it. The admirers of Messaien are clearly right: what they hear in his work is really there.

The difficulty of contemporary music, and, in general, of a great deal of mod-ern art and literature, is often ascribed to an attempt of the artist to direct his work entirely to professionals, to refuse to lower himself to the level of the mass public. On the contrary, composers, artists, and writers have always hoped for popular success—but on their own terms. Webern knew that his dream of hearing the postman whistling a twelve-tone row as he delivered the mail was utopian. Music in general has indeed become altogether less whistleable or hummable. I have heard friends whistle or hum tunes by George Gershwin and Harold Arlen, but I have never heard anyone whistle a tune by Andrew Lloyd Webber (perhaps I move in the wrong circles). In any case, I have not developed a theory that there is a conspiracy to force the works of Andrew Lloyd Webber and Stephen Sondheim on a helpless public to prevent the great musicals of Gershwin and Arlen from being revived. However, I do recall having actually heard a twelve-tone row whistled often on the Princeton campus back in the late 1940s when the Princeton Chapel Choir performed Schoenberg's *Survivor from Warsaw* with the New York Philharmonic. Dimitri Mitropoulos came to Princeton to rehearse the choral part, and started by telling the choir that he knew we hated the work but that we all had to suffer for the sake of modern music. The choir was surprised: as a matter of fact, no one hated the work, and some of us hummed and whistled the tune, but the role of martyr modeled on Savonarola was congenial to Mitropoulos, and the difficulty of modern music had already been elevated from the status of a problem to a myth.

The difficulty of contemporary music is more serious than that of contemporary painting, largely because you can look at a picture in a few seconds but you have to sit through a work of music for as long as it takes. Composers have faced the problem for a long time. In 1939, when Schoenberg took refuge from Nazi Germany for a year in Barcelona, he refused to allow a performance of his *Music for a Film Sequence* that Webern proposed for a concert of the International Society for Contemporary Music. "I have lived here for some months, and I have made many friends. I play tennis with them," he said. "What will they think of me when they hear this terrible music?"

There is a widespread misunderstanding about the taste of the public for classical music. It is not difficult music to which they object, but difficult music that is unfamiliar. The people who prefer to hear music that is easy to listen to are rarely the ones who are deeply concerned with what is called classical music, or who buy subscriptions year after year to orchestral and recital series. In fact, the most serious music-lovers are not particularly attracted by easy music even if they hate some of the difficult music that may be thrust upon them. The proposal to bring the alienated audience back to contemporary music by patronizing composers who write in a nice, agreeable style is impractical. "Listener-friendly" music—to use the current term—may not inspire noisy protests, but it also arouses no enthusiasm. Julian Lloyd Webber proposes, for example, to revive the music of Malcolm Arnold, a minor British composer who wrote the score to *The Bridge on the River Kwai*, and several serious orchestral works. Perhaps the general public would not mind sitting through a work by Arnold, but he inspires no passion except in a few English critics happy to find a native work that does not grate on their nerves with horrid dissonance. With Schoenberg or Boulez, on the other hand, who are still controversial, there may be a majority of music-lovers who hope never to have to listen to their works, but there is also a significantly large minority that passionately wants to perform and hear them.[3] The basic problem with Lloyd Webber's proposal, therefore, is not so much that interesting and original composers generally do not want to write "listener-friendly" music; the true stumbling-block is that few musicians have any passionate urge to play or hear that kind of music. It is a fallacy common to administrators in the music business—record companies, symphony orchestras, concert societies—that the public yearns for listener-friendly music. The only thing we can say is that the section of the public for whom music stopped with Tchaikovsky or Debussy does not want to hear any unfamiliar contemporary music at all, but if they have to sit through it, they prefer music that does not annoy them or to which they do not have to listen with any attention in order to grasp what is going on. The music of conservative modern composers, like Samuel Barber or Virgil Thomson (to name two who are safely dead), may not provoke outrage, but it has no more popular mass appeal than that of the most extravagant modernists.

VI

Accompanying Paul Griffiths' criticism of Lloyd Webber in *The New York Times* of March 22, a proposal similar to Lloyd Webber's was made by Peter Gelb in an article unusually obtuse even for the director of a large record company like Sony. (It is, no doubt, the policy of *The Times* not to print an attack on Philistinism without representing the Philistine point of view in the same issue.) The headline read "One Label's Strategy: Make It New, but Make It Pay." Like Lloyd Webber, Gelb has paranoid delusions of a conspiracy:

---

3. It is significant that when Pierre Boulez took over the New York Philharmonic and started to schedule many unfamiliar works, the subscriptions dropped from the 100 percent achieved under Leonard Bernstein, but that when he left a few years later, they had mounted back to over 95 percent—and, most important of all, the average age of the subscribers had fallen by ten years. And when Boulez initiated a two-week series at the end of the season called "Rug Concerts," for which the seats in the parterre were removed and young people could sit on the floor (like the Prom Concerts in London), fifteen hundred people were turned away every day, seven days a week. After he left, there was an attempt to continue the project, but it failed. Young music-lovers would come to hear Boulez only if they could sit on the floor, and they would not come for anyone less adventurous.

Attempts to commission or schedule accessible and emotionally stimulating new music were blocked by a cabal of atonal composers, academics and classical-music critics, who seemed to share one goal: to
confine all new classical music to an elite intellectual exercise with
limited audience appeal. By their rules, any new classical composition
that enjoys commercial success is no good.

This implies that difficult avant-garde music was played more often in recent decades than more conservative modern works "easy" to listen to and more successful commercially. That, of course, is quite simply false.

As for Gelb's "cabal" (the equivalent of Lloyd Webber's "politburo"), it never
existed.[4] Conductors and solo performers programmed works they liked to play.
Critics campaigned for works they thought had not been given a fair hearing. On
the rare occasions when a work unpopular with the public got performed by a
major orchestra, it was almost always because the conductor passionately wanted
to present it, sometimes against the advice of the orchestra's administrators.
Since many of the "difficult" works were complex and unfamiliar to the orchestra, the conductor had to fight, most often unsuccessfully, to get extra rehearsal
time. Like the Beethoven symphonies in the first half of the nineteenth century,[5]
the more complicated scores need to be performed several times over the years
for the musicians to be able to give a convincing, or even a clean, rendition. After
an initial performance, however, few avant-garde scores had a second chance until two decades or more had passed. The musicians and the conductor never
gained the experience to perform the work with the necessary freedom. Schoenberg once remarked: "My music is not modern, it is only badly played." When
Elliott Carter's piano concerto was presented for the first time by the Boston
Symphony (with an excellent pianist, Jacob Lateiner, but a conductor who had
no idea how to interpret the work), one of the members of the orchestra said to
the composer, "The trouble with your music, Mr. Carter, is that it doesn't make
any sense unless one follows your indications for the dynamics." Perhaps it was

4. Conspiracy theories are generally absurd. Some years ago a critic in *The New York Times*
wrote that there was a conspiracy to prevent the music of Hans Pfitzner from being performed. I remember wondering how one could join such a splendid conspiracy. Of course, the simple truth,
then as now, is that of the small number of people who were acquainted with the music of Pfitzner,
many of them did not care for it.

5. Berlioz reported that when Beethoven's Ninth Symphony was first attempted in Paris, it made
so little sense that the conductor, Habeneck, rehearsed it every day for a year before performing it
publicly: that must have been a rendition at least adequate. Only once have I heard a difficult modern work performed by an orchestra so familiar with every detail: the production of Berg's *Lulu*
complete for the first time, directed by Boulez in Paris; after ten performances and more than forty
recording sessions, the orchestra seemed to play by heart.

unreasonable in our time for the composer to expect his directions to be observed.

Since Sony is, after all, in the record business, Gelb has to decide what to record. He has cut down drastically on the standard classics: "particularly in the case of symphonic repertory," he writes, "it has become almost impossible to tell one modern performance on record from another." I am sure that this is an accurate and sincere expression of Gelb's perception. It seems sensible: if all performances sound alike to you, why bother to record a new one? What this confession hides, however, is the fact that with the backlog of old recordings that Sony inherited from CBS Records, remastering the old catalogue on compact discs at cut-rate prices can keep them busy for several years. Since the standard old classics are already in large supply, it becomes imperative to find new works. And these new works must not be difficult.

"As a major record label," Gelb insists, "we have an obligation to make recordings that are relevant." What does relevant mean? Gelb explains. "To me relevance means that people actually listen to our recordings. It is neither commercially rewarding nor artistically relevant for us to make recordings that sell only a few thousand copies." One thing should be made clear: it is perfectly possible to make a decent profit with a record that sells only a few thousand copies. Sometimes, indeed, it is more profitable to make lots of inexpensively produced records that have only a moderate sale than to spend a fortune on one recording that sells a hundred thousand copies and still loses money.[6] If publishers had refused any book which they thought would sell only a few thousand copies, most of the world's greatest masterpieces would never have been printed. A "relevant" recording, however, is simply one that sells in very large numbers. Relevant is not just profitable, but hugely profitable.

Sony wants to make money. That is not news, and it is taken for granted. Why, then, the jargon word "relevant"? Because Gelb wants to enjoy artistic pretensions along with his profits. He wants, as he says, "to succeed in revitalizing the classical-record industry and classical music itself." The revitalization of classical music is already under way: in a note to Gelb's article, the *Times* informs us that "Sony Classical currently boasts the No. 1 best-selling album in the world, James Horner's soundtrack for the film *Titanic*." This provides an ingenious solution to the problem of making the classical division of a company profitable: record pop music and call it classical. What is disarming about Gelb's article is that he seems to have no idea how silly he sounds. Making a profit needs no apology, but Gelb wants to gild his profits with aesthetics. That is why he becomes so defensive. He

---

6. When a producer at CBS Records pointed this out some years ago, he was taken to lunch by a vice-president who told him, "Don't make waves. This company likes large numbers."

writes: "Well, I am not afraid to admit that we are seeking success. We are seeking artistic and commercial success." If he were in earnest, he would try to deal with the reasons for the problem of finding an audience for classical music, and not invent substitutes for the music.

Indeed, the cause of our present difficulty can be laid right at the door of the recording industry. Since the 1930s, records have gradually supplanted concerts and radio programs as our principal means of hearing music. Throughout these years, the record companies steadfastly refused to make records freely or cheaply available for the schools, so that generations have grown up with no contact early in life with classical music. If the recording industry had had the foresight and the business sense of the tobacco companies, and tried to build a future market or an addiction for their classical product among children and teenagers, classical music would not feel itself under attack. Paul Griffiths was right in his *Times* article to claim that the only way to reinvigorate the state of classical music was through education: "We should resolve, most vitally, to encourage and enhance music in schools. Music teaches the ability to listen, which is fundamental to education." But most of the directors of the record industry wanted a quick profit without having to work for it, and with no thought of the years to come.

That is what "listener-friendly" music represents, a quick profit. The music which has endured—and, we may add, the art and literature, too—was rarely easy at first. With few exceptions, it met in the beginning with some incomprehension and even resentment. Throughout the centuries from Ockeghem and Josquin des Pres to Beethoven and Stravinsky, dedicated amateurs of music have wanted their music to be difficult.

VII

The most famous authors in Western culture are probably Dante and Shakespeare. The difficulty of reading Dante was formidable during his lifetime, and within a few years of his death Boccaccio gave public lectures in Florence to elucidate the *Divine Comedy*. It has not, I think, been sufficiently emphasized how hard it is to understand much of Shakespeare, both on the stage and in the library. Even for his contemporaries it must have been a challenge: he is considerably more complex than Kyd, Marlowe, and Middleton; even Jonson and Chapman are less formidable. The finest examples of that popular form, the nineteenth-century novel, make demands upon the reader, and with some novelists, like Flaubert, the demands are outlandish ("We need a lexicon," Sainte-Beuve complained in a review of *Salammbô*). The popular Dickens was not always an easy read, and his later novels are extremely tough.

In music, the initial difficulty of perception of the finest classical works is basic. Telemann is listener-friendly, considerably more popular during his lifetime than his contemporary Johann Sebastian Bach; by the end of the eighteenth century he was almost completely forgotten, while Bach's reputation has never ceased to grow. The minor Baroque composers have been revived and they provide period flavor, but the easier they are to appreciate, the less interesting they become in the long run. (One of the few concerts that I refused to sit out until the end was one devoted entirely to Albinoni, a composer significant only because he wrote a good theme that inspired a fugue by Bach.)

The most popular opera composer of the eighteenth century was Hasse, whose bland, facile style has completely disappeared from the repertory, while the tougher work of Gluck still survives. Mozart was considered difficult and even repulsive by his contemporaries (too many notes, too complex, too many ideas to follow); his easier and more popular contemporaries, Paisiello and Piccinni, are only musicological memories now. The difficulty of understanding Beethoven is well known: even at the end of the nineteenth century the late works were still contested, and the most famous piano teacher in Vienna, Leschetizky, advised his pupil Artur Schnabel not to play the last sonatas. In fact, I doubt if the enemies of contemporary music would sit through the Grosse Fuge if they did not know that Beethoven wrote it. Even as recently as the 1930s and 1940s, chamber music societies in smaller American cities would threaten to cancel concerts by the Budapest Quartet if they insisted on playing a late Beethoven quartet.

The opposition to Wagner is equally famous, but the innovations of Chopin and Schumann were also disliked and misunderstood. We may even say, paradoxically, that the greatness of these two composers, like that of Mozart, can only be understood historically when we realize how unacceptable they were at first hearing. Brahms, Mahler, Debussy, Richard Strauss, and the most important composers of the twentieth century are all resistant to easy listening. Perhaps the only major figures that won their audiences over at first hearing were Handel, Tchaikovsky, and the great masters of nineteenth-century Italian opera, Rossini, Donizetti, Verdi, and Puccini. In fact, Tchaikovsky was more misunderstood than is sometimes realized, and Verdi in the latter part of his life also became a less accessible composer with *Don Carlos, Otello, Falstaff,* and the second version of *Simon Boccanegra.* In some of the nineteenth- and twentieth-century music which presents few problems for the listener, however, the complexity of thought is sometimes replaced by the difficulty of execution. The immense popularity of Rachmaninoff's concertos is only partly due to the composer's melodic eloquence and mastery of sonority: a great part of their success comes from our awareness of the extraordinary technical demands made upon the pianist.

We must conclude that, for the most part, what the public generally wants is

difficult music that forces us to listen with undivided concentration and attention. At least, that is what the small public deeply devoted to classical music demands, and it is also partly true even of the somewhat larger public that likes
classical music, but whose attention span is not as great and whose interest is
only intermittent. The serious music that survives demands an intensity of listening antipathetic to many people: that is why it is an art for a minority—not
an elite, but a small although not insignificant number with a passionate interest,
like that equally small tribe, the lovers of poetry. This minority interest, however,
is deeply antipathetic to the record industry.

The problem for contemporary music is double: it is true that it demands
even more intensive listening to arrive at an understanding. Boulez is more
difficult than Rossini. There are historical reasons for this, of which the most important is the growing desire from the late eighteenth century on to eliminate
purely conventional material and to make every detail take on an individual and
personal significance. This makes it harder to relax one's attention while listening. However, the second part of the problem is more important: the replace-
ment of the experience of live music by listening to records.

In the 1930s, most lovers of classical music had still learned, at least in an elementary way, to play some instrument. The piano was the favored instrument,
and it enables one to understand the entire texture of art music. This is no longer
true: fewer young people learn to play, and the guitar has replaced the piano as
the most popular medium. Learning to play was an essential part of building an
audience for music, and it is not surprising that the public has grown smaller. If
the public for baseball consisted principally of people who had never played the
game, I doubt that it would be a popular sport. Most of the time, records have
replaced live performance as the primary way of getting to know music.

Listening to records is generally less gripping than hearing a concert or playing oneself. Walter Benjamin once wrote that the cinema was a medium for an
audience in a state of distraction. He was wrong about the movies: real movie-
buffs sit toward the front of a theater and immerse themselves in the screen as if
returning to the womb (perhaps the old custom of making out in the back rows
of the movie theater was more widespread in Benjamin's time.) But if he was
wrong about the cinema, what he said applies perfectly to listening to records
and to television. If beautifully played at a concert, the introduction to the last
movement of Mozart's Viola Quintet in G Minor can bring tears to my eyes, but
I have never wept at a recording. With records, there is always the chance of interrupting one's listening by leaving the room for a moment[7] or by conversation.

---

7. In the eighteenth century people attended the opera with similarly casual behavior. But at the
more private performances of chamber music, the listening was already more intense, and the intensity was gradually transferred to the concert hall.

We can achieve the same concentration with a record as at a concert, but it requires an effort of will. A recording tends to dilute and disperse the attention necessary for difficult music in the same way that watching a video in a room at least partly lighted is less intense than seeing a film in a darkened theater.

The panaceas proposed by Lloyd Webber and Gelb are makeshifts, and take no account of the process of listening and appreciation. Easily accessible music may have a quick success, but this does nothing to restore the intensity of experience which is the foundation of serious music. I do not know what music of today will survive into the future: great figures like Josquin and Monteverdi have been forgotten for centuries, only to be revived. History teaches us, however, that it is the art that is tough and that resists immediate appreciation that has the best chance of enduring and of returning. We must do all we can to foster it, to beg composers to pay no heed to the pressures of the music business but to listen only to their own inspiration.

VIII

Nevertheless, the problem of communication between the contemporary composer and the public is a real one, but any solution that suggests that someone is at fault is off the track. The public has a right to listen to what pleases it, the composer a right to compose as he feels. In most big cities, there is no reason to think that the public does not have access to the music it wants. The problem is how to enable musicians to make a living doing what they like to do, and this is not solved by having them play music they do not enjoy or compose in a style they have no faith in. Serious art music will survive as long as there are musicians who want to play it.

What is not understood in most of the debate is how taste is formed, and why music is difficult. Brahms once remarked that it would have been wonderful to be a composer at the time of Mozart, when writing music was easy. This nostalgia is profound, and it implies a real uneasiness which appears in all the arts in the mid-nineteenth century. The greatest French poet of the end of the century for most critics is Mallarmé, whose poems are so difficult that it is said that only foreigners can understand them—perhaps because foreigners read slowly, word for word, instead of skimming. Painting has become harder to read at first looking, music more difficult to grasp at first hearing. This is a fact of modern life. We cannot make the difficulty go away by trying to compose again like Mozart, write like Racine or Byron, or paint like Rembrandt.

It is not at all natural to want to listen to classical music. Learning to appreciate it is like Pascal's wager: you pretend to be religious, and suddenly you have faith. You pretend to love Beethoven—or Stravinsky—because you think that will make you appear educated and cultured and intelligent, because that kind of music is prestigious in professional circles, and suddenly you really love it, you have become a fanatic, you go to concerts and buy records and experience true ecstasy when you hear a good performance (or even when you hear a mediocre one if you have little judgment).

Berlioz detested the music of Bach: he did not want to enjoy it. Stravinsky despised Brahms, but came around to him at the end of his life. Not all composers are easy to love: Beethoven was more difficult than Mozart, Stravinsky harder than Ravel. Some composers, on the other hand, bring diminishing dividends over the years to their amateurs. One can revive a taste for Hummel or Saint-Saëns, but it is not nourishing over a long period. (A little Satie for me goes a long way: I am never in a hurry to return to him.) Those amateurs who love a composer are the only ones whose opinion counts; the negative votes have no importance. The musical canon is not decided by majority opinion but by enthusiasm and passion. A work that ten people love passionately is more important than one that ten thousand do not mind hearing.

Credits

Chapter 1: Originally published in *Prose*, Fall 1972.

Chapter 2: Originally published as "A Master Musicologist," *The New York Review of Books*, February 6, 1975.

Chapter 3: Originally published in *Keyboard Music*, ed. Denis Matthews (David and Charles Ltd., 1972).

Chapter 4: Originally published as "Rediscovering Haydn," *The New York Review of Books*, June 14, 1979.

Chapter 5: Originally published as "Love That Mozart," *The New York Review of Books*, May 18, 1972.

Chapter 6: Originally published as "Inventor of Modern Opera," *The New York Review of Books*, October 27, 1988.

Chapter 7: Originally published in *The New York Review of Books*, December 19, 1991.

Chapter 8: Originally published as "Did Beethoven Have All the Luck?" in *The New York Review of Books*, November 14, 1996.

Chapter 9: Originally published in *19th Century Music*, vol. 4, no. 1 (Fall 1980). © 1980 by The Regents of the University of California, reprinted by permission.

Chapter 10: Originally published in *Brahms Studies: Analytical and Historical Perspectives*, ed. George S. Bozarth (Oxford University Press, 1990). Reprinted by permission of Oxford University Press.

Chapter 11: A portion of this chapter was published in *The New York Review of Books*, Fall 1998, as a review of *Johannes Brahms: A Biography* by Jan Swafford.

Chapter 12: Originally published as "The Shock of the Old," *The New York Review of Books*, July 19, 1990.

Chapter 13: Originally published as "A Tone-deaf Musical Dictionary," *The New York Review of Books*, February 26, 1970.

Chapter 14: Originally published as "The Musicological Marvel," *The New York Review of Books*, May 28, 1981.

Chapter 15: Originally published as "Music à la Mode," *The New York Review of Books*, June 23, 1994.

Chapter 16: Originally published in the *Times Literary Supplement*, November 7, 1975.

Chapter 17: Originally published as "One Easy Piece," *The New York Review of Books*, February 1973.

Chapter 18: Portions of this chapter were originally published in *The New York Review of Books* ("Who's Afraid of the Avant-Garde?"), May 14, 1998, and in *Harper's* Magazine, March 1998.

Index